The
EVERYTHING
Accounting Book

Dear Reader,

A few years ago, a new client walked into my office with a bulging paper bag and a handful of cash. The bag held hundreds of receipts, some illegible or wadded up, and pages upon pages of different-colored check stubs. The cash was to pay his taxes.

This guy had absolutely no idea what kind of financial shape his company was in, but he figured he owed some taxes since he had money in his cash box. After spending weeks sorting through his paperwork (and that's a generous term), I told him the company was operating at a huge loss, but he could turn things around with a lot of attention and some basic accounting. The next tax season, he came to me with printouts in folders instead of torn receipts in a crumpled brown bag—and a profitable bottom line.

That's what this book is about: helping small-business owners succeed. Inside, I show you what you need to know to set your company on the path to profits (yes, there will be math!). From maximizing cash to minimizing taxes, I'll help you steer your business toward lasting prosperity.

Good luck,

Michele Cagan

The EVERYTHING® Series

Editorial

Publishing Director	Gary M. Krebs
Director of Product Development	Paula Munier
Associate Managing Editor	Laura M. Daly
Associate Copy Chief	Brett Palana-Shanahan
Acquisitions Editor	Lisa Laing
Development Editor	Katie McDonough
Associate Production Editor	Casey Ebert

Production

Director of Manufacturing	Susan Beale
Associate Director of Production	Michelle Roy Kelly
Cover Design	Paul Beatrice
	Matt LeBlanc
	Erick DaCosta
Design and Layout	Heather Barrett
	Brewster Brownville
	Colleen Cunningham
	Jennifer Oliveira
Series Cover Artist	Barry Littmann

THE
EVERYTHING®
ACCOUNTING BOOK

Balance your budget, manage your cash
flow, and keep your books in the black

Michele Cagan, C.P.A.

Adams Media
Avon, Massachusetts

To Ethan, who helped me get here on time.

An Everything® Series Book.
Everything® and everything.com® are registered trademarks of F+W Publications, Inc.

Published by Adams Media, an F+W Publications Company
57 Littlefield Street, Avon, MA 02322 U.S.A.
www.adamsmedia.com

ISBN 10: 1-59337-718-5
ISBN 13: 978-1-59337-718-2

Printed in the United States of America.

J   I   H   G   F   E   D   C   B   A

Library of Congress Cataloging-in-Publication Data
Cagan, Michele.
The everything accounting book / Michele Cagan.
p.   cm.
ISBN-13: 978-1-59337-718-2
ISBN-10: 1-59337-718-5
1. Accounting. I. Title.
HF5636.C24 2007
657--dc22
2006028132

This publication is designed to provide accurate and authoritative information with regard to the subject matter covered. It is sold with the understanding that the publisher is not engaged in rendering legal, accounting, or other professional advice. If legal advice or other expert assistance is required, the services of a competent professional person should be sought.
—From a *Declaration of Principles* jointly adopted by a Committee of the American Bar Association and a Committee of Publishers and Associations

Many of the designations used by manufacturers and sellers to distinguish their products are claimed as trademarks. Where those designations appear in this book and Adams Media was aware of a trademark claim, the designations have been printed with initial capital letters.

*This book is available at quantity discounts for bulk purchases.
For information, please call 1-800-289-0963.*

Contents

Top Ten Accounting Mistakes / x
Introduction / xi

Accounting Is More Than Numbers / 1
Tracking and Measuring Success **2** • Accounting Versus Bookkeeping **2** • Who Uses Accounting Information? **4** • Different Versions for Different Reasons **5** • Who's Who in Accounting **7** • How Accountants Can Help You **8** • Pick the Right Accounting Professional **11**

The Basic Accounts / 13
Accounting Starts with Accounts **14** • Understanding Assets **15** • A Look at Liabilities **16** • All about Equity **17** • Revenues, Costs, and Expenses **18** • How the Accounts Connect **20** • Debits and Credits **22**

Keeping Track of Transactions / 25
What Counts as a Transaction **26** • When to Record Transactions **26** • Setting Up Your Accounts **29** • Meet the General Ledger **33** • The Daily Journals **34** • It's All in the Posting **39** • Checking It Twice **41** • The Accounting Cycle **43**

Setting Up a System / 45
Get (and Stay) Organized **46** • Software Makes It Simpler **49** • Mapping Out Your Accounting Processes **50** • The Everyday Transactions **55** • Reconciling Your Accounts **56** • What to Keep, What to Toss **59**

The Accounting Equation / 63
Every Business Has Assets **64** • Breaking Out Asset Categories **64** • A Closer Look at Fixed Assets **68** • Liabilities Are What Your Company Owes **72** • Equity Means Ownership **74** • Assets Equal Liabilities Plus Equity **75**

Recording Your Revenues / 77

What Are You Selling? **78** • The Basics of Sales Transactions **79** • Develop a Sales Journal **82** • Simple Cash Sales **83** • Selling on Account **84** • Collecting Sales Tax **86** • Dealing with Special Sales Transactions **87** • When a Sale Is Not a Sale **90**

The Inventory-Cost Connection / 91

Inventory Transforms into Cost of Goods **92** • What Goes into Inventory Costs? **94** • Set Up Your Purchases Journal **95** • Four Ways to Value Inventory **96** • Extra Steps for Manufacturers **99** • Figure Out Cost of Goods Sold **100**

Standard Operating Expenses / 103

A Look at Expense Categories **104** • What Goes into Selling Costs **104** • Understanding Overhead **106** • All about Depreciation **109** • Don't Forget Amortization **111** • Employees Cause a Lot of Transactions **112** • Recording Expense Transactions **113**

Managing the Payroll / 115

A Big Pile of Forms **116** • All about Payroll Taxes **119** • Employee Benefits and Bonuses **121** • Calculating Take-Home Pay **122** • Payroll Tax Reporting and Filing **127** • Never Mess Around with Payroll Taxes **129** • Still Want to Do It Yourself? **130**

Always Know Your Cash / 131

The Importance of Having Cash **132** • Earning Profits but Out of Cash **132** • The Basics of Cash Flow **133** • Tracking Your Incoming Cash **135** • Recording Your Outgoing Cash **136** • Reconcile Your Bank Statement **137** • What to Do When Cash Runs Low **139**

Handling Customer Credit / 141

Why Sell on Credit? **142** • Establish Your Credit Policies **144** • Don't Give Credit to Just Anyone **146** • Creating Invoices and Account Statements **148** • Dealing with Collections **150** • Accounting for Accounts Receivable Transactions **152**

Controlling Purchase Costs / 153

Know What You Want Before You Buy **154** • Choose Your Vendors Wisely **155** • Getting Vendors to Extend Credit **157** • Creating Purchase Orders **159** • Dealing with Purchase Problems **160** • Review Their Invoices **161** • Recording Accounts Payable Transactions **161**

The End of Period Cleanup / 163

Accounting Periods **164** • The Working Trial Balance **166** • Making Adjusting Entries **167** • Accounting for Accruals **170** • Prelude to Financial Statements **173** • Closing the Books **174**

Preparing Financial Statements / 177

Three Major Financial Statements **178** • How These Statements Interconnect **178** • The Statement of Profit and Loss **179** • The Balance Sheet **184** • The Statement of Cash Flows **188**

Different Entities Mean Different Equity / 191

Meet the Business Entities **192** • Which One Is Best for Your Business? **192** • Accounting for Sole Proprietorships **194** • Accounting for Partnership Equity **195** • Distributing Partnership Profits and Losses **196** • The Corporate Equity Section **198** • Dealing with Dividends **201**

The Income Tax Impact / 203

Financial Statements Flow into Tax Returns **204** • Different Income Taxation for Different Entities **204** • Introducing Business Tax Forms **205** • Different Ways to Pay Yourself **208** • Your Payment Strategy Impacts Your Personal Taxes **210** • Tax Planning Strategies **213**

The Best Use of Your Financial Statements / 215

What Can Your Statements Tell You? **216** • Vertical and Horizontal Analysis **217** • Calculating Crucial Financial Ratios **221** • Nipping Problems in the Bud **226** • A Basis for Decision-Making **228** • Boosting Profitability and Positive Cash Flow **228** • When You Need Outside Funding **230**

More Ways Accounting Helps Your Business / 231
Know Your Costs to Set Your Prices **232** • The Break-Even Analysis **233** • Developing Pro Forma Statements **235** • Sticking to a Budget **236** • Financing Major Purchases **237** • Management Accounting **238** • The Importance of Internal Controls **239** • Using Internal Audits to Your Advantage **242**

Unique Issues for Specific Businesses / 243
Common and Not-So-Common Transactions **244** • Retail Is More Than Buying and Selling **244** • Manufacturers Produce Special Transactions **245** • Accounting for Your Home-Based Business **247** • Small High-Tech Companies **250** • Building Construction Transactions **251**

Retirement Plans / 255
The Best Tax Shelter **256** • Individual Retirement Accounts (IRAs) **258** • SIMPLE Plans **260** • Simplified Employee Pensions (SEPs) **262** • Keogh Plans **264** • Choosing the Right Plan for You **265** • Accounting for Contributions **266**

Common Small-Business Tax Snafus / 269
Don't Be Afraid of the IRS **270** • Employees Versus Contractors **271** • Salaries, Dividends, or Loans? **273** • Tracking Travel Expenses **277** • About Fringe Benefits **279** • Keeping Things Separate **280**

Appendix A: Glossary / 281

Appendix B: Small-Business Resources on the Internet / 284

Index / 286

Acknowledgments

Special thanks to my best friend, Jenny Thompson, who did so much to help me write this book. Thanks also to Jacky Sach, without whom I would never have had this wonderful opportunity.

Top Ten Accounting Mistakes

1. **Not knowing your true cash balance:** Due to things like automatic payments and bank charges, money that appears in your cash drawer and your checking account may already be spent.

2. **Extending credit without checking credit:** Until you collect some basic credit information about a customer, don't make on-account sales. A sale isn't much good if your company never gets paid.

3. **Mistaking profits for cash:** When you have a lot of credit sales, your company can post big profits without seeing any cash.

4. **Paying bills too soon:** If your vendors give you thirty days to pay them, take it. Unless you get a discount for paying early, paying your bills only when they're due improves your company's cash flow.

5. **Avoiding bookkeeping tasks:** Not recording and posting transactions regularly leaves you with a mountain of bookkeeping to deal with instead of a molehill. Plus, the time lag can act like a vacuum, where transactions disappear and never are recorded.

6. **Not hiring a payroll service:** The minor cost of hiring out this task provides a huge benefit for your company. It can free up your time and help avoid the financial penalties that go along with late and incorrect filings.

7. **Paying accidental dividends:** Every time a corporation owner takes money out of his business, it counts as a dividend. That can lead to a bigger personal income-tax bill.

8. **Not keeping personal finances separate from business:** Mixing up business and personal money can cause bookkeeping and legal problems.

9. **Setting prices too low:** Know your costs before you set product or service prices, or you run the risk of losing money on every sale. A simple break-even analysis can help you set prices at a profitable level.

10. **Turning over all the financial stuff to someone else:** Without an intimate knowledge of your company's finances, you can't make successful decisions. Even if you don't want to deal with the daily bookkeeping tasks, look at your financial statements every month to help you plan for profits and prevent potential problems.

Introduction

▶ The business world is full of endless opportunity to make it big, or crash and burn. Small businesses crop up every day, but very few of them last to see a second anniversary, even when their basic idea was a good one. In this world, the difference between success and failure is in knowing how to work the numbers. Those who learn to unlock the secrets of financial statements win; those who muddle through and leave the numbers solely to the "numbers guys" often lose their shirts.

From the outside, accounting seems daunting, overwhelming, and complicated. Some of it is, and that's the part you can leave to the professionals. For the rest, for the everyday stuff, all you really need to know are the basics—but you do need to know them. Especially in a company's earliest days, seemingly small financial decisions can present huge consequences. Making these decisions without an intimate understanding of your company's financial picture and the potential impact of each decision is like a crapshoot; they could work out, or they could kill your business with a single shot. Backed by insight and information, though, every decision can lead to prosperity.

When you get a firm grasp on the basic principles of accounting, you'll be able to monitor and control your company's financial position. Every business faces obstacles and suffers financial setbacks. Keeping your company afloat is hard; turning a steady profit is even harder. When you understand how to use accounting information to your advantage, you'll be more able to lead your company quickly back to a more profitable track.

That's how this book can help you. When you have a working knowledge of accounting, from daily transactions to formal financial statements, every crisis can be reduced to numbers—numbers you will know how to manage well. In addition to knowing the basics of bookkeeping, you'll be able to minimize taxable income without sinking your profits, maximize cash flow without skipping payments to creditors, and use your business to help you build personal wealth. After all, that's one of the main reasons you started your company.

The bottom line: You won't be able to proactively affect your company's bottom line without understanding all the numbers that go into it. You undoubtedly plan to stay in business, to grow your business, and to make some serious money. The information in this book can help you achieve those goals.

chapter 1

Accounting Is More Than Numbers

When you think of accounting, you may picture pages upon pages of columns of numbers. That image doesn't usually generate too much excitement. When you have your own business, though, those numbers come to mean the world to you. Then they aren't just random dollar amounts or boring statistics; they're your sales figures, your costs, and your profits. Once you know how to work with those numbers, and how to read the story they tell, you will be able to steer your business toward greater success.

Tracking and Measuring Success

When you first dreamed of starting your own business, you may have thought about happy customers, the luxury of being your own boss, or building a nice chunk of wealth for your family. All those things are possible, once your business starts to take off. Getting it to that point, though, means doing something that gives many people queasy stomachs: working with a lot of numbers.

Underneath every business success story—from the tiniest home-based business to the largest Fortune 500 corporation—are numbers and reports and some math. Behind many business failures is a failure to work with and understand these numbers. With a working knowledge of the basics, you can avoid that fate and watch your dreams come true.

You probably already do some basic accounting in your personal life: writing checks, paying bills, balancing your checkbook. Business accounting is not much different. In fact, it really just builds on those everyday activities and takes them a few steps further. Accounting gives you a way to figure out what those numbers mean in terms of your business, and it shows you how they work together to measure your company's financial health. It lets you track all the important numbers, such as sales and expenses. It helps you truly measure how well your business is doing, which may be quite different than how things appear on the surface.

Accounting Versus Bookkeeping

Accounting and bookkeeping are related in the same way as recipes and ingredients. Ingredients are the raw materials you need to create a meal; bookkeeping provides the raw materials you need to develop useful financial reports. A recipe takes that pile of ingredients and tells you how to transform it into that tasty meal; accounting helps you create reports that can help you make your business successful.

In theory, there's a wide gap between bookkeepers and accountants, but in reality the lines are often blurry. By definition, a bookkeeper compiles and records information. An accountant analyzes that information, and then presents it in a more useful format (such as specialized reports), explains what all the numbers mean, and makes future recommendations. As more tasks are performed by computer programs, specific tasks become intertwined and harder to separate.

You cannot have accounting without bookkeeping; bookkeeping is a crucial part of the whole process. You can, however, have bookkeeping without accounting. Just as you can eat carrots without making soup, you can do bookkeeping without performing any full-blown accounting tasks.

The Ins and Outs of Bookkeeping

Bookkeeping is really just what it sounds like: keeping the books. That includes every facet of recordkeeping, from writing a check to recording it to marking it off when it has been cashed to making sure it was cashed for the right amount. In fact, every time money is involved—even if it has not yet changed hands—there is something to record. Sometimes you have something to record even when there is no money involved, such as when two companies barter services instead of paying each other.

Bookkeeping is by far the most labor-intensive and time-consuming part of accounting. It is also one of the most important parts, because without it there would be no way to keep track of your business finances, let alone see how well your company is really doing. Many new or small-business owners let bookkeeping slide (at least initially), maybe because it does take so much of their very precious time, or maybe because they just don't like working with numbers. Then, at the end of the year, they take huge sacks of paper over to the tax preparer and wait for him to tell them how the business is doing. The answer often is "not good," and by then it can be too late to do anything about it.

Keeping your books thorough and current will help you avoid that scene, and it may also save you a lot of money at the end of the year. Yes, it takes time, and you probably do not have tons of time to spare. You can get around that by using some simple business bookkeeping software, or by hiring a part-time bookkeeper. At least in the very beginning, though, it's good to do some of it on your own, so you can get a good feel for how your business finances work and develop a better understanding of how everything fits together financially.

By starting with the small, clear steps of bookkeeping, you will be able to make the giant leaps of financial analysis and forecasting more easily. It's like starting out in the mailroom and working your way up to the president's office: you learn the ins and outs of everything along the way, giving you a better ability to understand virtually every facet of the company.

Accounting Ties It All Together

Accounting covers a lot of ground, from the framework supporting all the bookkeeping tasks to the final analysis of what all the numbers mean and what to do next. This science sets the rules for figuring out which events will be recorded by the bookkeepers, dictates exactly how and when that information will be set down, and most important, communicates all of this in a useful way to the people who need to know it.

That communication is both simple and complex. It includes standard reports, called financial statements, that everyone from business owners to bank managers can read. Accounting also provides the tools for analyzing those numbers—not just how they all add up, but what they mean and how they can be used to make a difference going forward.

Who Uses Accounting Information?

Accounting information is used by virtually everyone, in every job, at home and at work. Every time you get a bank statement or a credit card bill, it's accounting information. Every time you look at your homeowners' association annual budget, it's accounting. Every time you verify the charges on your dinner check, and add on a tip, it's accounting. When you do your taxes or fill out college loan applications, you are supplying accounting information. That's the everyday-life version. The business version is equally pervasive.

Most people use accounting information in their jobs every day. Whether you are ordering supplies, taking customer orders, buying stamps, or preparing the payroll, you are dealing with accounting information. All of these seemingly small pieces of accounting data add up to one big picture of how a company (or a household) is doing.

On the inside of a business, the people most likely to use that big-picture information are the owners, chief financial officers, and the accounting department. When it comes to outside users, the list is much bigger, especially for small-business owners. This varied group includes:

- Bank loan officers
- Tax authorities (federal, state, and local)
- Anyone who might offer credit (such as a supplier)
- Potential and existing investors

These different users all have different reasons for wanting to see the numbers. A bank loan officer wants to see that you have enough cash, not too much debt, and sustainable income. A tax authority wants to make sure that you have not miscalculated your taxable income or your income tax bill. Creditors look for a lot of the same things that bankers want to see, especially the cash-related figures. Investors tend to look for two separate things: current income that could be paid out in dividends, and the capacity for long-term growth that will cause their investment value to grow as well.

Different Versions for Different Reasons

In addition to you, there may be a lot of people who want to see how your business is doing. This includes your own employees, who may need to track particular numbers to get their jobs done; your accountant, who needs the numbers in order to prepare your tax returns; and the IRS, which needs the numbers so it can collect whatever taxes you or your company may owe. These people don't all need the same information, though, and may not need it in the same form.

When you're looking over the financial results for your company, you'll probably want to see a lot more detail than you would be willing to show outsiders. For example, while you would report your total sales on your tax return, you wouldn't really want to send in a breakdown of which customers bought what. That information doesn't help the IRS determine whether you figured out the right tax payment. It can, however, help you figure out things such as whether your company is relying too heavily on sales to a single customer.

Give Them What They Want

You've got a bunch of people asking you for financial statements, but they all want something different. What do you do? First, look at who's doing the asking. If it's a tax authority, you have to give him the numbers in the format requested; the same goes for your loan officer. These guys may look at hundreds of financial statements every week, and they need them to be consistent.

For people on the inside, or consultants that you've hired, you can prepare special versions or just make do with what you already have. With most accounting software packages, though, it's pretty easy to pick and choose what information you want on each report. For example, you can run a report with just the current numbers, or run it to include both this period and last period for comparison purposes.

A good rule to remember if you fill out your own tax forms is this: Don't report more than the forms ask for. Fill in all the requested numbers, and stop. Don't explain, and don't add details. When you provide extra information, you could be flagging your return for audit. Audits are not necessarily bad—they could decide you did everything correctly—but they are generally not pleasant.

When the Numbers Are Different

You've probably heard the phrase "two sets of books," usually involving an agent and an arrest warrant. The truth is, though, that some companies keep one set of books for tax purposes, and another for everyday accounting. While there may not be two separate physical ledgers, some accounts have two sets of balances and different transaction streams.

Why bother with that? For tax purposes, you have to follow IRS requirements, even when they don't make perfect sense for your business. Even some flexible areas, such as certain expense calculations, may work differently for book purposes (meaning your internal books) and tax purposes (meaning what you put on your tax return). The biggest reason for having different numbers here is taxes: When it comes to income taxes, you want to show the lowest possible income because that means the lowest possible tax bill. For your own purposes, though, you may want to use the most realistic numbers, even if those would have left you with a bigger tax burden. It's fine to do that, as long as you let anyone who needs to know (such as your loan officer, who will see both versions) that you've done it.

For small businesses, it's just plain simpler to track one set of numbers. Since you have to do certain things for the IRS, it's easiest to use those figures for your own books. If you decide you'd like to see how things would have worked out if you had used a second set of numbers (a different inventory number, for example), you can always figure that out on the side.

Who's Who in Accounting

The world of accounting is populated with lots of players. There are the people who put the numbers together, the people who analyze and report on those numbers, and the people for whom those reports are compiled. Having a handle on who does what can help you get a handle on your role, as well as who may best be able to help you when you decide you want assistance.

In the business of accounting, there are three basic flavors: public, private, and government. Public accounting professionals sell their services to (as you might guess from the name) the general public. Private accounting is also called in-house, and covers the accounting staff of one company. Government accounting professionals (again, no surprise here) work for the government—from the tiniest county seat to the U.S. Government Accountability Office (GAO).

There also are different types of accounting professionals, such as bookkeepers and accountants and tax preparers and auditors. Some specialize in one distinct area, such as bookkeeping or income tax returns, and others perform a wide variety of services.

Certified public accountants (CPAs) provide the highest level of services to the public, due in part to their additional education, experience, and testing requirements. CPAs jump through a lot of hoops to earn and maintain state certification, including stringent continuing education requirements that ensure they will always know the most current information and issues.

How Accountants Can Help You

When you are just starting out in business, having a professional accountant on your team can make your life as an entrepreneur a lot simpler. Without a background in business accounting or finance, it's easy to get the numbers wrong, or sometimes even overlook certain numbers altogether. Also, when it comes to setting up an accounting system, getting it right from the start is a must, even if you use the most basic do-it-yourself software package. Trying to change it after the fact is pretty tough, if not impossible.

Once your business is up and running, you'll find many more reasons to have an accountant. From creating more useful reports to going over the numbers with you to helping you make plans for next month or next year, having her available to walk you through the finances frees up your time so you can focus on the business of running your business.

Then comes tax time. Whether it's sales tax, payroll taxes, or income taxes, having an experienced professional deal with the paperwork will remove a huge headache-producer from your life. Plus, on top of your time savings, you could end up saving money. Tax mistakes can be pretty costly, in part because late filings are subject to fees and fines. Also, professional income tax preparers really know their way around deductions, which can reduce your company's income tax bill from a shade tree to a sapling.

When You're Just Starting Out

Hundreds of new businesses crop up every day in the United States, and every year thousands of them fold. A lot of the time, those failures could have been prevented easily with better financial planning and management, two areas where an accountant can help. In fact, if you hook up with an accountant during the planning stage, he will be able to point out potential pitfalls before they show up, and help you figure out ways to prevent or deal with them.

ALERT!

While you may be comfortable with the CPA who's been doing your personal taxes, he may not be the best person to deal with your business taxes. The two types are very different, and someone well-versed in personal returns may not have a lot of experience in small-business returns. That can lead to an unnecessarily high tax bill on your business income. It's very important to make sure that whoever takes care of your business taxes knows the ins and outs of a business return.

If you've started working on a business plan (something no new business should be without), you know there are pages upon pages of numbers involved. When it's your first business plan for your first business, coming up with those numbers is a daunting task. First, you have to figure out how much it will cost to get your company off the ground and where that money is coming from; without enough startup cash, your business may not even make it past the planning stage. Then you have to estimate what your sales and expenses (among other things) will be over the next couple of years. Experienced accountants won't even blink when you ask them to help you come up with these numbers; it's their job.

These are some other things that accountants can do for startup businesses:

- Help you choose the best business structure (like corporation or limited liability company [LLC])
- Introduce you to bankers
- Set up your accounting system
- Teach you how to use your accounting system
- Show you different ways to keep initial costs down
- Help you get all the necessary tax ID numbers

Once Your Company Is Up and Running

After your company has been around for a few months, you will have a better feel for the way your business flows. You'll also know by then which things you like to do yourself, which things you feel you have to do yourself, and which things you cannot wait to pass off to somebody else. A lot of the time, what falls into that last category are routine bookkeeping and paperwork tasks.

Once you know how to do tasks, and what the results of your work should look like, you may be ready to stop doing them yourself. That's the time to consider bringing in a bookkeeper, whether you have enough volume to put her on your regular payroll or just enough to bring in an independent bookkeeper once a month. That person could handle all the detailed data entry, freeing up your time for other projects. You'd still have the ultimate responsibility for reviewing and understanding the final numbers, but without the time-consuming process of having to come up with them.

Payroll is another labor-intensive job that many small-business owners farm out. Many bookkeepers and accounting firms offer this service, and there are also dozens of dedicated payroll service providers. Most companies offering payroll preparation services can do everything from writing paychecks to filing all the necessary payroll tax returns. All you have to do is provide signatures and money, and record the grand totals in your books (or have your bookkeeper do it).

Speaking of taxes, having a business opens up the gate for a lot of different tax returns. In addition to payroll taxes, there are income taxes (both for your company and for you) and sales taxes. Some businesses (such as gas stations) are subject to specialized taxes, and have to file extra returns. Accounting professionals can help you figure out which returns are required for your business, prepare them for you, and provide you with detailed filing instructions so you don't miss any deadlines.

Looking Toward the Future

An experienced accountant can provide invaluable help as your business grows. She can help you build on any success you have achieved so far; help you turn around a business that's struggling now but has a lot of potential for success; and help you figure out the best ways to grow your company and what you need to have in place before that expansion begins. The latter includes obtaining adequate financing, which is crucial to success. Your accountant can help you figure out how much cash you really need to get things going, as well as the best source of funds.

Pick the Right Accounting Professional

Once you decide you want some help, your next step is to figure out what level of help you're looking for. Doing that will point you toward the right kind of professional. You may use a mix of professionals—for example, a bookkeeper may handle the day-to-day data entry, and a tax professional may help you at year-end; you may do all of the basic bookkeeping in-house but hire out the payroll processing.

Many new and small businesses forge close relationships with their accountants. The most important elements of this relationship are confidence and trust: you must feel confident that you are getting sound advice and that you can trust your accountant with a lot of confidential information.

The Money Factor

As you would expect, higher-level services such as tax planning cost more than lower-level services such as bookkeeping data entry. Higher-level professionals may offer lower-level services, but there's a pretty good chance that they will charge more than the going rate, even if they do charge less than their standard rate. If you need soup-to-nuts help, consider a full-service firm with different levels of employees for which the firm bills different rates. That way you can get bookkeeping rates from your CPA firm for that level of service, even though you pay higher fees for the higher-end services.

Straight bookkeeping generally costs between $30 and $60 per hour; on a monthly contract basis, you could expect to pay between $250 and $600 per month. Payroll services (which you should absolutely consider using) typically charge their fees based on the number of employees you have and how much of the process you expect them to perform. An average small business with four employees that has its payroll firm do everything from preparing the checks to making the tax deposits to filing all the year-end paperwork could expect to pay somewhere around $500 per month (plus the cost of actual payroll and taxes).

CPAs and accountants charge relatively high hourly fees, and some may have graduated fee structures based on specific tasks. Reporting and similar tasks are likely to fall at the lower end of that scale, but exactly where they fall could also depend on the complexity of both your business and the volume of reporting requirements. Bankruptcy services, business advice and planning, tax advice and planning, and other consulting services all fall at the high end of the scale. There can be a lot of variety here, but expect the numbers to start at about $150 to $250 per hour, ranging to $750 to $1,000 for a business tax return. On the plus side, every dime you spend here is fully deductible on your company's income tax return.

FACT

In most cases, CPAs charge more for their services than do any other professionals in the accounting industry. As more letters attach to their names, such as CIA (certified investment adviser), the fees climb even higher. In exchange for those higher fees, though, you will benefit from their extensive experience and unique insights.

Your Comfort Factor

Choosing an accountant involves more than opening a phone book and calling around for prices. This person may become intimately involved in your business. You want to choose someone that you can trust, both to lead you and your company in the right direction and to honor the confidentiality of sensitive and sometimes personal financial information.

Equally as important as all that, though, is looking for someone you genuinely like. You should feel secure asking questions about anything that could affect your company. You should feel free to also bring up questions about your personal financial business, especially because it will be intertwined with that of the company. Your accountant should be someone with whom you'd enjoy sharing a meal or catching a ball game. At the same time, you must feel confident enough in her advice to follow it—and when you disagree with that advice, you also should feel comfortable saying so.

chapter 2

The Basic Accounts

Your business is unique, but it still has a lot in common with other businesses when it comes to accounting. Every business deals with the same account types, and most deal with a core set of similar accounts. Overall, except for some specialized accounts here and there, your company's basic accounts will look a lot like the ones described in this chapter.

Accounting Starts with Accounts

As you might expect, an accounting system is made up of accounts. Here accounts really serve as a way to group information, much like a filing system. For example, everything that happens with cash gets run through a cash account, and those ten receipts for stamps will all show up in the account for postage expense.

Although there are some basic rules to follow when it comes to accounts (as you'll see later in this chapter), any grouping that would be meaningful to you can become an account. There are some standard accounts, and some standard account names, that you will find in almost every bookkeeping system. There are also plenty of specialized accounts, unique to particular businesses, that will not really apply anywhere else. For example, a florist would not need a "ketchup and mustard" account, and a hot-dog vendor would not need a "glass vases" account.

Permanent Versus Temporary

Every account falls under one of two main categories: permanent or temporary. Permanent accounts include assets, liabilities, and equity accounts, and they stay in place from year to year, accumulating information the whole time. Temporary accounts include revenues, costs, and expenses, and they carry the information of only a single accounting period (however long that may be).

FACT

In the world of accounting, net activity has nothing to do with fishing or tennis, and everything to do with math. When you net accounts together, you combine their balances (positive and negative) to come up with how much they're worth as one lump. So if account A showed $10 and account B showed -$5, their net activity would be $5.

At the end of every accounting period, the temporary accounts get rolled up into permanent accounts. Then they are zeroed out to start the new period with a clean slate. What's the point of this? Permanent account balances are measured at a particular time; for instance, the cash balance on March 3, 2007. Temporary accounts are measured for a period of time, such as racking up $10,000 in sales during February 2007. Those temporary accounts need to be reset so you can begin tracking them again, but their overall net activity needs to be permanently added to the records by way of the permanent accounts.

Account Numbers

There is no part of accounting that doesn't involve numbers, and the accounts themselves are no different. In addition to a descriptive name, you will assign an account number to each. This cannot be done haphazardly, or it will wreak havoc on your records. Believe it or not, accounting is supposed to simplify how you deal with your business finances; doing everything according to tried-and-true systems can make everything so much easier.

This is the basic accounting convention. Asset account numbers start with 1, liability accounts with 2, equity accounts with 3, revenue accounts with 4, cost accounts with 5, and expense accounts with 6. Depending on how many accounts you have overall, you would add anywhere from one to ten digits to that first one. For example, if you have hundreds of accounts, you could use a three-digit account numbering system: Your cash account might be number 101, your inventory account 120, and your first fixed-asset account 150.

Understanding Assets

Assets are those things that your business owns, from the cash in your desk drawer to the file cabinet in the backroom to the delivery van in the driveway. It does not matter whether they are big or small; all that matters is that your company owns them and that they have monetary value. For that matter, they do not even have to be physical things: patents and copyrights, for example, count as assets even though you can't touch them. Also, anything your company has a legal right to get, such as future payment from a customer, is accounted for as an asset.

Since there are so many different kinds of assets, they get split into categories to make the accounting less cumbersome. There are four commonly used groupings, which are pretty standard across businesses:

- Current assets
- Investments
- Fixed assets (also called "property, plant, and equipment")
- Intangible assets

Current assets include anything that is expected to be turned into cash or used up within one year, such as inventory or cash itself. The investments category contains long-term holdings that are not really used in the normal course of business, such as mutual funds or municipal bonds. Fixed assets also have long lives, and they are regularly used to support regular operations; examples include trucks, desks, and computer systems. Finally, intangible assets are long-term assets that really have no physical form but are still worth money to the company, such as a patent or a trademark.

A Look at Liabilities

Every dime your business owes, no matter to whom or for what reason, is a liability. Owing someone a product (such as a magazine subscription) or a service (such as insurance coverage) counts as a liability as well.

Although there aren't as many kinds of liabilities as there are assets, liabilities also get broken out into groups. In your accounts you will have current liabilities and long-term liabilities. What differentiates them is when you have to pay them: Anything due within one year counts as current, and any debts that stretch further out than one year go into the long-term group. In most cases, current liabilities tend to be created through daily business activities (like purchasing inventory), and long-term liabilities tend to be loans.

For product-based companies, the biggest chunks of liabilities are usually the same: the business loan and the accounts payable. Service businesses tend to have the least debt, since they usually cost less to start up and don't have to maintain stocks of inventory. Service company debts often tend to be in the form of work for which a customer has paid in advance; a good example of this is lawyers who work on retainer. These liabilities often have names such as "unearned revenue" and virtually always belong in the current liabilities category.

When you look at a list of accounts, you will notice that most liability accounts have the word "payable" in their name. The rest of the name helps you determine just what that liability is payable for, such as sales tax payable or loan payable. The most unspecific name is accounts payable, which acts as a holding account for all the money you owe to all of your vendors in one big lump.

All about Equity

Equity represents how much of your company is really yours and not owed to someone else. Think of it in terms of your house: You own your house, but the bank probably has a claim on part of it, too, in the form of your mortgage. Here your house is your asset, your mortgage is your liability, and the part of your house that you truly own (the difference between its value and your outstanding mortgage balance) is your equity. It's exactly the same for business. You have your assets, you owe your liabilities, and you own your equity stake.

Equity does have a slightly tricky angle; its makeup depends on what type of business structure you choose for your company. As you will learn in Chapter 15, the different business structures include sole proprietorships, partnerships, limited liability companies, and corporations. The structure of your company dictates how the equity looks for accounting purposes and exactly what types of equity accounts will appear in your books.

The main split among equity accounts, common to all business types, is in which direction the capital is flowing. There are equity contributions, which means owners put more of their own cash into the company. There are equity withdrawals, which means owners take money out of the company, but not as regular salary. Finally, there is the temporary profit or loss that becomes a permanent piece of the equity account. As you might expect, profits increase your equity, while losses decrease it.

FACT

It's possible, and not uncommon, for new businesses to end up with negative equity after their first year or two in business. This happens when early losses are greater than your initial capital investment. Having negative equity shows that your business is struggling, but you still may be able to turn things around if you have some cash and a workable idea for boosting revenues.

Revenues, Costs, and Expenses

New and small-business owners tend to track their profit-related accounts more than any others. There's a good reason for this: Without pretty consistent profits, no business can survive for the long haul.

There are three numbers that go into figuring out profits: revenues, costs, and expenses. Every business has revenues (hopefully) and expenses (definitely). Only product-based businesses have costs. In the profit equation, you start with revenues, then deduct costs and expenses. When the result is positive, you have profits. When it's negative, your company has sustained a loss for the period.

ALERT!

It's very easy to confuse costs and expenses; after all, they seem like the same thing. In accounting, costs refer to the amount of money you have to spend to buy or make a product that you plan to sell to someone else. Expenses, on the other hand, exist whether you buy or make or sell anything.

In the profit equation, a product-based company with costs will see an additional and crucial subtotal called *gross profit* (when expressed as a percentage, it's called *gross margin*). That number represents the revenue left over once you take out the direct costs of the products you are selling. The gross profit tells you how much you have available to cover all the rest of your expenses, ideally leaving some net profit at the end.

Fine-Tuning Your Gross Profit

There are two components that go into your gross profit: the price you charge your customers for a product, and the amount it costs you to buy that product from your supplier. While you do have some control over costs, such as switching vendors, that control is pretty limited. Prices, on the other hand, are set completely at your discretion. The bigger the gap between your price and your cost, the higher your gross profit will be. The trick is to set your prices as high as possible without scaring off your customers; sales at slightly lower prices are much better than no sales at all.

FACT

Gross margin percentages vary widely by industry. Some have very high margins, of more than 50 percent; others have very tight margins of 10 percent to 15 percent. It really depends on the type of item you are selling, and how much markup the customers are willing to bear. For example, the margin on luxury items is normally much higher than the margin on groceries.

To figure out how much of your sales are going toward general expenses and profits, divide your gross profit by your sales to get the gross margin percentage. Here's an example: Suppose your sales are $20,000 and your costs are $15,000. That would give you a gross profit of $5,000 ($20,000 minus $15,000). Now take that gross profit of $5,000 and divide it by the sales of $20,000 to give you your gross margin percentage; in this case, 25 percent. That means 25 percent of every sales dollar is available to cover your expenses.

If you are in a low-margin industry, keeping a close eye on expenses is a good way to ensure bottom-line profitability. The other way is to generate a very high level of sales volume, but that can be harder to pull off. Especially for new or small businesses, strict expense management can make all the difference between profits and losses.

Expenses Mean Tax Deductions

When tax time rolls around, many small-business owners begin searching everywhere for receipts and invoices not yet accounted for. They try to remember every trip they made in the name of the company, every meeting they attended, every client lunch. They do this to make sure that every one of their expenses makes it into the accounting records for the year, and for good reason: Every dollar of expense translates into a reduction of income, and less income means a lower tax bill.

More things count as deductible expenses than you might think. For example, if you have to take courses to maintain a professional license, save the invoices and deduct those fees. When you drive to visit customer sites, every mile you travel goes toward deductible expenses (the mileage rate varies from year to year based on federal law). Other commonly overlooked business expenses include reference books, alarm systems, bank charges, and dry-cleaning of uniforms.

How the Accounts Connect

At some point, every type of account will interconnect with each of the others. Assets will be used to pay for expenses. Inventory products bought on account involve both assets and liabilities. Product sales hit both cost and revenue accounts. Owner withdrawals deplete both assets and equity. Every single transaction your business conducts involves at least two accounts, sometimes more, and they most often are of different types.

In addition to that, though, the accounts have to be in specific balance. The company's total assets must be exactly equal to its combined liabilities and equity. To get to that balance, the net result of combining the revenue, cost, and expense accounts must be folded into the equity account.

The Formal Connection

Periodically, you (or your accountant) will produce financial statements for your company. These statements are formal reports that lay out exactly

what has been going on for the preceding period, and where things stand right now.

There are three main financial statements that you will create: the balance sheet, the statement of profit and loss, and the statement of cash flows (you will learn about these in more detail in Chapter 14). The balance sheet provides a snapshot of your assets, liabilities, and equity on a particular date. The statement of profit and loss informs you of your revenues, costs, expenses, and business results (the profit or loss) for a specific time. Finally, the statement of cash flows shows you how the money came into and went out of your company during that same specific period; this statement typically includes every account type, because they all have some relationship with cash.

The Everyday Connection

For many small businesses, daily transactions include three types of accounts: revenues, expenses, and cash. These are the accounts that will be involved in the vast majority of transactions, and your checkbook will often be the first place that transactions are recorded. Bring products into the picture, and liabilities become an everyday account as well. Even though you won't necessarily see a daily entry in your equity accounts, they are impacted by every revenue and expense transaction.

At the most basic level, though, the connections among the accounts are what keep your business flowing. You use a combination of liabilities and equity to purchase assets. Assets are your company's resources, and you use them to create revenue, some directly and some indirectly. For example, there's a clear link between inventory and revenue production, but your computer also can bring in revenue. You can use your computer to create invoices, design promotional flyers, keep your books in order, even learn more about your industry and find new ways to bring in customers. Expenses also go directly toward revenue production; you can't run a company without phones and electricity and pens. Those revenues and expenses come together, hopefully with revenues greater than expenses, to create additional equity.

Debits and Credits

One of the most basic—and most confusing—concepts of accounting is debits and credits. That is usually one of the first things taught, and one of the later things that clicks, in basic accounting courses. The debit-credit scheme, though, is at the bottom of every accounting system. Once you have a grasp on how debits and credits work, you will understand much more easily how the whole system works.

Every single accounting transaction has a debit side and a credit side, and the two have to be equal. The word "side" here is crucial: in old-fashioned, traditional manual accounting systems (where each account looks like a T), all debits go on the left and all credits go on the right.

Here's the tricky part. Some accounts are increased by debits; some are decreased. In the same way, some accounts are increased by credits, and others are decreased. Whether a debit acts like an addition or subtraction completely depends on the type of account you are working with. Check out the following table to see which accounts work in which ways.

Account Type	Debit	Credit
Asset	Increase	Decrease
Liability	Decrease	Increase
Equity	Decrease	Increase
Revenue	Decrease	Increase
Expense	Increase	Decrease

Sometimes It's the Opposite

There are some accounts that act completely the opposite of the other accounts in their group. For example, there are asset accounts with normal credit balances, and sales accounts with normal debit balances. These special accounts are called contra accounts, because they act contrary to the norm.

Although contra accounts may seem puzzling, they serve a very clear purpose. They can help you separate certain kinds of transactions from their "parent" account, giving you a clearer picture of what's really going on. Sometimes that breakdown is very important and can impact your future business strategies and policies.

For example, suppose your company sells sweaters. Most of those sales will be final, but there are bound to be some returns. If you just lumped those returns into your sales account, sort of like negative sales, you would have no way of knowing later on how much you sold altogether and how much was returned. Instead, you would just see one lower sales number with no breakdown. For planning purposes, though, it's important to know what percentage of your sweater sales resulted in returns. An expected percentage might not cause you to take action, but a much higher percentage probably would.

Breaking Down a Transaction

As you've already learned, every transaction has both a debit and a credit component. That does not mean that it has a plus and a minus (although that may happen sometimes), or that one account balance will go up while another goes down (which may also happen). It means that there will be a left-side impact and a right-side impact. How those affect the accounts involved depends wholly on what kind of accounts they are.

For example, suppose you write a check to pay the company's electric bill. That transaction would result in a debit to electricity expense and a credit to cash. Your electricity expense is increased, and cash decreased. If you change that transaction a little, the account impact changes, too. Suppose you paid that electric bill with a credit card; you would still debit electricity expense, but now the credit would go to credit card payable, a liability account. In that case, the expense account increases, and so does the liability account (because now you owe more).

A month later, you pay that credit card bill. That transaction includes a debit to credit card payable and a credit to cash. Credit card payable, the liability account, gets decreased with a debit (the payment reduced your balance). The cash account, an asset, is decreased as well, but this account is decreased with a credit entry.

chapter 3

Keeping Track of Transactions

Accounting is all about recording transactions, kind of like a financial diary for your business. Depending on the type of business you have, you may have hundreds of transactions every day, or just a few every week. The trick is to keep current and record your transactions as you go along. Once you know the what, where, and when of recording transactions, you will be able to keep your books up to date very easily.

What Counts as a Transaction

A business transaction takes place when an event that can be measured in terms of money has occurred. There are dozens, probably hundreds, of events that happen in any business on any given day that have no monetary effect: opening the mail, talking on the phone, and writing letters, for example. Turning those occurrences into transactions takes only one thing, and that is money. If that envelope held a customer check, you have a recordable transaction. If that phone call resulted in a sale, you have a transaction.

Most companies have the same general transactions, and those get repeated all the time. Common transactions include:

- Making sales
- Collecting money
- Paying bills
- Paying employees
- Paying taxes
- Receiving inventory
- Buying equipment

Every transaction affects changes in specific accounts, changing what you owe or what you own. When you record a transaction, you have to know which accounts are affected, and how; when the transaction took place; and its dollar value (even if no money has changed hands yet).

When to Record Transactions

In accounting, as in most other things, timing is everything. That applies to transactions themselves, in two different ways. The first involves the day the transaction actually took place (for example, you buy a box of copy paper and tell the store to bill your company). The second comes into play when money changes hands (you send out a check for that paper). These two things may happen at the same time (for instance, if you paid for the paper while you were still in the store), but equally as often they won't. The trick is knowing at which time you'll record the transaction, and that depends on the accounting method you decide to use for your business.

You have two distinct options to choose from for your overall accounting method: cash or accrual. The cash method, more commonly used by small businesses, means you record transactions only when money changes hands. Using this method, you wouldn't write up that paper purchase in your books until the day you wrote the check. The accrual method, which some companies have to use, requires that you record transactions as they occur regardless of the money factor. Under this method, you would write up the transaction on the day you got the paper, then use a second transaction to record the payment.

Cash Accounting

When it comes to choosing an accounting method, cash wins hands down over accrual. It's easier to understand: you record transactions when cash changes hands. It gives you a little leeway at year-end to minimize taxable income: you can pay a bunch of expenses early to reduce your profits and your tax bill for this year, and you pay taxes only on the cash you have actually received this year. Plus, it's simpler to keep your books; since all transactions involve cash, you need to write out only the accounts involved in the entry.

FACT

When you use cash accounting, virtually your entire bookkeeping system can be run through your checkbook. As long as you record every check you write and every deposit you make, you will have most of your daily accounting chores taken care of. Typically, the only extra recording comes in when you pay cash for some expenses (such as stamps).

There is a drawback to this much-preferred method, though. It doesn't track your revenues and expenses as they happen—only when there's a payment. Knowing exactly when the original transactions occurred could come in very handy for planning purposes, because you would know definitely the actual period in which the expense was incurred or revenue earned.

In addition, there are some companies that cannot use cash accounting, according to IRS regulations. If your company has inventory, you can't use cash accounting. You also can't use this method if your company is formed as a C corporation, or if your gross revenues are more than $5 million a year (a very good problem to have). If you aren't sure whether your company can use the cash method, check with a tax accountant.

Accrual Accounting

Using the accrual accounting method is a bit more complicated than the cash method, but it can provide you with better information. Keeping your books in this way requires double-entry accounting, which means you always have to specify which two accounts (or more, when applicable) are affected by any transaction. This is different from the cash method, because in that case, it is assumed that no matter which account you write the transaction to, the other one is the cash account.

The basic rule of accrual accounting is to record transactions as they happen, even if no cash is involved. You record every revenue as it is earned, and every expense as it is incurred. The underlying accounting principle here is called the matching principle: you match revenues and expenses to the period in which they actually took place.

With the accrual method, the noncash entries are the ones that impact your bottom line. Their purpose is to record revenues and expenses right now. When you do pay those expenses or receive those customer checks, those transactions have no effect on your profits, since the transactions involve only assets and liabilities.

When you buy supplies on account, you record the transaction on the day you bought the supplies. When you make a sale to a client, you record the sale that day, even if your invoice doesn't ask him to pay you for another thirty days. Of course, when the cash does eventually change hands, you will have another transaction to record. Having to record those extra entries is one of the drawbacks of accrual accounting. The other drawback has a bigger impact on your bank account: you have to pay income taxes on revenues you have earned, even if you have not yet been paid.

Setting Up Your Accounts

Every accounting system needs accounts, and every account will fit into one of the standard account categories (such as assets or revenues). When you start out in business, it can be difficult to anticipate every single account you are ever going to need. Instead of trying to do that, it's better to focus on core accounts that are common to virtually every business. Then you can add on the more specialized accounts you need to run your company.

FACT

There's a standard system for numbering the different types of accounts, and it's embedded into virtually all packaged accounting software. As long as you follow the standard numbering convention, your reports will print correctly. If you choose to make up your own account numbering system, you may have to reset every report within the program.

When talking about accounts, you tend to use their names: cash, postage expense, payroll. In the accounting system, though, you will assign distinct numbers to each account. The combination of the number and the name serves as a unique identifier for each account and can help avoid recording transactions in the wrong accounts. Once you have all your accounts named and numbered, you will list them in account number order; that listing is known as the chart of accounts, and it will come in handy when you are getting started.

Similar and Different Accounts

Almost every company uses the same standard accounts for its assets and liabilities. The differences mainly come in with equity, revenues, costs, and expenses, because these are more dependent on the type of business you have.

Your equity setup depends entirely on your business structure. Sole proprietors have a single capital account and owner withdrawal accounts; the withdrawal accounts are often split out into personal categories, so owners can track things such as personal deductible expenses and estimated income tax payments more easily. Partnerships have one capital account and at least one withdrawal account for each partner, so there will be at least two of each of those accounts. Corporations' equity is completely different, made up of at least one stock account and an account called *retained earnings*. (For more information about equity accounts, see Chapter 15.)

QUESTION?

Do I have to deal with sales taxes?

That depends on the laws in each state where you do business. In some states, only products are taxable; others impose sales tax on services as well. Many states have varying sales tax rates for different types of items. Check with the state sales tax office in any state where you have sales to learn its requirements.

Revenue accounts should match your major products or services. Sometimes, revenues are also broken down into taxable and nontaxable sales to make things easier when it comes time to file your sales tax return. Your cost accounts will match your revenue accounts; if your product revenues are split up, your cost accounts will be, too. As for expenses, some are common to every business (such as phone and electricity), while others may be unique to your industry (waiting room magazines, for example).

Assigning Account Numbers

Even among the same types of accounts, there's a method to the numbering scheme. In the asset section (where the numbers all start with 1), cash always comes first; if you have three cash accounts, those would be your first three listed accounts. Then come other current assets, in their order of liquidity. Accounts receivable would come before inventory, for instance. After you've numbered all current assets, start on the fixed assets;

most of the time, the first entry here gets number 150. Each fixed asset is listed separately and usually alphabetically. The final entry in the fixed-asset group will be the accumulated depreciation account. If you have intangible assets, they come next, followed by their accumulated amortization account.

Account numbers for liabilities (which start with 2s) work basically the same way. Current liabilities come first, usually starting with accounts payable. When you switch to long-term liability numbering, start with account number 250 to show a clear segregation; that will be useful as you begin to add accounts, because it will be easier to figure out where they go. The specific equity accounts (all starting with 3) differ based on your business entity, but the numbering scheme remains the same. You start with the capital itself, whether it's a partner's capital account or total shares of stock outstanding. That is followed with drawing or dividend accounts, then prior and current earnings.

Your revenue accounts will start with 4s. Depending on your type of business, you may have several revenue accounts, or merely one. If you sell both services and products, you have to separate them for accounting purposes. However, you may want to further break down sales for your own tracking purposes; for example, taxable and nontaxable, or clothing and accessories. Cost accounts (which start with 5s) track your sold inventory, no matter what kind of products you sell. If you've decided to split up your sales accounts, you may want to mirror them with the connected product cost accounts. Expenses (which all start with 6s) are often just listed in alphabetical order, allowing enough room in between to insert new categories as necessary.

A Sample Chart of Accounts

A complete chart of accounts could fill several pages, so here you will see more of a skeleton version to give you the basic idea. This setup is for a retail company that sells two products only: hammers and nails. The company is set up as a sole proprietorship.

Chart of Accounts

Account Number	Account Name	Account Type
100	Cash	Asset
110	Accounts Receivable	Asset
120	Inventory—Hammers	Asset
121	Inventory—Nails	Asset
130	Prepaid Expenses	Asset
150	Fixed Assets	Asset
180	Accumulated Depreciation	Asset
200	Accounts Payable	Liability
210	Payroll Taxes Payable	Liability
220	Sales Taxes Payable	Liability
250	Long-Term Loan Payable	Liability
300	Rob Smith, Capital	Equity
350	Rob Smith, Withdrawals	Equity
400	Sales—Hammers	Revenue
401	Sales—Nails	Revenue
450	Sales Returns	Revenue
500	Cost of Goods Sold—Hammers	Cost
501	Cost of Goods Sold—Nails	Cost
610	Accounting & Legal	Expense
615	Advertising	Expense
630	Depreciation	Expense
640	Insurance	Expense
645	Interest	Expense
660	Payroll	Expense
661	Payroll Taxes	Expense
670	Rent	Expense
675	Repairs & Maintenance	Expense
680	Utilities	Expense

Most companies will have more accounts than this, and some of these basic accounts may be split out in a more meaningful manner. For example, you may have three cash accounts: cash on hand (also known as petty cash), regular checking, and payroll checking. Those would require three separate accounts in your chart.

Meet the General Ledger

The general ledger is like a file cabinet for all your accounts. Each account gets its own page, and every entry that affects that account is recorded there. In that way, the general ledger acts as a summary of your journals, which are books where all the transactions originally are recorded. Rather than duplicate the line-by-line entries, you will transfer daily or weekly totals (depending on your transaction volume) to each account's general ledger page.

For accounts that attract lots of volume, you can use subsidiary ledgers to hold more detail, and use summary totals from there to fill out your general ledger. You will also use a subsidiary ledger to keep track of the detail that makes up your accounts receivable and accounts payable accounts. The accounts receivable ledger contains a page for each customer that your company extends credit to; the accounts payable ledger has a separate page for each vendor that lets your company buy on credit.

What a Ledger Page Looks Like

The general ledger serves to sort transaction information by account, and that includes specific details. To keep things consistent, the necessary pieces of information are recorded in columns. That way, if you need to go back to look up something for a particular account, the information is laid out for you in a uniform way, making it easier to find.

The basic columns in a general ledger include things such as the date, the dollar amount of the debit or credit, posting information (which you'll learn about later in this chapter), and a brief description of the transaction. For example, the page for postage expense in the general ledger might look like this:

Postage Expense					
Date	Description	Journal	Debit	Credit	Balance
3/04/06	sent package to client	CJ2	15.60		15.60
3/16/06	bought stamps	CJ2	37.00		52.60

CJ2 stands for Cash Journal, page 2

Checking the Balance

While some accounts, such as expenses, tend to have mainly debit or credit entries, there are others that have a mix of both (such as cash). When an account has both debit and credit entries, it's very common to make mistakes in the balance column, and that can affect reports going forward.

Every once in a while, add all the entries in each column to get a total at the bottom (this is called footing the columns). Then combine the debit and credit columns to make sure that their total matches the total balance column (this is called crossfooting). If they don't equal now, there is a mistake somewhere in one of the columns, probably the balance column. Recheck your math in the balance column to find and correct the mistake.

The Daily Journals

When accounting was strictly a pencil-and-paper gig, journals were books containing pages and pages of transactions. Because that was the place where all transactions were first recorded, journals are called the books of original entry. Now, most journal work is done using a computer, making the old paper journals nearly obsolete.

Inside a journal, you can find a chronological listing of your company's daily transactions. Each entry contains a full picture of one transaction, and this is the only place where the transaction appears as a whole. In addition, journal entries typically include a description, something for you to look back at should questions arise.

Most companies tend to have the same transactions over and over. For the transactions that take place more frequently, such as sales, you can use one of the standard special journals (in this case, the sales journal). There are four special journals that you may use: sales, purchases, cash receipts, and cash payments (also known as disbursements). Transactions that don't occur very often are recorded in the general journal, a kind of catchall for things that don't really fit anywhere more specific. The general journal is also the place for adjustments and closing entries (for the temporary accounts).

What a General Journal Page Looks Like

A journal page looks like a transaction diary, detailing everything that took place during the business day. A standard journal entry contains at least three lines: one for the debit account, one for the credit account, and one for the transaction description. An entry can have more than one debit and more than one credit. As long as the total entry balances, meaning that the debits equal the credits, you can have as many of each as necessary to completely record what took place.

When you write up a journal entry, always write the debit account flush left in the column. That line (or lines, if there are multiple debit accounts) comes first. The next line contains the credit side of the entry. When you write the credit account, always indent toward the right, to indicate the shift.

Most general journals have five columns. The first is for the date of the transaction, which may not match the date on which you record the transaction. The second is for the account names affected by the transaction, or an explanation of what took place. Third comes the posting reference, where you would write down the account number after you posted this information to the general ledger (posting is covered in detail in the next section). The last two columns hold the debits and credits. You can't have both on the same line, and the total debits must equal the total credits.

General Journal Page				
Date	**Account & Explanation**	**Post Ref**	**Debit**	**Credit**
02/04/06	Rent Expense		$650.00	
	Cash			$650.00
Paid ABC Holdings rent for February 2006				

The Sales Journal

If you have a business, you have sales, and hopefully a lot of them. Sales transactions are among the most frequent for any business, and that earns them a special journal. The point of the sales journal is to minimize your task by getting rid of some of the labor involved in manual bookkeeping. Where the general journal requires at least three lines for every entry, a single line is all you need to record sales transactions in the sales journal.

Because it's the sales journal, you already know that every regular transaction will hit the sales account as a credit. There also is only one choice for the debit side: accounts receivable. If you have a buy now, pay later arrangement with the customer, accounts receivable will get the debit. If you got paid at the time of the sale (whether it was actual cash or a check or major credit card), the debit account would be cash, and that would be entered in the cash receipts journal instead of the sales journal. Here's what a couple of typical entries in the sales journal would look like:

The Sales Journal				
Date	**Account to Debit**	**Invoice No.**	**Post Ref.**	**Amount**
02/14/06	Bob Jones	151		185.60
02/15/06	Donna Reed, n/60	152		355.50

In the second line, the n/60 refers to special sales terms for this customer.

The customer name is the most crucial part of the transactions you enter in the sales journal. Without that, you wouldn't know whom to bill or for how much. If the terms of a sale are different from the norm for that customer, you should enter that in the journal as well. For example, if you usually let Donna Reed pay you thirty days after a sale, but this time you told her that she could take sixty days to pay, make sure to record that information when you book the transaction; otherwise, thirty days from now, you may not remember that deal.

The Purchases Journal

Product-based companies have to get the things they sell from somewhere, whether it's in the form of finished goods or raw materials. The companies you buy your inventory from are your suppliers, and you count as their customer. In most cases, these types of supplier relationships involve buying on credit. That's where the purchases journal comes in so handy. It's like the flip side of the sales journal; every debit goes to the inventory account, and every credit goes to accounts payable.

Most companies use the purchases journal only to record transactions that involve inventory. However, some also use this to record any type of purchase made on account, whether it's for inventory or equipment or office supplies. If you use your purchases journal as a catchall, you will need an extra column to identify your debit account.

Although the purchases journal is used mainly to track inventory purchases, other items that are included in inventory costs may be recorded here as well. These items may include things such as sales tax or freight (to have the products delivered to your company). If you track these costs separately but still want to enter them in your purchases journal, you simply need to include extra debit columns, dedicated to these inventory add-ons.

Again, the point of the purchases journal is to save you time and effort, allowing you to record transactions with a single-line entry. Since on-account purchases are made regularly and frequently (for product-based companies), the use of a special journal is called for. When you do pay cash for your purchases, do not record them in your purchases journal; rather, write them up in the cash disbursements journal. This is similar to cash sales going into the cash receipts journal rather than the sales journal.

Purchases Journal (with extra columns)						
Date	Account to Credit	Post Ref	A/P Credit	Purchases Debit	Sales Tax Debit	Freight Debit
2/12/06	Ken's Crafts		181.55	140.00	16.55	25.00
2/13/06	Lou's Lampshades		200.00	200.00		

The Cash Journals

Since cash is involved in more, and more diverse, transactions than any other account, it merits two special journals. The cash receipts journal holds all transactions for which cash is debited; the cash payments journal carries all the transactions for which the cash account is credited. That's because any time you receive cash, it increases your cash account; and cash, an asset account, gets increased by a debit. Whenever you pay cash, it decreases your account, calling for a credit entry.

FACT

To avoid potential problems with having numerous debits and credits recorded in the same place, early accountants began the practice of putting cash transactions into two separate journals. When you use this system, you don't have to worry about whether a number should be added or subtracted, because they all go the same way.

The cash receipts journal comes with several credit columns, because cash can come in from different sources. Typical columns include sales, accounts receivable, and a miscellaneous column to hold any other accounts. Similarly, the cash payments journal comes with some standard debit columns, such as accounts payable and purchases, plus a catchall column. However, if you find yourself paying a particular expense with cash very frequently (or collecting cash from an unusual source frequently), you can always add your own special column. Anything that cuts down on your data entry demands is a good thing!

The cash journals look very similar to the other special journals; only the column headings are really different. Both cash journals have the standard columns of date, account to debit or credit, and posting reference. Then they have columns for the usual debit or credit accounts (for instance, accounts receivable and sales in the case of cash receipts), followed by a general account debit or credit column, and the cash column. In the cash receipts journal, the cash column is for debits; in the cash payments journal, the cash column holds only credits.

It's All in the Posting

The journals are where all the daily bookkeeping activities take place. Periodically, that information is transferred to the ledger to update each account. That transfer is called *posting*, and it's a critical part of the full accounting process.

With computerized systems, the posting process can be performed automatically, as soon as transactions are recorded. Some programs give you the option of real-time posting or periodic posting (meaning some time later); which you would use depends on your transaction volume and computer capacity. For manual bookkeeping systems, though, periodic posting is the only way to go, even if you do it every day at closing time.

Posting manually is a pretty straightforward process. You start with the first new journal entry and see which accounts are involved. You record the debit part of the transaction on the appropriate account page in the general ledger, marking down which journal page the transaction came from. Then you go back to the journal page, and indicate the account number to which you posted the information. Repeat the process for the credit side of the entry. If there are multiple debits or credits in a single transaction, post each line item separately to the general ledger.

Posting from the Special Journals

Using special journals doesn't only cut down your journal entry time; it also saves you a lot of posting time. Unlike posting from the general journal, where you must individually post each line item from every transaction, special journals allow for summary posting. At the end of every period or every page, you calculate the column totals, then post the totals to the appropriate general ledger accounts.

For example, instead of posting each line in the sales journal to your sales and accounts receivable general ledger accounts, you simply post periodic lump-sum totals. That helps make your busiest accounts easier to manage. How often you make this summary post depends on your transaction volume and how often you want to know where your accounts stand. At the very least, you must post the totals at the end of the accounting period.

ALERT!

Before you post column totals, make sure to crossfoot your columns. This will help you root out any errors before they hit the general ledger, where they may be much more difficult to track down. Ideally, you will foot and crossfoot every time you complete a journal page, as well as at the end of an accounting period.

Posting to the Special Ledgers

Accounts receivable and accounts payable both hold summary information for a lot of underlying accounts. Accounts receivable includes everything your customers owe you, and accounts payable includes everything you owe to your suppliers. Chances are, though, that you have a lot of different customers and use at least a few different suppliers. For each, you have to track the individual balance, and that would get extremely unwieldy if you tried to fit it all on the main general ledger account pages.

For that reason, both accounts receivable and accounts payable have special subledgers. Where the general ledger holds detail information for each separate account, the subledgers hold the detail data for each customer and vendor account. Rather than posting specific transaction information to the general ledger, you first post transactions involving accounts payable and accounts receivable to the special subledgers. Then you make a summary entry to the general ledger accounts.

In addition to verifying the journal column balances before you make that summary posting to the general ledger, you must also make sure that your subledger totals agree with those general ledger account balances. For example, the total of all of your customer account balances must equal the total accounts receivable balance; likewise, the total of your individual vendor balances has to tie to the accounts payable balance.

Checking It Twice

With all those numbers floating around, mistakes are inevitable. One way to catch mistakes (though this is by no means foolproof) is to prepare a report called a trial balance. A trial balance is basically a listing of every account and its balance, with debit balances on the left and credit balances on the right. The total debits are supposed to equal the total credits, but they sometimes do not balance on the initial run-through. If your debit and credit balances are out of whack, you know there is a mistake in there somewhere.

ALERT!

When you uncover an accounting mistake, you can't just erase it or cross it out; you have to write up a correcting journal entry to put the affected accounts back in the right balance. These entries are recorded in the general journal and identified as correcting entries.

The trial balance can also help you find wrong balance accounts. These are accounts with the wrong side balances; for example, an asset account with a credit balance, when all asset accounts should have debit balances. In most cases, the error is caused by either a simple misposting or math mistake.

Different Kinds of Mistakes

With so many accounts, and so many different places that the numbers show up, it is literally impossible to be completely error-proof—even when you're using a computerized accounting program. There are also many different kinds of possible mistakes; catching and correcting them depends on the type of mistake made.

The most common accounting mistakes include:

- Math errors (such as adding a column of numbers incorrectly)
- Using the wrong account in a journal entry
- Mixing up the debits and credits in a journal entry
- Posting to the wrong ledger account
- Posting the wrong dollar amount to the ledger account
- Posting a debit as a credit (or vice versa)

Some of these mistakes keep your trial balance from balancing; others don't, and those errors are much more difficult to spot. For example, posting the wrong dollar amount to the ledger account will upset the balance, but posting the right dollar amount to the wrong ledger account will not. When you have been doing the accounting work for a while, you will become familiar enough with the accounts to notice when something seems out of whack, even when your trial balance balances perfectly.

Finding and Fixing Mistakes

If your trial balance doesn't balance, the first thing you should do is add up both the debit and credit columns again. A lot of the time, that will solve the problem. When that quick fix doesn't work, it's time to move on to step two.

Step two is figuring out the difference. You can do that by subtracting the debit column total from the credit column total. If the difference is divisible by nine, that usually indicates a transposed number. Double-check the numbers you've picked up from the ledger; one of them will probably have been copied incorrectly. When that difference isn't divisible by nine, check to see what happens when you divide it by two. If that comes out to an even number, or a number that seems very familiar, it's quite likely that a debit has been posted as a credit (or the other way around) in one of the accounts. That calls for a quick look through the general ledger to find the account with the misposting. Other times, a completely wrong number gets picked up, such as posting an amount from one journal entry to an account from the next. Correcting this usually takes going through both the ledger and the journal until you locate the mistake.

Other types of mistakes—the ones that won't knock your trial balance out of balance—are nearly impossible to find without a solid acquaintance with your accounts. You will really only notice that an account balance is off when you know approximately what that balance should have been. That just takes experience in doing the books.

Transposed numbers are among the biggest headaches in accounting. A transposition error occurs when you inadvertently switch the order of the digits in an amount, such as recording $19 as $91. It also happens if you skip a zero at the end, recording $450 as $45, for instance. Transposition errors always result in a difference that can be evenly divided by nine.

Fixing mistakes depends on where they occurred. Mistakes made in the journal entry phase require a correcting entry in the general journal. To do that, you have to identify the accounts involved, and the amount by which each is off; then you write up an entry that makes up the difference. For example, suppose you debited insurance expense for $50 instead of debiting interest expense for that amount. To correct the error, you would debit interest expense for $50 and credit insurance expense for the same amount. For a posting error, you can simply add a line on the ledger page to correct the balance and include an explanation for the entry.

The Accounting Cycle

You now know about the bulk of what goes into the accounting cycle (the process that starts with a transaction and ends with financial statements). In fact, the entire accounting cycle can be summed up in eight basic steps. The first three have been covered in detail in this chapter; the other five will be explained more fully in Chapters 13 and 14.

1. Write up transactions in the daily journals.
2. Post journal entries to the appropriate ledgers.

3. Prepare a trial balance of all general ledger accounts.
4. Create your working trial balance, complete with adjusting entries.
5. Enter those adjusting entries into the general journal and post them to the general ledger.
6. Prepare your financial statements.
7. Close out your temporary accounts.
8. Create a postclosing trial balance.

The five new steps have to do with end-of-period wrap-up. Those steps are designed to give you financial statements to analyze and a clean accounting slate to go forward. Then the accounting cycle begins all over.

chapter 4

Setting Up a System

The easiest way to keep your accounting under control is to put a system in place. All of the numbers you have to track came from somewhere, need to go somewhere else, and need to be easy to find two years from now. The most important aspect of your system is that it's easy for *you* to create and maintain. Make it simple and stay on top of it so all of the day-to-day stuff will flow that much more smoothly.

Get (and Stay) Organized

By now you have probably realized that accounting involves dozens of forms, hundreds of other pieces of paper, and thousands upon thousands of numbers. Keeping track of all of that information can be tricky. Having a system in place that tells you how to fill out every form, what you need from every piece of paper, and where each of those numbers goes makes the whole thing easily manageable. The hard part is putting the system in place.

It sounds obvious, but the first things you need to keep your accounting data organized are a file cabinet and some clearly labeled file folders. You should keep one set of files for your vendors, another for general expenses, and a third for customers. In addition, you need to set up a file for each asset and liability that shows up in your books. Finally, you also need to maintain files for your tax returns. Believe it or not, just having a place to put each piece of paper (and there will be a lot of them) makes your job much easier.

That physical organization is just one piece of the puzzle, though. You also need to come up with procedures for your accounting tasks. Having a single standard way of doing things will streamline your tasks and make it much easier when you turn over the job to someone else. Daily transactions can pile up quickly if you don't enter them in the journals automatically as they occur. Your accounts won't tell you anything if you haven't posted to them recently. Finally, you can't produce even rough financial statements if your general ledger isn't up to date. Developing a routine is pretty much the only way to get a handle on this considerable work; without one, the book-keeping can get away from you before you know it.

Easy Retrieval

One of the most important features of your setup is how easy it is to retrieve documents when you need them—and you will need them. Having the most organized file cabinet on the planet won't help you if you don't file your paperwork on a pretty regular basis. Being in business generates a lot of paper, and you will have times when you need to find an invoice or a receipt *right now.* Sometimes it's only frustrating to have to search around for a document, but at other times it can cost your company money.

Suppose your company is selected for audit by the IRS (a situation that comes up a lot for small businesses but is not nearly as scary as you might imagine). The IRS asks to see your receipts for travel, meals, and entertainment for the year. If you can't find all the backup documentation, part of your expense deduction could be disallowed. If the IRS discounts some of your expenses, that increases your taxable income, which means a new tax bill, usually accompanied by penalties and interest.

FACT

There are times when missing a receipt or two won't be a problem with the IRS. As long as you have most of your receipts, and they're all pretty similar, you probably won't lose the deduction for a couple that have been misplaced.

Here's another scenario. A customer sends you a purchase order asking for fifty yellow sweaters at $20 apiece. You pack and ship the order and send an invoice for $1,000. The customer calls back, angry, and claims he ordered orange sweaters for $10 each. He says he'll keep the order if you knock off $500; otherwise he's sending the whole thing back. If you can't find his original purchase order, you have no way of proving that you filled the order correctly. If you let him keep the order, you'll be out $500; if you don't let him keep it, you will lose this sale, probably lose the customer, and pay for shipping costs twice.

To avoid situations like these, it's crucial to keep your files organized and up-to-date. It should be easy for anyone to find the paperwork you need (in case you aren't there to pull it). In addition to potentially saving your company some hard-earned money, being organized will help save your most precious resource: your time.

Staying on Top of Recordkeeping

To keep your records properly, you have to follow the standard recordkeeping order of tasks. Going out of order can mess up your books and will require a lot of correcting work at the end of the accounting period. Since one of the goals of your system is efficiency (which includes not having to do the same thing twice), following the right task sequence is critical. For example, you have to write up journal entries before you post to the general ledger, and you must prepare a trial balance that balances before you can move on to the next accounting period.

Until your accounting chores become automatic, it helps to keep a calendar of which tasks need to be done at which times. You usually back into this chore calendar: first you figure out your deadlines for government filings (such as sales tax or income tax), then work backward to figure out which tasks need to be done by then. For example, if you have to file a sales tax return on March 31, you need to verify your total taxable sales before that. The other factor that will come into play is your transaction volume. A high transaction volume requires more daily work just to stay current; companies with low transaction volume (fewer than twenty transactions per week) can implement a weekly schedule.

It's very easy to let the bookkeeping lapse, especially when you are doing it yourself. This is where many small-business owners get in trouble, but that trouble is easy to avoid. There are some bookkeeping tasks that you deal with every single day: You close sales, write checks, make bank deposits. What is neglected is journal recordings and postings, which may give you some extra time right now but will leave you with a real time crunch at the end of the accounting period.

The key is to do whatever you have to in order to keep up with the bookkeeping. When you don't, you face a potential loss of money and a definite loss of time. It's much harder to get things straight when an error occurred months ago; it's even tough to remember the details of transactions that happened as recently as last week. However, when you make it a practice of at least recording journal entries every day or two, you'll be able to re-create transactions much more easily. On top of that, your business does have deadlines to comply with, mostly tax-related. If your bookkeeping isn't up to date, you risk late filing (and that sets off interest and penalties) or filing with incorrect numbers (which means you'll have to file an amended return, which may be subject to interest and penalties).

Software Makes It Simpler

The easiest way to get your bookkeeping done is to have someone else do it. That's not always practical (especially from a cash-flow perspective) and not always a good idea for someone trying to get a handle on his business finances.

FACT

Simply using a computer does not mean you have a computerized system. For example, typing your entries into a Microsoft Excel spreadsheet is not the same as using dedicated accounting software. While the spreadsheet will help with some of the math, it will not take care of any posting or reporting tasks on its own.

In the beginning, using accounting software may seem very awkward and time-consuming, but that will pass. Once you get used to the program, the entries will practically enter themselves. Most of the more popular versions try to make information entry as simple as possible, with their screen forms looking a lot like the paper kind. For example, entering the information to pay a vendor shows up looking like a check from your checkbook; entering sales takes the form of a standard invoice.

Unless you have an overwhelming reason not to, using accounting software is really the way to go. That said, you still need to know what's going on behind the scenes—such as how journal entries work, and what posting does. Without this base of knowledge, you may be able to get by with the software, but your accountant will probably have a lot of fix-it work to do at year-end (and that can add a lot to your bill). When you understand the basics of accounting and bookkeeping, you will be able to take full advantage of your software and all its features.

How Software Can Help You

There are probably dozens of reasons why a computerized system makes more sense than a manual one, but these three should be enough to convince you:

- It won't make calculation mistakes.
- You'll never have to post transactions to the ledger.
- Reports can be generated automatically.

Using accounting software will save you countless hours during the year, and that time can be better spent on building your business. On top of that, the programs give you instant access to account balances and special reports. If you want to know how much your biggest customer owes and how long the amount has been outstanding, all you have to do is click your mouse a couple of times and print a report. These programs are very versatile, and many even come with enhanced report capabilities that allow you to customize virtually any information you need, with just a click of the mouse.

Which Program Should You Use?

When it comes to selecting accounting software, there are only two factors you have to consider: which one your accountant can work with, and which is the easiest for you to work with. Other than that, there is not much difference in how they perform. There are folks who swear by Peachtree, and others who love their QuickBooks (these are the two programs most commonly used by small businesses).

Before you buy the full version of any accounting software, which generally costs $150 to $250, ask the manufacturer for a trial version. Most trial versions give you full functionality, but only for thirty days; after that, you either have to buy the full version or switch to something else. Ask your accountant which program she uses for her small-business clients, and try that one. If you like it, stick with it; if not, try something else (your accountant will still be able to work with you at tax time). As soon as you find software you can work with comfortably, buy it.

Mapping Out Your Accounting Processes

You can start to develop your regular accounting procedures by separating your tasks by expected frequency: daily, weekly, monthly, quarterly, or yearly. General accounting chores will fall into each category, but tax-related tasks typically come up no more than monthly.

Every business will have unique needs, and your task schedule can be tailored to match whatever your company requires. Until you have a good feel for how things flow, though, the schedule laid out in this chapter is likely to be suitable.

To keep on top of your regular recordkeeping, enter transactions in the journals daily. Post to the ledgers at least weekly; if your company has a high transaction volume, post transactions more frequently. Once transactions have hit the ledgers, file the corresponding paperwork so you'll be able to easily locate any documents you need.

ALERT!

Some accounting and tax chores may differ depending on your company's legal structure. For example, some corporations have to file quarterly reports, whereas partnerships and sole proprietorships almost never do. Sole proprietors and partners, though, have to pay personal quarterly tax estimates; corporate owners or shareholders may not.

Daily and Weekly Tasks

For many small businesses, the first five items on the following list will be daily tasks; the rest will be weekly. However, only you can judge your company's transaction volume and tailor the schedule accordingly. For example, with a very light transaction volume, you may want to shift more items to your weekly list.

1. Sort your mail into action piles (such as bills to pay and orders to fill).
2. Inspect and stock any incoming inventory orders, and record the purchase transactions in your purchases journal.
3. Process any new customer orders, record all sales transactions, and mail out any new accounts receivable invoices.
4. Gather the day's cash and checks, make up a deposit slip, and put any necessary entries in your cash receipts journal (and checkbook).

5. Pay any invoices that are due or for which you can get an early payment discount.
6. Record any checks that you've written in your cash payments journal.
7. Record any cash transactions in the appropriate cash journal.
8. Record any other transactions of the day in the appropriate journals.
9. Post all journal transactions to the ledger accounts.

Monthly Tasks

In addition to whichever daily or weekly tasks fall at the end of the month, make time to deal with all the recordkeeping and tax-oriented month-end chores. These tasks are often more complex than journalizing and posting transactions, and may take some time to accomplish, especially when you're first getting started. Using accounting software can reduce your time factor for some things (such as report preparation), but even with that help, these tasks can take longer than what you've done so far.

When you want to see fully accurate financial statements under the accrual accounting method, you first must write up adjusting entries to get your accounts exactly up to date. Adjusting entries cover income- and expense-related transactions that fit into this accounting period, even though the cash exchange took place (or will take place) in another period.

The most important job you have at month-end is to make sure all your accounts have correct balances. For some accounts, you will perform reconciliations, which means you will match your general ledger account balance with something else to verify its accuracy; if they don't match, you can find and fix the error. For example, every month, you have to reconcile your cash accounts with corresponding bank statements (just as you do with your personal checkbook); also, you have to make sure that the accounts receivable subledger total balances with the accounts receivable account in the general ledger. While you're in the accounts receivable ledger, prepare account statements for any customer with an outstanding balance.

When you think all the accounts are accurate, prepare a trial balance to make sure your general ledger is in balance. If you want to look at rough financial statements for the month, you can create them once your trial balance balances. Once you have all the reports you need, you can close out your books for the month (unless you use different accounting periods for your company, such as quarters).

Once all your regular monthly accounting tasks are complete, you can turn toward tax responsibilities. Which chores you have to do depends completely on your business; you may not have to deal with monthly tax issues at all. If you have employees, you may be required to make a monthly payroll tax deposit (see Chapter 9). When your company has taxable sales, you may have to file a monthly sales tax return along with payment (see Chapter 6), depending on the state law and your company's sales volume.

Quarterly Tasks

On the recordkeeping front, your quarterly tasks won't be much different than regular month-end tasks (unless you close your books only quarterly). If you've got the time, you may want to take a look at how close your actual revenues and expenses are to what you've expected. For example, if you prepared a budget at the beginning of the year (or as part of your original business plan), you can compare your real-life results to those estimates.

F A C T

Estimated taxes for owners are always due in April, June, September, and January. The only difference for corporations is that they have a December due date instead of January. Each of these due dates falls on the fifteenth of the month. If the fifteenth falls on a weekend, the due date shifts to the following Monday.

From the tax side, the end of a quarter usually brings a lot of responsibilities. First, if your business structure is anything other than a C corporation, or a limited liability company (LLC) taxed like a C corporation, you and any co-owners must file personal quarterly estimated federal and state income taxes. C corporations must file their own quarterly estimated income taxes. (See Chapter 16 for a discussion of both.) In addition, most companies with employees will have to file payroll tax returns each quarter, sometimes along with payment. Finally, you may have quarterly sales tax reporting obligations, depending on your state law.

Annual Tasks

As you might expect, the list of year-end chores is pretty long. On the accounting front, you have to do the following:

- Pay every bill that you want to be able to deduct in the current year (for cash basis)
- Prepare adjusting entries (see Chapter 13)
- Verify your trial balance
- Create comprehensive financial statements (see Chapter 14)
- Set a budget for the upcoming year
- Close out your books for the year
- Set up your journals and ledgers for the upcoming year (only for manual systems)

Turning to taxes, the list is just as long, but many of the chores can be grouped together. First, the payroll responsibilities (see Chapter 9): In addition to all your normal payroll filings, you must provide a personal tax statement to each employee. A copy of each of these, along with a summary report, has to be sent to the federal government. The annual federal unemployment tax return is also due at this time. (State requirements for payroll reporting may vary.) If you paid any nonemployees during the year (for job-like work), you have to send them personal income reports as well, and copies of those along with a summary statement to the IRS.

Year-end is also income tax time. You will have to prepare both the company tax returns and your personal tax returns (in that order), for both the state and federal governments. As you'll learn in Chapter 16, these forms can get pretty complicated, and it may be easiest to enlist the help of a qualified professional.

The Everyday Transactions

Most companies have the same types of day-to-day transactions, and almost all of these involve revenue and expense accounts. Each of these common transactions involves some kind of document, whether it's an invoice, a receipt, a check stub, or some cash register tape. From these source documents, you can record your company's transactions in the journals.

Following, you'll see a glimpse of a typical day's transactions for a small retail business. For each transaction, the standard source document is clearly identified, along with instructions for recording the journal entry. Because this company has inventory, it uses the accrual method of accounting, which includes the following transactions.

1. Accept inventory delivery of twenty umbrellas at $5.00 each, purchased on account from Bella's Umbrellas.
2. Write check number 126 for $178.00 to Union Electric to pay utility invoice in full.
3. Write check number 127 for $550.00 to Rain Gear, Inc., to pay for last month's delivery of galoshes.
4. Write check number 128 for $68.66 to Verizon for phone service.
5. Buy lunch for $7.65 in cash.
6. Buy stamps for $39.00 in cash.
7. Write up deposit slips for $130.00 in cash, $167.50 in checks, and $233.50 in Visa and MasterCard receipts for the day's sales, including $26.54 in sales tax.

The source document for the first transaction is the invoice that comes with the delivery. This transaction is recorded in the purchases journal, with a $100 debit to inventory purchases and a $100 credit to accounts payable. The accounts payable portion must include the name of the vendor. For transactions two through four, the source documents include both the invoices paid and the check stubs (or the check register). All are recorded in the cash payments journal, as each includes a credit to cash. In transaction three, the debit is utilities expense. In transaction four, the debit is to accounts payable, with a notation of the vendor name. For transaction five, the debit is to telephone expense.

The next transaction, number five, is a trick: your lunch does not count as a business expense. If you used company cash, you have to debit owner withdrawals and credit cash in the cash payments journal; if you used your own pocket money, no entry is needed. The source document for transaction six is the receipt from the post office. The debit side of the journal entry is postage expense, but the credit depends on which cash you used. If it was your pocket money, that counts as an owner contribution, and the credit is to your equity account; record this in the general journal. If it was the company's cash, credit the appropriate cash account using the cash payments journal. Finally, the source document for transaction seven is the deposit slip. This entry goes in the cash receipts journal, with a debit to cash and a credit to sales.

ALERT!

Be aware that paying business expenses with personal money, or vice versa, can spell trouble when your business structure is a corporation or LLC. Mixing funds like that can invalidate your business structure and cause quite a legal mess. Instead, take the extra step of writing a check to the business, then using those funds for whatever the company needs.

Reconciling Your Accounts

The best way to verify your account balances is to reconcile them with outside (meaning outside that account) information. Reconciling accounts simply means making sure they are in agreement with something else. Doing that assures the accuracy of your books, or lets you find and fix mistakes. In most cases, only balance sheet accounts will be reconciled, though any adjustments usually involve a revenue or expense account.

Although you can probably find a way to reconcile almost any account, the most common ones to tackle are cash, accounts receivable, inventory, and accounts payable. That doesn't mean you won't verify any of your other ledger account balances, but most of them won't require full-blown reconciliation throughout the year.

These procedures have to be done whether you use a computerized or manual accounting system. However, using accounting software also cuts down on the work burden here. In fact, most programs have special features for account reconciliation and devoted cash reconciliation modules.

The Cash Reconciliation

Cash account reconciliations (also called "bank recs") are the ones most commonly performed. You probably do this every month with your personal checking account. This procedure isn't much different, except that you may end up with journal entries that you need to record. In this process (there is a full example in Chapter 10), you start with two sources of information: a cash account from the general ledger and the corresponding bank statement.

For a checking account, your cash balance and the balance on the bank statement won't match; they are not supposed to. The main reason for the difference is timing: The bank statement stops on a certain date, and your cash account keeps going. You will have written checks and made deposits since the bank's cutoff date. In addition, the statement may list bank fees and other charges or interest earned; that information probably has not hit your cash account yet. Then, of course, there's the possibility of errors on either side, which must be corrected promptly. The bank grants you about sixty days to notify it of its errors; if you don't do it in time, it may not adjust your account (especially when the adjustment would be in your favor).

Maintain a separate cash account in the ledger for every bank account your company has. Mixing them together in your books makes it nearly impossible to reconcile any of them. Linking each bank account to a distinct ledger account streamlines the reconciliation process, making your accounting job much easier.

Timing differences don't require any additional bookkeeping work. Items on the bank statement that you have not recorded yet, such as fees, require journal entries. The same goes for errors on your side; they require journal entries as well.

Accounts Receivable Reconciliation

Reconciling your accounts receivable mainly involves making sure the overall total of the customer ledger matches the balance of the general ledger account. These two sources are supposed to equal exactly, to the penny, but they often don't (particularly in manual systems, but sometimes even in computerized ones). It's very common to make adjustments to customer accounts in the subledger without doing the same in the journals or the main account, and that will cause some differences.

FACT

Customers will tell you their invoices or statements are wrong. They'll try to take discounts they don't deserve, or ask you to remove finance charges. When they call, it's easiest to make a notation on their file in the subledger and change their balance on the fly. The follow-up— a formal journal entry and posting—are easily overlooked during a busy day.

To find and fix these differences, start in the customer ledger. Look for any entries that seem haphazard or look like account corrections. Then go back through your cash receipts journal (where customer payments are recorded) and your sales journal (where on-account sales are recorded) to see if these entries have been written up. Any that have not been recorded require journal entries and posting at this point.

Inventory Reconciliation

No matter how careful you are in recording your inventory as it moves in and out, it will virtually never match up exactly with a physical item count. There are several reasons for this mismatch, including damage, theft, and simple calculation errors. In any case, when you want to know where your inventory really stands, a physical count is usually the first order of business. When a physical count and a ledger account disagree, the physical count wins.

Once you have taken inventory, you can make any necessary adjustments in the general journal. Then you need to post to your ledger accounts to update them as well. If you have an inventory subledger (very common for companies with varied or extensive inventory), update the individual items also.

Accounts Payable Reconciliation

To make sure your accounts payable is accurate, you have to reconcile its general ledger account with the total vendor subledger. As with accounts receivable, these two sources can get out of balance if you update an individual vendor account without going through all the regular bookkeeping steps. An imbalance can occur when a vendor invoice doesn't mesh with your purchase order or when a vendor's account statement doesn't have the same balance as your subledger file.

Once you've straightened things out with the vendor, you can turn to your accounts. Errors on the vendor's part won't impact your bookkeeping at all. Any changes that you need to make to update your accounts require journal entries and posting to both the subledger and general ledger accounts.

What to Keep, What to Toss

Accounting is full of paperwork. To keep your office from being overrun, you need to know which papers you can safely toss, because there are some your company is required to hold on to for a pretty long time.

The government, through various agencies, sets schedules for how long your company has to maintain specific types of documents. Those requirements change a lot and can differ from state to state. Your insurance company may also require you to hold on to certain pieces of paperwork, especially if you have insured specific items in your policies. In addition to all the outside requirements, though, there are some documents that you should hang on to for the long run. Since there is no single unchanging comprehensive set of rules for record retention, common sense has helped develop some generally accepted standards. You can also check with your accountant to find out if there are things he wants you to keep.

FACT

The biggest must-keep stack comes courtesy of the IRS. It requires everyone to maintain all the information related to an income tax return for three years after the return was filed. That's because the IRS has three years to select a return for audit under normal circumstances (though it has extra time for cases such as suspected fraud).

For long-term storage records, you can collect all the information pertaining to a single closed year and box it up. Make sure to label the box on all sides (so you don't have to go digging through a pile to see if that's the box you need), and store it somewhere safe and dry. That will at least keep your file cabinet free for the current stuff.

One-Year Documents

There are some paper records that you need to hang on to for only a little while. The exception to this guideline is when a specific document may be needed to settle a legal claim. Otherwise, these documents will probably never see the inside of a long-term storage box, and clearing them out helps free up room for incoming paperwork. Here's a list of papers you can get rid of after one year:

- Bank account reconciliations
- Duplicate deposit slips
- Receiving documents
- Postal delivery records (such as return receipts)
- IRS Forms I-9 (keep for one year after employee termination)

Three- to Five-Year Documents

The next group includes documents to keep for at least three years, maybe four or five. After that, you can shred them and send them to the landfill or have a document bonfire. The exception, of course, is any that you will need to settle a pending legal claim.

- General business correspondence
- Employment applications (hired or not)
- Expired insurance policies
- Petty cash records
- All supporting documents for income tax returns
- IRS Forms W-4 (four years)
- Occupational safety logs (five years, kept for OSHA)

Seven-Year Documents

There's a long list of paperwork that you should keep around for at least seven years. These items are often packed up and sent to long-term storage in boxes with like documents. When their time is up, you can get rid of the whole box without having to go through the individual papers.

- Accounts receivable ledgers
- Customer invoices
- Accounts payable ledgers
- Vendor invoices
- Purchase orders (to vendors)
- Payment vouchers
- Bank statements
- Canceled checks (most; some will fall in the forever group)
- Contracts (seven years after *expiration*)
- Employee records (seven years after *termination*)
- Inventory records
- All payroll and payroll tax records

Keep These Documents Forever

There are some pieces of paper that will be around indefinitely, at least for the life of your business. These should be stored somewhere waterproof and fireproof, somewhere they aren't likely to be destroyed by accident. For the more critical documents, such as deeds and asset titles, you may want to invest in a safety deposit box or similar vault-type storage to ensure their safety.

- Chart of accounts
- General ledgers
- Cash ledgers
- Critical correspondence
- Asset depreciation schedules
- Year-end financial statements
- All journals
- Business licenses
- Loan documents (even after they're paid off)
- All property records (deeds, titles, appraisals, bills of sale, improvements, etc.)
- Workmen's compensation documents
- Income tax returns
- Independent auditors' reports (from accountants)

In addition to those documents, you should pull out and save certain canceled checks. These include checks you wrote to pay tax bills, for asset purchases (down payments, for instance; not ongoing loan payments), legal claim settlements, and others of like importance.

chapter 5

The Accounting Equation

One of the foundations of accounting is the accounting equation: assets equal liabilities plus equity. The three pieces of that equation can define your company. They tell you what you have, what you owe, and how much of your business you truly own. You could not run your company without them, because they are the tools you use to generate revenue.

5

Every Business Has Assets

No matter how small your business, no matter what industry your company is part of, your company has assets. From a computer used to prepare customer invoices to a 20,000-square-foot processing plant, every single thing your company owns is an asset, as long as you can assign a dollar value to it.

Some assets are physical, such as computers, file cabinets, and delivery vans. Others are legally binding promises, such as accounts receivable, which is the money owed to your company by its customers. Still others seem to exist more on paper, though they may also have tangible form, such as the company checking account or prepaid expenses (for example, a year's worth of insurance paid in advance). Regardless of the form it takes, anything with monetary value that your company owns or owns the rights to (such as the right to collect money from customers who owe it) counts as an asset.

Assets appear on your balance sheet, which is one of the key financial statements produced at the end of each accounting period. On this report, your assets will be split into different types to make analysis easier. The order in which you list them on the balance sheet typically matches the way they appear in your chart of accounts.

Assets do more than just show up on reports, though. They are the resources your company uses to produce revenue, and revenue is what keeps your company alive. Your business cannot bring in sales without assets, and while this connection is more clear for product-based businesses, which could not produce a dime of revenue without inventory to sell to their customers, it's true for service companies as well. At the very least, you have to have cash to pay your expenses and to help get the word out that your company exists. Service companies also need basic tools to provide service to customers: a hair stylist needs a chair, scissors, and styling tools; an accountant needs a computer and a lot of file cabinets.

Breaking Out Asset Categories

The accounting way to separate assets into categories uses liquidity as the measure. Anything that is expected to be converted to cash within one year of your balance sheet date is considered a current asset; all others are plunked down into one of the long-term categories. Long-term assets fit one of three types: long-term investments, fixed assets, and intangible assets.

FACT

Liquidity refers to how easy it would be to turn an asset into cash. Your checking account counts as cash, making it 100 percent liquid. As for your other assets, think about how long it would take to turn them into cash if you absolutely had to. For instance, inventory should move pretty fast, but your customized delivery van might take a lot longer to sell.

Even within these broad categories, the assets have a particular pecking order. For example, your current assets (which you already know are liquid) have a liquidity pecking order. Cash is already cash, so that always come first; prepaid expenses, on the other hand, have a fixed use-up date, which usually makes them the last current asset listed. Fixed assets have their own ranking system as well, but this is based on how long you expect them to last (a.k.a. their useful lives).

Current Assets

Current assets include anything that could be or that you expect to be changed into cash within a year of the date on your balance sheet. These assets are listed in their order of liquidity, from cash down to the current asset that you expect would take the longest to convert to cash (usually prepaid expenses). Here are the most common current assets, in order of liquidity:

- Cash, which includes every cash account plus any cash you have on hand
- Accounts receivable, which is money your customers owe to you for sales to them
- Inventory, which includes anything you will resell regardless of the form it's in now

- Short-term investments, such as stocks or bonds that you plan to cash out within a year
- Prepaid expenses, which are expenses paid in advance of use, such as insurance or rent

Long-Term Investments

When your company is doing well and you have extra cash lying around, you may choose to invest that money so it can earn even more. Any investments that you make and plan to hold on to for more than a year fit into the long-term investments category. These investments could include stocks, bonds, and high-yield CDs; they also can include things such as buildings that you are holding for investment purposes only.

ALERT!

Long-term investments often provide current earnings, such as interest or dividends. Those earnings have to be included when you figure out your profit or loss for the period. Since they aren't regular revenues, they are reported separately, usually as "other income" at the very bottom of the statement of profit and loss.

Long-term investments are often used to finance expansions, minimizing the amount you would have to obtain from outside sources (such as bank loans). Instead of withdrawing the cash, and hoping to be able to put it back in when it's needed, many small-business owners instead invest that surplus cash, then sit back and watch it grow.

As your expansion plans get closer, and you think the time is coming to liquidate those investments, you should shift them over into the short-term investments. When you expect to sell them within the upcoming year, they transform into current assets for the balance sheet.

Fixed Assets

Any physical asset that your company owns and does not intend to sell falls into the fixed-asset category. Fixed assets range in size, useful life, and purpose. A $40 office chair counts as a fixed asset just as much as a 15,000-square-foot storage facility. The point is that they are both part of what the company needs to have in order to produce revenues, and you plan to keep them around for a long time. Fixed assets can include things such as:

- Land
- Buildings
- Building improvements
- Vehicles
- Office furniture
- Equipment
- Computer systems

Fixed assets also come with a unique contra account, called accumulated depreciation. This account fits in the asset category but has a normal credit balance (which is what makes it a contra account). It holds all of the depreciation expense ever taken on the connected assets. Depreciation expense tracks the declining value of assets and lets you take that decline as a tax-deductible expense, but spread out over the entire life of the asset. You'll learn more about calculating depreciation in Chapter 8.

Intangible Assets

Some companies own assets without physical form that they plan to hold on to for the long haul. These are called intangible assets, and some companies couldn't succeed without them. In order to count an intangible as an asset, your company must own it or the rights to it, and it has to have a measurable dollar value.

Some of the more common intangible assets include patents, copyrights, licensing agreements, trademarks, franchise rights, leaseholds, and goodwill (the most intangible of them all). Goodwill can be the most confusing asset, because it really exists only in perception and can be measured only when a business is purchased. The goodwill asset represents the reputation of a company—its good name. It comes into accounting play only when someone buys a company for more than it would be worth by the numbers alone.

Like fixed assets, intangible assets have useful lives over which they decline in value, at least for accounting purposes. This decline is called amortization, and it counts as a tax-deductible expense. Since intangible assets can be hard to pin down, their useful lives are considered to be their legal lives or forty years, whichever is shorter. Amortization can be held in a separate contra account, called accumulated amortization, or simply be deducted directly from the intangible asset balance; the choice is yours (or your accountant's).

ALERT!

It can be very hard to value intangible assets that haven't been purchased. For example, when you write a screenplay, you hold the copyright. That copyright is your intangible asset, and it's worth something, but that something can be hard to put a number on. Ask an experienced business accountant to help you assign a value.

A Closer Look at Fixed Assets

Fixed assets take more work than other assets, from both a real-life maintenance perspective and from the accounting viewpoint. The more substantial fixed assets, from vehicles to factories, can require a lot of planning, drawn-out purchase arrangements, and the burden of long-term liabilities to go along with them.

Since so much can go into fixed assets, there are a lot of guidelines to help you deal with them for accounting purposes. Some of the guidelines come from the IRS, and you may have to use them when you do your business tax return. Others come from generally accepted accounting principles (GAAP). The combined rules cover everything from what to include in the price of your asset to the method of calculating depreciation to how to write up the journal entry when you eventually dispose of the asset. Broken down, these rules are really pretty straightforward.

Calculating Fixed-Asset Costs

For the more basic fixed assets, such as file cabinets and desks, the costs are easy to determine. When you start adding in things such as down payments and trade discounts, as you would with a fleet vehicle, for instance, the accounting gets just a little trickier. The basics, though, are the same for every fixed asset you have. The accounting rule here is called the cost principle, which means that you will value your fixed assets based on what you paid for them, never on their market value (or how much they are "really" worth). That cost, though, includes absolutely everything you had to pay to get that asset ready for work. Of course, there's the price tag of the asset itself, but you add to that things such as sales tax, delivery charges, installation, setup fees, and training on how to use the asset (common with equipment).

> If you have to do something to your property so the asset will work properly, whatever you pay for that goes into your total asset cost. For example, if a machine needs to be set on concrete and you have a tile floor, the cost to have a concrete slab put in counts as part of your asset cost.

Say your company needs a computer network. The system itself costs $11,000 for all the hardware and software. The installation and network management training tacks another $2,500 onto your bill. The computer company offers you a 5 percent discount on the system if you'll sign a one-year service contract for $500, which you do. There's 6 percent sales tax on the system only, and a $100 delivery charge. Before you can take delivery, though, you have to set up a climate-controlled room to house your server, and that costs $3,000. You pay a cash deposit of $300 on the room, another cash deposit of $1,100 on the computer system, the full price of the service contract, and the rest is payable over three years.

All those costs except for the service contract go into the cost of your computer system asset. That makes your asset value equal to $16,677. The system is $11,000 less a 5 percent discount, bringing it to $10,450. Sales tax (at 6 percent) on that comes to $627. You also add on the $2,500 setup fee, the $100 delivery charge, and the $3,000 room work. Here's what the general journal entry would look like:

General Journal Entry				
Date	Account & Explanation	Post Ref	Debit	Credit
01/3/06	Computer System		$16,677.00	
	Prepaid Service Contract		$500.00	
	Cash			$1,900.00
	Long-Term Loan Payable			$15,277.00

Purchased computer network system with cash deposit and three-year loan, plus one-year service contract for cash.

Depreciation Basics

Depreciation is one of the accountant's favorite expenses: it reduces your taxable income (and your tax bill) without taking up any of your current cash. This expense represents the loss of value over time of your fixed assets. To qualify for depreciation, the asset has to be kept by your business (and not be for resale), and it has to have a useful life of more than one year.

FACT

Land is the one fixed asset that is never subject to depreciation. Whatever you paid for it in the first place is the value that sticks with it until you're ready to sell. That's because in the accounting world, land never deteriorates and never declines in value.

There are a few different ways to calculate depreciation (as you'll learn in Chapter 8), but the journal entry to record it is the same no matter how you've come up with the numbers. It always involves a debit to depreciation expense and a credit to accumulated depreciation. The accumulated depreciation account does just what its name implies: accumulates all of the depreciation expense taken from year to year (the expense account itself is temporary and is closed at the end of each accounting period).

When you deduct accumulated depreciation from a fixed asset, the result is that asset's book value. Book value equals the original cost of the asset minus its current accumulated depreciation and usually bears no resemblance to its market value.

Getting Rid of Assets

You may hold on to some assets for the life of your business; others will come and go. For those assets you don't keep forever, there are guidelines for figuring out your gain or loss on the disposition. The gain or loss will happen whether you sell the asset or just trash it; either way, the transaction has some impact on your overall bottom line. Part of the resulting journal entry takes the asset and related accumulated depreciation off the books; the rest goes to gain or loss.

ALERT!

Asset sales may involve trades. For example, you might sell your old van to another company for a combination of cash and some equipment. These transactions can be tricky to record, so get advice from your accountant before writing up the journal entry.

When you get rid of an asset, the difference between what you get for it and its book value will be your gain or loss. When you simply trash a fixed asset, its remaining book value will count as a loss. For example, suppose your landscaping company has a broken-down lawn mower that you've decided to take to the dump. You bought it for $2,500 and it has $2,200 of accumulated depreciation on the books, giving it a book value of $300. You would debit accumulated depreciation for $2,200 and loss on disposal of equipment for $300, then credit the fixed asset for $2,500.

Selling it, though, could go either way; plus, you have an extra account to work with, the cash account. Say you sell that same lawn mower for $500. Now you have a gain of $200 ($500 minus $300 book value). Your journal entry would include a $500 debit to cash, the same $2,200 debit to accumulated depreciation, and $2,500 credit to the fixed asset, but now you would also credit the gain on sale of equipment account for $200. On the other hand, if you sold that asset for $100, you would have a loss of $200, and the entry would change again. Now there would be three debits: $100 to cash, $2,200 to accumulated depreciation, and $200 loss on sale of assets; then you still credit the asset account for $2,500.

Liabilities Are What Your Company Owes

Most businesses owe something to someone. Whether you take out a bank loan to start the company, use a company credit card to pay for expenses, or buy your inventory from vendors on account, your company will show liabilities on the balance sheet. Even if you borrow your startup money from a family member or friend, it still counts as a liability on the company books.

FACT

Some very small service companies may not have any liabilities. When there's no inventory, no payroll, and no company credit card, there really aren't any debts to mount up. Unless there's some major change in the business—for instance, you hire employees or start selling products—your balance sheet may remain liability-free, and that's fine.

Like assets, liabilities are split into categories for easier financial statement analysis. The division for liabilities is somewhat simpler, though, as it's purely time-based. Any obligation that will be due within the next twelve months counts as a current liability. Debts that are expected to remain outstanding for more than a year are considered long-term liabilities. For financial statement purposes, you count the current portion of a long-term liability (meaning the payments your company is scheduled to pay this year) along with the current liabilities; the balance of the loan remains in the long-term group. That's it—no other rules and no other categories.

Most of your current liabilities will be those that occurred during your normal course of business. Buying inventory on account leads to accounts payable debt, for example, and paying employees prompts payroll tax liabilities. On the other hand, most long-term liabilities (other than any startup loans) come about as the result of fixed-asset purchases, and those are not typically everyday occurrences once your business is up and running.

Money Isn't All You Can Owe

In addition to owing money, there's another kind of liability your business can have: it can owe products or services to customers. This liability comes about when you get paid in advance for something, and you have a legal obligation to either fulfill your part of the bargain or give the money back. Until you complete your part of the deal, whether performing services or delivering products, there will be a liability on your books. Most of the time, unearned revenue fits in with current liabilities.

Any kind of company can have unearned revenues. Common examples include a lawyer who works on retainer, a retail shop that lets customers use a layaway plan, and a cabinetmaker who gets a down payment before starting work. In each of these cases, the business gets the money up front, before the full transaction is finalized, which means the company still owes something to the customer and is contractually obligated to provide it.

Once you fulfill your end of the deal, your unearned revenue will transform into regular revenue, courtesy of an adjusting journal entry (see Chapter 13). If you perform part of the service or deliver some of the product, only a portion of the unearned revenue will be adjusted.

The Interest Factor

Most long-term liabilities, and some current ones, come with an expense tacked on to them: interest. Loan payments typically include both a principal and an interest portion (just like your home mortgage payments); the same may go for current liabilities such as credit card payments.

When your payment combines these two different features, you have to deal with both in your journal entries. For example, suppose you're making a $100 payment on the company credit card bill, and there's an $18 interest charge on the statement (almost all credit card companies first apply payments to interest, then balance). That payment would result in a $72 debit to credit card payable ($100 – $18), an $18 debit to interest expense, and a $100 credit to cash. Here's what your journal entry would look like:

	Cash Payments Journal						
Date	Account/ Description	Accounts Payable	Purchases	Loan Payable	Credit Card Payable	Miscellaneous	Cash Credit
3/1/06	Interest Expense				72.00	18.00	100.00

For long-term loans, you may need an amortization schedule to figure out how much of your payment goes to principal and how much to interest. In this example, suppose you have a long-term loan on the books. Your monthly payments are $158.05. You look up this month on your amortization schedule and see that the current interest expense portion is $38.50. That leaves $119.55 ($158.05 – $38.50) to apply to the liability account balance. The journal entry would look almost the same as the one above, but with two exceptions: the numbers would be different, and you write the debit in the loan payable column instead of credit card payable.

Equity Means Ownership

When you first start a business, you (along with any co-owners) put some of your own assets into the company. Those original contributions form the first entries in your equity account and get your business on its way. Adding resources into the company is one way to beef up your equity account, whether it comes from you and other involved owners or from silent investors.

Any asset you put into the business increases your equity stake. The most common contributed asset is money, but all other personal assets being used exclusively by the company count as well. Contributed assets can be anything from a laptop computer to a backyard shed to a pickup truck that now bears your company logo. For major assets like that pickup truck, it's important to retitle the asset in the company name to avoid any problems down the line, such as the IRS questioning ownership.

The other way to grow the equity is by keeping some of the profits inside the business. Many small-business owners like to take out profits as soon as they're earned; after all, they've had to pay tax on the money, and want to enjoy the benefits. If you're planning to expand your company, though, leaving some of those profits inside is a great first step. It can also make your company more attractive to prospective lenders, as banks are often more likely to make a loan when they see there is substantial equity at stake.

Though equity is about ownership no matter what type of company you have, the accounts you use depend entirely on your business structure (as you'll see in detail in Chapter 15). Sole proprietorships and partnerships will have a separate owner's equity (or capital) account for each owner, along with a corresponding withdrawal account for each. The owner's equity account is a permanent account, and contributions are made directly into this account. The withdrawal accounts are temporary and are folded into the owner's equity account at the end of the accounting period, along with that period's net profit or loss.

Corporations don't have equity accounts geared toward individual owners. Instead, they have accounts for each type of stock they issue to represent the contributed capital. Unlike sole proprietorships and partnerships, no other accounts are folded into these. Earnings at the end of the period are held in an account called retained earnings. Owner withdrawals are a much more formal affair, and here exist only in the form of dividends; the dividends account is temporary and is rolled into retained earnings at the end of the period.

Assets Equal Liabilities Plus Equity

This equation, which is at the very core of accounting, expresses one of the biggest accounting basics: everything must remain in balance. Changes in one side of the equation require changes in the other.

The form of this equation comes from the basic idea that assets are financed with a combination of liabilities and equity. You can pay for your assets by using existing capital, by raising additional capital, or by borrowing funds. The transactions will be different, but the accounting equation will remain in balance no matter which way you go. For example, when you use existing capital to finance an asset purchase, you are spending resources you already have. That transaction results in a debit to the new asset and a credit to whichever asset you used to buy it (such as cash or a traded-in vehicle). Although individual asset balances are affected, the total asset balance is not, and the equation remains in balance.

The same balance holds true when you raise new capital to purchase an asset. Your asset account and your equity account will increase by equal amounts, maintaining the balance. Financing your assets with debt acts exactly the same way: assets increase, but so do liabilities. As long as each individual transaction has equal debits and credits, your books will be in balance, and the accounting equation will be true.

chapter 6

Recording Your Revenues

The goal of every small business is to rack up revenues. After all, revenues are the first step on the path to profits. When it comes to recording revenues, though, it's not quite as simple as ringing up a sale. There are different types of sales transactions and different accounting methods to use. With all the variables surrounding a single sales transaction, the accounting can seem overwhelming, but each really involves just a few basic steps to get the entry recorded and your business another step closer to profitability.

What Are You Selling?

When it comes to recording your revenues, what your company sells plays a big part in how transactions are written up. There are basically three things you can sell: products, services, or a combination product and service. The main transaction differences are with cost of goods sold (for products only) and sales tax (which depends on your state's laws).

No matter what you sell, your journal entries will always have the same foundation. That includes a credit to the sales account and a debit to one of your receipts accounts (either cash or accounts receivable). Those two accounts are certain, for every sale you'll ever make. For service-only sales, the transaction usually ends there; the only exception is if your company sells in a state that taxes service sales.

With product sales, you may also write up an entry to reflect what you sold. As you'll see in Chapter 7, every product sale involves inventory moving out the door; when an inventory item is sold, it becomes a cost of that sale. Inventory systems that track the movement of every item all the time, called perpetual inventory, require a product-based journal entry for each sale you make. That means every time you write up a basic sales entry, you also create an entry that debits the cost of goods sold account and credits the inventory account (to show the increase in cost and the decrease in inventory).

ESSENTIAL

When it comes to recording product sales, especially if your company uses a perpetual inventory system, accounting software really earns its keep. These programs create the second entry automatically, as well as updating your inventory item records with every sale.

Sales tax just adds an extra line item (and some extra money) into your basic sales entry. On top of a debit to cash or accounts receivable and a credit to sales, you will have an additional credit to your sales tax liability account. The trick is to make sure your debit entry includes the sales tax amount to keep that entry balanced.

The Basics of Sales Transactions

There is one thing all sales transactions have in common: a credit entry to the sales account. The rest depends on the particular circumstances surrounding the transaction, and there can be a lot of variation in those circumstances.

ALERT!

Remember, companies with inventory generally must use the accrual method of accounting. Even if your business sells a combination of goods and services, the inventory issue is the deciding factor. That means every sale—even if a sale doesn't involve any inventory—has to be recorded, whether or not you've been paid yet.

For instance, the way your company makes sales has an impact on your transactions. Sales can be made for cash, resulting in a debit to cash; or on credit, resulting in a debit to accounts receivable. Then there's the "when" factor to consider: companies using the cash method record sales only when actual cash is received, whereas companies using the accrual method record sales in the moment regardless of payment. Finally, your inventory method plays a part in transactions as well. If your company uses a perpetual inventory system, every entry for a product sale must have a corresponding entry for cost of goods sold. Under a periodic inventory system, though, no cost of goods entries are recorded during the accounting period, resulting in a single-entry sales transaction.

The method variables (inventory system and accounting method) are stable factors. Once you've chosen a method, it dictates that part of the entry every time. For example, if you use the cash method, you cannot ever record a sales transaction until you've been paid. Under a perpetual inventory system, you have to book a cost of goods transaction for every single inventory item you sell. The cash or credit issue may vary, because it depends on the actual sales transactions.

Cash or Credit

There are two major differences between cash sales and credit sales: timing and risk. With a cash sale, you get paid on the spot with currency, checks, or credit cards; with credit sales (where your company extends the credit), you get a promise that your company will be paid some time in the future. Cash sales provide different levels of risk, ranging from none for actual cash to possible risk for credit card sales and customer checks. With credit sales, you run the risk that the customer won't pay on time or that he won't pay at all.

In either case, when you complete a sale you need to keep a record of it. With a cash sale, the standard source document (where you can find the details of the transaction) is the sales receipt, which contains such information as the date, amount, and description of what was sold. For credit sales (not credit card sales; those are treated like cash sales), the source document is an invoice. Invoices include all the same information as sales receipts, plus a bit more, such as:

- Customer name and contact information
- Customer account number
- Credit terms and due date
- Customer's purchase order number (where applicable)
- Invoice number

To keep your records straight, use prenumbered sales receipts and invoices, and use them in order. That makes for much easier tracking, both now and down the line.

Cash or Accrual Method

Companies using the cash method of accounting record sales only when cash has been received. Companies using the accrual method of accounting record sales when they take place; the cash part requires a second journal entry at the time of receipt. This doesn't mean that cash-method companies can't have credit sales, or that accrual method companies can't have cash sales; these transactions happen all the time, and they get slightly special treatment (as you'll learn later in this chapter). The accounting method dictates only when you count the revenue, not how you got it.

While you'll want to keep track of every transaction, the accounting method tells you when to book the journal entry. It may seem unimportant whether you record a transaction now or four weeks from now, but sometimes that timing can make a very big difference. Take year-end, for example: Under the accrual method, you have to report all the income you earned for the year to the IRS and pay tax on it whether or not you've gotten the money. Using the cash method, though, you have to report and pay tax only on the cash you've actually received. A $2,500 sale made on credit on December 31 counts as this year's taxable income under the accrual method, but not under the cash method.

Periodic or Perpetual Inventory

Inventory adds an extra layer of complication to accounting in general; it's much easier to do the accounting for a service business than a product-based one. At the most basic level, inventory may add extra journal entries to your sales transactions. Here's the theory: With the perpetual inventory method, you write a journal entry every time inventory items are bought or sold; with the periodic method, you don't. Practically speaking, though, you want to keep close track of your inventory for dozens of reasons, some much more important than journal entries, as you'll learn in Chapter 7.

ALERT!

For your own peace of mind, use a perpetual inventory system only if you're using accounting software or have very limited inventory. This system isn't terribly complicated to do manually, but it is extremely time-consuming. Unless you have only one or two inventory items that are incredibly easy to track, go periodic or go computerized.

From an accounting perspective, the difference between the two methods comes down to how many journal entries come with each sales transaction. With periodic inventory, you make no entry at the time of sale, so there's just the sales side of the transaction. With perpetual inventory, two journal entries are required every time you sell a product: one to record the sale, and one to move the product out of inventory.

Develop a Sales Journal

When your company has a high sales volume, creating a separate sales journal can cut down on your bookkeeping time substantially. High sales volume is relative, but a good rule when you're first starting out is at least ten sales transactions per day. Once you hit that threshold, trying to enter every sale in your general journal can demand too much of your time—time that could be better spent trying to increase sales.

A classic sales journal is devoted solely to credit sales. This cuts down on the amount of entry work for each transaction while still allowing you to specify the customer involved in the sale. Especially when you work with a manual accounting system, using this special journal will save you lots of time (not to mention helping to protect you from sore wrists and fingers). You can find dedicated sales journals in most office supply stores, or you can create your own if you need some customized columns.

A bare-bones sales journal includes columns for the date, transaction description, and your invoice number, as well as a debit column for accounts receivable, a credit column for sales, and a miscellaneous catchall column. However, if your sales transactions typically involve more than just a debit to accounts receivable and a credit to one general sales account, adding some additional dedicated columns can save you even more time. Extra columns you might want to use include:

- Sales tax payable
- Sales discounts
- Different sales accounts (like parts revenue and service revenue)
- Delivery charges

As soon as you complete a journal page, foot all of your columns (i.e., add up the numbers in each separate column). Then add together the totals of all your debit columns; follow that with a summary total of all the credit columns. For your journal page to be in balance, the total debits must equal the total credits. When the columns balance, it indicates that your entries were recorded correctly.

ALERT!

Cash sales are generally recorded in one daily lump in a separate special journal called the cash receipts journal. When you have mainly cash sales, peppered with just a couple of credit sales, you can use a combination sales and cash receipts journal.

Simple Cash Sales

Cash sales are simpler to record than credit sales in two very important ways. First, you don't have to bother recording the transaction in a customer's account on top of the general account. Second, there's no second step to the transaction; with credit sales, you have a second transaction to record when the cash is finally received. In addition to that, it doesn't matter whether you use the accrual method or the cash method: when you have a straight cash transaction, you record it right then and there. Remember, cash sales include every sale in which the customer pays right away, even if it's by check or credit card.

Cash sales are typically recorded in one giant journal entry at the end of each day. The special journal for these transactions is called the cash receipts journal. A standard entry involves a debit to cash and a credit to sales. Other accounts may factor in, though, such as sales tax payable. When those other accounts are used more often than not, you can include special columns for them in your cash receipts journal.

When you get to the end of your journal page, foot all the columns; then make sure your combined debit columns total equals your combined credit column totals to ensure that your journal remains in balance. Once you know your journal page is in balance, you can post the column totals to the appropriate general ledger accounts. If your journal includes a miscellaneous column, though, you have to post the individual line items to the various accounts in use.

To keep your bookkeeping life as simple as possible, make sure your deposit slips match your journal entries exactly. If you record $862 in cash sales on Monday, deposit $862 on Tuesday. That way you have an easily traced trail from your sales to your bank deposits, which can come in handy should any questions arise. When you have other items to deposit, such as customer payments on account or vendor rebates, you can use separate deposit slips or simply indicate the alternate source on your cash sales deposit slip.

The easiest way to keep track of your cash sales is to deposit every penny you receive, whether the customer pays with cash, check, or credit card. This way, your revenues equal your deposits, which simplifies record-keeping. Don't use cash from sales to pay for expenses before the money ever hits the bank; that can cause unnecessary confusion when you're trying to write up your journal entries.

Selling on Account

When you extend credit to your customers, there will be a lag between the time of the sale and the time you get paid. Credit sales by nature allow customers to buy now and pay later. That can help you increase your sales, particularly with commercial customers. Although it would be nice if everyone paid you in full and on time, there will be some customers who pay late or never. As you'll learn in Chapter 11, there are some simple steps you can take that will help minimize this potential problem.

If you decide to extend credit, it's up to you to know who owes you how much at any given time and to communicate that information to your customers. After all, no matter how honest and trustworthy your customers are, they can't pay if they don't know how much they owe you. To keep track of individual customers' accounts, use an accounts receivable subledger (or customer ledger). This ledger is simply a book that holds a separate page for each customer account; on those pages, you record all the activity that relates to each particular customer. The sum of all your individual customer balances must equal the balance in the accounts receivable account in the general ledger (a.k.a. the accounts receivable control account).

The Mechanics of a Credit Sale

When you make a sale on account, no cash will change hands at the time of the sale. Instead, you'll present the customer with an invoice detailing the transaction, and he will offer you the implicit promise to make payment on some later, agreed-upon date. The basic journal entry, which will be recorded in your sales journal, is fairly simple: a debit to accounts receivable and a credit to sales. Unlike cash sales, you cannot record credit sales in one big lump; they must be recorded individually so you can properly account for each customer's purchases.

In the description column of your sales journal, you'll write the customer name and account number. If the customer has issued a purchase order for this transaction, you can record that information in your description column as well. Make sure to also record your invoice number for easy reference later on.

Posting to the Ledgers

Accounts receivable transactions require posting to two different ledgers. Complete individual sales data for the transaction has to be posted to the appropriate customer accounts in the customer ledger. Then summary information (column totals from each completed journal page) is posted to the accounts receivable and sales general ledger accounts, as well as any other accounts included in the transactions.

FACT

A customer statement is a document containing summary information for that customer's account. It includes a list of all transactions for the period, such as new invoices and payments received. The statement ends with a balance due, which is the total amount you expect to receive from that customer.

Posting to the general ledger accounts requires very minimal information: the date, the dollar amount, and the sales journal page (typically numbered SJ1, SJ2, and so on). Posting to the customer ledger, though, requires a more comprehensive transfer of information. After all, that is where you'll get the data you need to bill your customers. There you'll include the date, transaction amount, and sales journal page, as well as the invoice number and the customer's purchase order number (when applicable). Any information you would like to include on the customer's monthly statement should be included on his ledger page.

Credit Sales, Cash Accounting Method

There are many companies that use the cash method and extend credit to their customers (very common among small service companies). This is where recordkeeping and revenue-tracking purposes go their separate ways. Under this circumstance, you still want to record the accounts receivable transaction; otherwise, you'll have no way of remembering who owes how much to your company. You can't really record the sale, though, because no cash has changed hands yet.

Don't let this detail throw you. You can still record everything the same way it's explained in this chapter with one small exception: unpaid sales will go into a pending sales account rather than your regular sales account. The pending sales account will appear in your sales journal, and that's the account you'll post your credit sales to when you make them. When cash comes in, you'll have to make a double entry: the first part records the debit to cash and the credit to accounts receivable, and the second part records the transfer from pending sales to actual sales.

Collecting Sales Tax

If you sell products, you probably will have to deal with sales tax. In fact, even if you provide only services to your customers, you may still have to deal with sales tax, although that's still more the exception than the rule. Either way, sales tax tends to be pretty straightforward: you collect it from customers, then send it in to the state along with a brief sales tax return.

From an accounting perspective, the sales tax that you get from customers has nothing to do with revenues, and the sales tax that you pay to the state has nothing to do with expenses. Yes, you collect sales tax as part of a sales transaction, but that part of the transaction has absolutely no impact on your statement of profit and loss. Instead, this is a balance-sheet-only transaction affecting two accounts: sales tax payable and cash. At the time of sale, you debit the cash account and credit sales tax payable as part of the overall sales transaction; when you send in the payment, you debit sales tax payable and credit cash, just as you would for any other payable account.

Whether sales tax comes into play is a state issue. You can learn about your company's specific sales tax requirements by contacting your state's revenue collection office. There you will find out which items are subject to sales tax, how much tax you have to collect, which form you have to fill out, and when you have to send it in (along with the cash you've collected).

In some cases, though, you may not have to deal with sales taxes at all, no matter what you're selling. The most common reason for this is called the resale exemption. That means if you are selling products to someone who is going to resell them to someone else, you don't have to deal with sales tax; only the company that sells the product to the end user does. To cover your company, make sure to get resale certificates from your customers; state sales tax authorities often check up on this.

Dealing with Special Sales Transactions

Some sales transactions involve more than just a debit to cash or accounts receivable and a credit to sales (and maybe sales tax payable). These special transactions are handled a little differently than the standard fare. Examples include sales that involve discounts, time sales (such as layaway plans), and retainers (common with service providers).

The basics of these transactions are the same old thing; they simply involve an extra line or two in the journal and little extra posting. If these types of transactions are commonplace for your company, you can add dedicated columns to your sales journal to cut down on entry writeup.

Sales Discounts

Many businesses offer discounts to their customers, usually to increase sales and speed up customer payments. Some very common sales discounts include:

- Early payment (for credit customers)
- Bulk buying
- Coupons
- Special customer incentives (such as buy one, get one free)

Regardless of the reason, though, sales discounts reduce your overall revenue. To keep track of sales discounts without losing track of your full sales, you record them in a separate contra account called sales discounts. Sometimes the discount will be recorded at the time of the sale (for instance, with coupons and incentives). Other times, it will be recorded when you get paid, since you won't know at the time of sale whether an early payment discount will apply.

Time Sales

Some companies let customers buy pricier products using a layaway plan. Basically, they give you a deposit in exchange for your holding a particular item for them. They continue to make payments, usually according to a set schedule, until they've paid the full price of the item (including any sales tax). At that point, the sale is considered final: they've paid in full, and you've turned over the merchandise.

To record these transactions, you need to have a special general ledger account. The account can be called something like "layaway sales." However, this account won't go in the revenue section of your chart of accounts; instead, it goes in with the liabilities. That's because until the sale is complete, you owe the customer something. The entries until the time the sale is final will involve a debit to cash, and a credit to this layaway sales account. When the sale becomes final, you'll record a debit to cash and a debit to layaway sales (which together should equal the amount of the total sale), and a corresponding credit to your sales account.

FACT

Because time sales involve inventory, trying to figure out when to record the sale isn't a factor. Companies with inventory have to use the accrual method of accounting, and that means the sale counts as a sale only when it becomes final.

Using Retainers

Many small service businesses, such as lawyers and contractors, use the retainer system. The client pays a lump sum up front to cover upcoming services provided by the company. As work is performed, the balance in the retainer goes down; when it hits an agreed-upon balance, the client replenishes it.

How you treat this transaction depends on which accounting method you use for your company. Using the accrual method, the retainer is initially booked to cash (debit) and a special account called unearned revenue (credit). The unearned revenue account is a liability account, because you legally owe your client either the service you promised or the money he paid. As you begin to provide the service, measured in whatever chunks you and the client have agreed upon, you begin to debit unearned revenue and credit sales. These chunks can be measured in portions of a project completed, milestones met, or straight time. Whatever measurement you use, no revenue is recorded until you actually provide some services.

Under the cash method, the entire retainer is taxable upon receipt; if you end up refunding any portion of it, you get an expense deduction at that time. However, you still have to keep track of the unused portion, for you owe your client the full amount of services he paid for or his money back.

When a Sale Is Not a Sale

Sometimes a sale does not stay a sale. This can happen when a customer returns whatever he bought, or a trade customer asks for a special allowance on wrong or substandard merchandise.

At some point, you have probably returned something to a store (or at least tried to). It either turned you down flat, allowed an exchange, or actually gave you your money back. As soon as that money was back in your hands (or credited to your credit card), that original sale was no longer a sale; it transformed into a sales return. The same holds for your company's sales: when a customer brings (or sends) something back and you give her a refund, that counts as a sales return transaction. Sales returns are measured in their own account, separate from your general sales account.

E ALERT!

For your company's protection, put some standard procedures into place to prevent fraudulent returns. For example, require an original receipt in order to process a refund, or set a time limit (maybe three or six months), after which no refunds will be allowed.

For cash customers, you return "cash" in whatever form the customer paid you: cash or a store credit for an actual cash; a credit card credit for a credit card payment. A refund for a check depends on the timing. If the check has cleared (usually measured in a certain number of days from receipt), the customer can get cash or a store credit on the spot; otherwise, your company policy may require the customer to make an exchange rather than get a refund. For credit customers (not credit card customers), you can simply deduct the amount from their account balance, based on a common document called a credit memo (short for memorandum).

chapter 7

The Inventory-Cost Connection

If you sell any kind of product, you have inventory. That inventory starts out as an asset, hanging out on your balance sheet—that is, until you sell it. Once you sell a product, it jumps out of the asset category and into costs, where it makes its way to your income statement. The journey involves some journal entries and some math, but this trail guide will greatly simplify the trip.

7

Inventory Transforms into Cost of Goods

Whether you are a manufacturer, a wholesaler, or a retailer, you sell some kind of product. When you sell some kind of product, first you have to create or buy it. The products you have on hand, the ones that you intend to sell to your customers, make up your inventory asset. Your inventory can include finished merchandise (such as a desk), raw materials (wood to make the desk), or anything in between. If your company makes products, you are a manufacturer, and your inventory has to go through a few steps before it makes its journey to the sales floor.

FACT

If you have a consignment shop, the consigned merchandise you're selling does not count as inventory for you. Since your company never actually owns the goods, they never show up as inventory or cost of goods sold on your financial statements.

As soon as you sell one of your products, it stops being part of your inventory and turns into a special kind of business expense known as cost of goods sold. At that point, it also makes the transformation from a balance sheet item to a piece of the profit-and-loss puzzle. In accounting, though, the conversion of inventory to cost of goods may not show up in the books immediately, depending on the inventory system you choose to use. Also, as you'll see in a later section in this chapter, there are four different ways to compute the value of your inventory once you know exactly how much you have on hand.

Periodic or Perpetual?

In accounting, you have a choice between two basic inventory systems: periodic or perpetual. Their names describe how they work. In a periodic system, you figure out the value of your system periodically; with a perpetual system, you update your inventory every time you make a sale.

The system you use will dictate how you record product sales. In the periodic system, you record a simple, one-step entry that includes only the revenue part of the entry. In a perpetual system, each sales entry has two parts, one that addresses the sale and one that addresses the shift from inventory to cost of goods. With perpetual inventory, you will always have a pretty good idea of your current inventory value. When you use a periodic system, though, you can really only tell what you have when you take a count.

Although it seems that you would know your inventory to the penny at all times using the perpetual system, that's not always the case. In reality, some inventory just disappears; some breaks, some goes bad, and sometimes people just make entry errors. That's why both systems require at least an annual physical inventory-taking, where you count every single item you have available for sale.

Three Stages of a Manufacturer's Inventory

Manufacturers make things and then sell them. Throughout that process, everything they haven't sold yet is inventory. For manufacturers, though, not all inventory is equal; in fact, not all inventory is necessarily even created yet.

It takes time to make things, and your creation schedule may not neatly match the financial accounting calendar. At any point in time, manufacturers usually have three different kinds of inventory on hand:

- Raw materials
- Work in process
- Finished goods

Raw materials aren't necessarily things like rough diamonds or full tree trunks. In accounting, this term really just means the things you need to make your product (which could include rough diamonds or full tree trunks). Anything that goes into creating the final goods counts as part of your raw materials inventory, from beads to marble to glue to fabric. Work in process is any item you've started making but just haven't finished yet. Finished goods are anything that's ready to be shipped out.

What Goes into Inventory Costs?

The whole point of your inventory is selling it. The point of selling it is to make some money. In order to actually make a profit by selling your inventory, you have to know how much it *really* costs to make every item so you can set your prices accordingly. Otherwise, you could actually lose money on every single product you sell.

For resale operations, such as retailers and wholesalers who buy and sell complete merchandise, figuring out that total cost is more involved than you may think. Manufacturers—companies that actually make the products from scratch—have a lot more math to do to get to their true inventory costs.

Total Product Costs for Retailers

In the retail trade, you get merchandise from your suppliers and sell it as-is to your customers. If it comes in a box, you sell it in the box; if it comes blue, you sell it blue. Your role in the product process is just to make your display look appealing enough to attract customers and get them to open up their wallets. Even with that tiny role in the product's life, you still have a few numbers to add up to get to your total product cost.

At the base of this little calculation is the price you paid for the product. Add on to that any sales tax you had to shell out, as well as any delivery charges you paid to get the product to you. If you got some kind of discount—for instance, for early payment of your invoice—deduct that from your inventory cost. Now, you've got the basic equation:

Total inventory cost = total item price + sales tax + delivery charges – discounts.

Once you have that overall total amount, divide it by the number of units you bought to get the per-unit cost.

So, suppose you bought 500 DVDs for $10 each—a total of $5,000. You paid 5 percent sales tax, which came to $250. It cost you $50 to have the DVDs delivered to your door. Finally, you paid the invoice within ten days, which got you a 2 percent discount on the original price, for a savings of $100. Your total inventory cost for these 500 DVDs comes to $5,200, calculated like this: $5,000 + $250 + $50 – $100. That makes your total unit cost $10.40 per DVD ($5,200 divided by 500 DVDs).

Product Costs for Manufacturers

When your company makes the products that it sells, figuring out the product costs is a little trickier than copying a few numbers from an invoice. First, you need to know exactly what went into making the product.

Second, you need to know how much you paid for each component that goes into your finished product. This part works the same way as it does for retail goods; you add up the item cost, the sales tax paid, and any delivery charges, and then subtract any discount you received. Divide that overall total by the number of units you received to get a unit cost for each component.

If you were just buying and selling finished goods, your job would be done there. Since you are creating new products out of the component parts, though, you have another couple of steps to tackle.

Set Up Your Purchases Journal

To make recording inventory purchases as painless as possible, use a special purchases journal to write up these entries. Like the other special journals, the purchases journal is set up so that you don't have to keep writing the same account names over and over again; instead, you can just write a number in a prelabeled column. A classic purchases journal contains at least a column for inventory purchases (debits), accounts payable (credit), and a miscellaneous catchall for any other accounts occasionally involved in these transactions. If you find that most of your purchase transactions include other accounts rather frequently, you can set up dedicated columns for those accounts as well. Some common examples include shipping and purchase discounts.

The majority of inventory purchases are made using credit (see Chapter 12). That's because these purchases are usually regular and sizable, even for small businesses, and also because these are virtually always business-to-business transactions. The companies you buy your inventory from are called your vendors. As you write up your purchases in the journal, make sure to include the name and account number of the particular vendor (your account number for the vendor, rather than the other way around).

When you get to the bottom of a journal page, total each column. Then add the total of your debit columns, followed by your credit columns. The total debits must equal the total credits for your journal to be in balance. When you post from your purchases journal to the ledgers, you can post totals for all the dedicated columns to their corresponding general ledger accounts; items entered in a miscellaneous column must be posted individually to the appropriate general ledger account. In addition, individual transaction information must be posted to each applicable vendor account in the accounts payable subledger (also called the vendor ledger).

Purchases journals traditionally are used only to record purchases of inventory that you expect to resell. If your purchase volume is fairly low and doesn't really merit its own journal, you can use a combination purchases and cash payments journal. Just make sure to use a dedicated column for your inventory purchases.

Four Ways to Value Inventory

There are four ways to keep track of how much your inventory is worth:

- Last in, first out (LIFO)
- First in, first out (FIFO)
- Average cost
- Specific identification

The method that works best for your business depends on what type of inventory you keep. When you offer more than one kind of product for sale, you can use a different inventory valuation method for each, because what makes sense for one may seem somewhat ridiculous for the other. This section can help you figure out which version will work best for your company.

Because different methods will give you different outcomes, prevailing accounting principles make you pick a method and stick with it. If you need to make a change, you have to have a good reason. You also may have to recalculate prior years' numbers to show the impact of the change, and you have to stick with the new method going forward. You cannot keep switching your inventory valuation method to make your numbers come out better.

The LIFO Method

Using the LIFO method makes a lot of sense when your most current merchandise is the first to fly off the shelves. This happens with books on the bestseller list, newly released DVDs, and the latest fashions. LIFO follows that pattern, turning the most recently received inventory into the merchandise that just got sold.

When you use LIFO, your inventory system (periodic or perpetual) can make a difference in the end-of-period value of your inventory asset. Here's why: Under a perpetual system, you track the cost of goods for every single sale, and you would use the most immediate cost at the time under LIFO. When you value the inventory only periodically, those costs are lumped together and only the most recent (at the end of the period) would be included.

FACT

LIFO is a favored valuation method among tax accountants. In periods of rising prices (and when have we really seen anything else?), the LIFO method gives you the highest cost of goods sold, and that translates into the lowest taxable income. Lower taxable income means lower income taxes, and that is what tax accountants like.

Here's an example of how the LIFO method works, under both inventory systems: On January 1, XYZ Company bought ten units for $10 each. On January 15, it sold six of those units. On January 17, the company purchased another ten units, but this time it paid $12 each. The company sold another eight units on January 20, and bought ten additional units on January 22 for $13 each. Finally, on January 31, the company sold nine units, leaving a grand total of seven units in stock. Under the periodic inventory system, the ending inventory would have a value of $70, and the cost of goods sold would equal $280. That $280 is made up of ten units at $13 each, plus ten units at $12, plus three units at $10; you simply count up the sold units backward.

The result under perpetual inventory is different, because you calculate the cost at the time of every sale rather than once at the end. For that first sale, the cost of goods sold would be $60 (six units times $10). For the second sale, it would be $96 (eight units at $12). Then for the third sale, the cost would be $117 (nine units times $13). That would come to a grand total of $273 for cost of goods sold, and inventory would ring in at $77 at month's end.

The FIFO Method

Inventory with a limited shelf life naturally follows the FIFO pattern. That includes things such as fresh food and flowers but can also include standard stock items such as classic movies. Under FIFO, every time you sell a product you use the earliest inventory price on the books to cost it out.

The majority of products follow this pattern, making FIFO one of the most popular inventory valuation methods. Another plus of this method is that your inventory will always be measured using the most current costs, virtually the same as its upcoming replacement value. Also, in contrast to the LIFO method, you will get the same ending inventory valuation regardless of whether you use a periodic or perpetual system.

Here's an example of how the FIFO method works, using a periodic inventory system: On January 10, ABC Company bought a hundred units for $20 each. By the end of the month, it had sold sixty units. Then, on February 12, the company purchased another hundred units, this time for $25 each. By the end of March, ABC Company counted thirty units still in inventory. Under the FIFO method, the cost of goods sold for the quarter (January through March) came to $3,750: a hundred units times $20 plus seventy units times $25. The company's ending inventory was valued at $750—the remaining thirty units at $25 apiece.

Average Cost Method

The average cost method (sometimes called the weighted average cost method) works well for companies that sell a large number of very small, identical items. Think of a hardware store, with bins of nuts and bolts and nails and screws. Trying to assign a specific cost to each would just drive you crazy. It's much easier to treat each unit as part of a whole.

The main drawback of the average cost method is the math: Every time you buy more inventory, you have to recalculate the average cost. If you use accounting software, you may not even notice that the recalculation has taken place. With a fully manual system, though, get ready to pull out your calculator.

Specific Identification

The specific identification method works well with unique or uniquely marked inventory items. A one-of-a-kind designer dress would be perfect for this method, and so would a Honda Accord with its unique vehicle identification number. Here, every time you sell a product, you remove that specific unit from inventory. Whatever you paid for that particular item now becomes the cost of goods sold number, no math, no fuss.

Extra Steps for Manufacturers

Not only do manufacturers need extra steps to figure out their product costs; they also have to deal with three distinct types of inventory: raw materials, work in progress, and finished goods. Raw materials inventory includes any untouched building blocks that you will eventually use to create your products. Work in process includes partially made products, whether they're in the very earliest stages of production or almost to the end. Finished goods include products that are ready to be sold right now. Each of these distinct inventory groups will be valued, using one of the four valuation methods discussed in the previous section.

In addition to more steps, manufacturers' product costs also have more components. Not only do you count the physical pieces that go into the final product; you also count the work it takes to create that product, as well as some more indirect creation expenses. These three pieces of the cost puzzle are split out as follows:

- Direct materials
- Direct labor
- Manufacturing overhead

Direct materials include the basic raw materials you need to make your product: wood to build tables, flour to bake cakes, rubber to make tires. Direct labor includes the wages of the people who actually make your products. Manufacturing overhead involves things that you need to create your finished goods but that can't be directly linked to the process. Common costs included here would be such things as lubricants, the electricity it takes to run the machinery, and factory supervisors' salaries. You include these indirect costs because your products couldn't be made without them.

Figure Out Cost of Goods Sold

In order to figure out your profit or loss for a period, you need to know several key figures. One of the most crucial is the cost of goods sold; with that number, you can calculate your gross profit and begin to get down to the bottom line. Unlike other numbers (such as total sales or postage expense), the total amount of cost of goods sold can't just be plucked from a ledger account. Instead, it has to be figured out based on activity in the inventory accounts.

With accounting software, you may be able to get an automatic, preliminary cost of goods sold with a click of your mouse. That number will need to be adjusted based on your ending inventory numbers, but it can give you a good idea of where the final figures will fall.

To get to your true cost of goods sold, you need to know the exact amount of inventory on hand at the end of the accounting period; that's your ending inventory. The only way to get that number is to take a physical inventory—that's right, you have to count every piece of inventory you have. That number may come pretty close to your book inventory, if you use a perpetual inventory system, but it won't be exactly the same.

That ending inventory is just one part of the cost of goods sold equation, albeit a very important part. To get to your cost of goods sold, you also need to know your beginning inventory (which will equal the prior period's ending inventory) and your total purchases for the period. The combination of beginning inventory and purchases gives you a subtotal called "merchandise available for sale," which is basically everything you could have sold during the period. From that subtotal you subtract your ending inventory, which represents what you have left on hand. The result there lets you know how much was sold during the period—your cost of goods sold.

Taking the Inventory

At least once a year, as part of your accounting tasks, you have to count, weigh, or measure every piece of inventory that your company has on hand. On that day (or those days, depending on how much inventory you have), putting a hold on everything else will make this not-much-fun task flow more smoothly. That means don't buy anything or sell anything until you're done taking the inventory. This will make your inventory-taking task much easier and more accurate.

Get yourself a big, fat notebook. Designate at least one page for every separate item of inventory you have. Then start counting and writing. Only include salable items in your total count; if you don't think you can sell it, it shouldn't be counted as viable inventory.

When you come across a box that is supposed to contain one or more items, open it to see what's inside. That may sound like overkill, especially if you have been the only one handling the merchandise, but it's still a good idea. For one thing, if the box hasn't ever been opened, you have no way of knowing whether the item is in one piece, or even whether it's the right item. If the box has been opened, it may now contain fewer items than it started out with (you can't expect to remember every time you took something out of a box), or something could have broken since the last time you looked.

Then there's mold, water damage, freezing, overheating—probably dozens of things that could impact the state of your inventory. Add employees to the mix, and you open up the possibility of inventory walking out the door. Granted, you probably hire only employees whom you trust not to sneak out with a wide-screen TV. However, even the most trustworthy employees may not think twice about grabbing a six-pack of soda from the back, or taking home some blank CDs.

The point is, unless you take the time to go through your inventory and count every piece, you won't truly know what you have on hand. To get an accurate picture, you need a physical count. That accuracy will flow through to your statement of profit and loss to give you your bona fide bottom line.

Cost of Goods Sold for Manufacturers

Manufacturing companies have an extra twist added into their cost of goods equations. Although there's a lot of different inventory here, only finished goods ever make it into the hands of customers. To get to your cost of goods available for sale (those total finished goods), you first need to know how much was made—that's called the cost of goods manufactured.

ESSENTIAL

For manufacturers, cost of goods manufactured plays the same part that purchases do for retailers. That number tells them the dollar amount of finished goods that were added into inventory during the period, just as if they had purchased the products already complete.

To get to the cost of goods manufactured, you start with your work in process inventory from the beginning of the period. Add to that the current manufacturing costs: all the direct material, direct labor, and manufacturing overhead from this period. That gives you the total costs associated with work in process. Now deduct your ending work in process inventory. The final result here gives you the total cost of goods manufactured during the period, also known as the total finished goods you've added to that branch of your inventory.

To get to your costs of goods sold, start with the finished goods inventory from the beginning of the period. Add your cost of goods manufactured to that to get your total goods available for sale. From that subtotal, subtract your ending inventory number for finished goods. The bottom-line grand total gives you the cost of goods sold.

chapter 8

Standard Operating Expenses

Unlike your personal expenses, every business expense is tax-deductible to some degree. The list of what counts as business expense is vast, and probably includes some things you wouldn't expect. When you have a good working knowledge of business expenses, it will help you develop a better picture of your company's profitability and help you manage your tax bill. It can also save you some money: When you know what your accountant will be looking for when he does your taxes, you can come in completely prepared.

A Look at Expense Categories

One of the oldest business clichés is this: You have to spend money to make money. Expenses are the standard costs of doing business, and there's really no way around them. On the plus side, expenses are tax deductions, and that means a lower tax bill for your company at year-end.

Expense accounts all have normal debit balances, which is the exact opposite of revenue accounts. In fact, there are very few times when you will ever see a credit entry in an expense account. Those rare occasions would be to correct mistakes, to reverse an accrual from an earlier period, or to close out the account. Any other credit postings are probably mistakes, which you need to correct with adjusting entries.

Like most everything else in accounting, there are so many different expenses that it's easier to group them than just look at one very long list. The most common division is between selling expenses and overhead, which is typically called "general and administrative" expenses on financial statements.

ALERT!

Don't confuse standard business expenses with product costs, even when the word "cost" is used. Unlike product costs, which are directly tied to products, expenses exist even when not a single product is bought or sold. Also, even though both types are incurred with the hope of producing revenue, expenses can exist all on their own.

What Goes into Selling Costs

Selling costs include just what you would expect: any expense involved in selling your products or services that tie in directly with sales. For example, sales commissions would count as a selling cost, as would shopping bags and delivery charges (when you deliver something to your customers). Those types of costs don't exist without sales, so they vary directly with your sales.

Other types of selling costs, such as advertising and promotions, are not dependent on sales. Rather, the opposite is true: you hope that spending more on advertising and promotion will drive up your sales. Even though the connection is not as clearly defined, it does exist, making these types of expenses part of selling costs as well.

FACT

There is no accounting rule that requires you to split out your selling costs. If they don't make up a large part of your total expenses, you can leave them in with your general expenses. However, if they are high enough for you to want to track them separately, you can make a selling costs category within your general expenses.

When you choose to highlight your selling costs separately, they will be the first expenses listed on your statement of profit and loss. That's because they are more closely linked to sales than are your other expenses, so they appear on the statement closer to the revenue section.

Direct Selling Costs

Selling costs take two forms, direct (or variable) and indirect (or fixed). Direct sales costs come into play only when a sale takes place. For instance, shopping bags are a common selling expense, but you would not incur this expense unless you sold something to put into that shopping bag. The sale drives the expense.

Examples of direct selling costs include:

- Shopping bags
- Gift boxes and wrapping
- Packaging materials
- Freight charges
- Order fulfillment
- Sales commissions

Indirect Selling Costs

Indirect selling costs are those expenses that are necessary to generate sales but do not vary based on sales. You have to pay these expenses even if you don't sell a single thing. However, it can be pretty hard to generate sales without them, making them well worth the cost.

The most common indirect selling costs include sales salaries, advertising expenses, promotional costs, and travel. Essentially, any cost you incur while trying to convince customers to buy your product can count in this expense category. You may include meals and entertainment here as well; many business owners take clients and potential clients to lunch, or conduct business over golf. Be aware, though, that these particular expenses (the meals and entertainment) are not 100 percent deductible for tax purposes.

ALERT!

Don't confuse sales salaries with sales commissions. Sales salaries are paid to the sales staff regularly, regardless of whether they generate sales or how much they sell. Commissions are paid only when a sale has been made: no sales means no commissions.

Be careful, too, not to go overboard with the mostly social expenses. This is an area more closely monitored by the IRS than others, because there can be a fine line between the personal and the business aspects of these expenses. While traveling to Hawaii to meet with a store owner who may begin stocking your sunglasses counts as business travel, staying an extra two weeks and bringing the whole family along does not.

Understanding Overhead

A lot of people throw around the term "overhead" without really knowing what it means. It's often considered a catchall for anything that's not a direct product cost, and that's partly correct. Sometimes it's called fixed expenses, and that's also only partly correct. The true definition is this: Overhead includes any expense your company would incur even if it never sold anything. Those expenses could be exactly the same every month, or never really the same; they're fixed in the sense that you have to pay them to stay in business, but the dollar amount can change. What overhead does not include are direct and indirect product costs—anything that varies in relation to sales.

This category is where you'll find the unexpected expenses, things you may not think are tax deductible. Here are some of the most common overhead expenses that new and small-business owners forget to include:

- Business-related books and magazines (one-time purchase and subscriptions)
- Donations (such as providing T-shirts for a softball team)
- Tolls, parking, and mileage (for any business travel, no matter how far)
- Professional dues (association memberships, for example)

Some overhead expenses come with special rules, courtesy of the IRS; the two most likely to impact your small business are entertainment and home office expenses. Others, such as depreciation and amortization expenses and payroll, come with a side order of math (payroll is complicated enough to get a whole chapter, right after this one).

Home Office Expense

Many new and small-business owners do at least part of their work from home. If you were to rent office space, all of the expenses associated with that would be fully deductible; the home office deduction lets you record the same types of expenses for your business. However, you can deduct only part of the total expense, because part of your home is for personal use. Typically, your deductions can include a portion of your mortgage interest and property taxes, rent payments, utilities (not phone), security system, insurance, and general maintenance and repairs.

In order to qualify for this deduction, you have to use part of your home regularly and exclusively for business purposes. You also have to use that spot as your principal place of business for whatever tasks you do there; for example, if you always do your billing from home, that counts. It also counts if you normally meet with customers there, or if it's actually a separate structure on the same property (such as a shed).

ALERT!

You can use the home office deduction only if you file Schedule C for your business income. That form is for sole proprietors and single-member LLCs only. For other business types, the associated expenses may be included with the company's regular expenses. Talk to your accountant for advice on how to treat these expenses.

Once your home office qualifies, you have to figure out how big it is in relation to the rest of your house. You can do that using square-foot measurements. For example, if your workspace is 100 square feet and your whole home is 1,000 square feet, you can deduct 10 percent of the common expenses. Expenses that apply only to the office space (such as special wiring or repainting) will be 100 percent deductible. Expenses that don't apply to that space at all—for instance, the cost of painting your kid's bedroom—aren't deductible.

Entertainment Expenses

Entertainment expenses come with a lot of limitations. For one thing, you can deduct only half of the total expense when you take clients out to lunch. Small gifts, $25 or less per person, can be fully deductible, though—and make just as big an impression on your customers.

FACT

Here's an entertainment loophole: Give gifts to a company instead of to a person. When you do that, the gifts are 100 percent deductible, with no $25 limit. Instead of giving five guys $60 theater tickets and only getting a $125 deduction, give them to a company and deduct the full $300.

As you might expect, these types of expenses are audit favorites, so save your receipts and document the business purpose whenever possible. Even if you lose track of some, you'll likely be able to keep the deduction if the lost receipts were for less than $75 each, a fairly new easing of the IRS receipt rules. You are, however, *required* to keep an entertainment expense log that includes the date, place, dollar amount, client name, and business purpose of each event.

All about Depreciation

Depreciation is the accounting way of measuring the wear and tear on your fixed assets. Although it has no impact on cash, it is part of your expenses. That means it lowers your company's net income, which means lower taxes. When you buy assets, you don't get to deduct them right away, even though they have taken up a portion of your cash or increased your liabilities. Taking depreciation expense allows you to deduct that asset over time, as you use it to help produce revenues.

FACT

You can choose to depreciate all or part of your newly acquired assets for tax purposes, under a rule called the Section 179 deduction. Instead of depreciating them over time, you can book an expense for the total fixed assets purchased during the year. Two catches: the deduction can't cause an overall loss, and it can't be more than the IRS limit for that tax year.

Although there are several different ways to depreciate assets, the two most used by small businesses are the straight-line and tax (or MACRS) methods. Both are acceptable for use on your business tax return. You can use one method for book purposes and another for tax purposes (though you have to report that fact to the IRS), but it's easier to keep your books and tax records the same way. MACRS, or modified accelerated cost recovery system, lets you take bigger depreciation deductions sooner than does straight-line (that's where the "accelerated" comes from); overall, though, the total depreciation over the life of the asset will be the same.

Whichever method you choose, you'll need some basic pieces of information to get started: the asset cost, purchase date, useful life, and what percentage is used exclusively for the business. If the asset won't be used 100 percent by the business, you can depreciate only the portion used by the company. For example, if you have a laptop that you use both for business and personal reasons, you must estimate the percentage of business use; if the business use is 80 percent, you can only deduct 80 percent of that year's total depreciation calculation for the business.

MACRS Depreciation

MACRS is what the IRS wants businesses to use for calculating depreciation. Under this method, all assets are lumped into categories, and each category comes with a specific depreciation schedule. For example, all office furniture is considered seven-year property, while all computers are considered five-year property; each property class comes with its own preset annual expense percentages. You can download a complete copy of the table from the IRS Web site (*www.irs.gov*).

In most cases, you'll use the "half-year convention" table. The basic point of this table is that no business buys all its assets on January 1. The half-year convention assumes that all new assets were purchased at mid-year and gives them all 50 percent of the full depreciation for the first year; it then allows for the full-year expense going forward. You'll notice that the tables have an extra year built in; three-year assets have four years of percentages, five-year assets have six years of percentages, and so on. That's to account for the half year at the end of the asset's life, to make up for the missing half year at the beginning.

Here's how MACRS depreciation works. First, figure out which category your asset belongs in, according to the IRS chart. Then you look up the percentage for this year in the asset's life. For instance, if it's the second tax year you have the asset, use the percentage for year two. Finally, multiply the total original asset cost by the percentage from the chart. If the asset isn't used exclusively for business, you have to take an extra step and multiply the business-use percentage by the depreciation amount you just calculated.

Straight-Line Depreciation

Straight-line depreciation is usually an acceptable option for most assets, even though the IRS typically prefers MACRS. Although this method gives you a lower depreciation expense up front, the annual deduction remains steady over the life of the asset and gives you bigger deductions than MACRS in later years.

ALERT!

When it's allowed, a lot of new business owners prefer to use straight-line depreciation for assets purchased in the early years. That's because new businesses often sustain losses early on, and bigger depreciation deductions aren't necessary to keep income taxes low. In later years, when profits start growing, the extra expense helps keep the tax bill to a minimum.

The calculation for straight-line depreciation is straightforward. Take the total original cost of the asset and divide that by the asset's useful life (usually taken from the MACRS asset class listing). The result is the annual depreciation expense, which is the number you'll use every year except the first and last. For those years, you can go with 50 percent, to mimic the half-year convention, or figure out the true proportion. For example, if you bought the asset in February, you could multiply the total expense by 10/12 for the first year; you would use 10 instead of 11 because March would be the first full month the asset was in use.

Don't Forget Amortization

Amortization expense is similar to depreciation, except it works only for intangible assets. This expense measures decline in the value of those assets over time. How do intangible assets decline in value? Well, they don't wear out or rust, but some of them, such as patents, have specific end dates. Others, such as licensing agreements, come with clear useful lives.

The running total of amortization expense is held in a contra account, which generally is called accumulated amortization. The reasoning here is the same as it is for depreciation: this allows you to see the original value of the asset separately from how much of it has been "used up." For amortization, though, you actually have another choice, which you don't have for depreciation: you can record amortization directly to the intangible asset account.

Also unlike depreciation, amortization can only be calculated on a straight-line basis. This means that each period, the exact same amount is booked to expense until it's all used up. If your company bought a patent for $15,000 that had fifteen years left until expiration, you would amortize $1,000 per year for fifteen years.

FACT

You can't amortize any intangible asset over more than forty years, even if it has a much longer legal or useful life. If the asset's useful or legal life is shorter than forty years, though, you have to use that shorter time span when you figure out the expense.

Although it may seem as if amortization won't apply to your company, it probably will. The most common amortization expense for small business is startup costs. While you're doing all the things you have to do to get your business started, there's no actual business for which you can deduct those expenses. Instead, you have to lump the expenses into an asset and amortize them over five years. Expenses you would typically put into this account include legal fees, business licenses, incorporation fees (or the equivalent for LLCs or partnerships)—any expense you incur to create the company.

Employees Cause a Lot of Transactions

Employees are often the single biggest expense a company can have. Not only that, they also bring on a lot of transactions and add more accounts to your system, as you'll see in Chapter 9. First, you have to pay them, and that's usually a big expense in itself. On top of that, though, your business is responsible for extra taxes and some insurance. Finally, your company has to comply with all local, state, and federal requirements, most of which are in place to protect your employees, and some of which come with a price tag.

You also may incur some employee-related expenses that are voluntary. Most of these will actually come with two costs—money and time—but may bring you better and more loyal employees. Those extras include things such as paid holidays, sick days, and vacation days; health, dental, and vision plans; life insurance; and retirement plans. To keep up with the accounting and filing duties required by these benefits, many small businesses turn to payroll services, which is an added but very cost-effective expense.

To escape the extra costs and responsibilities that come with employees, a lot of new and small businesses enlist independent contractors. This can save you a lot of money and a lot of headaches. If you decide to go this route, check out Chapter 21, which explains the many advantages and potential pitfalls of using independent contractors instead of employees.

Recording Expense Transactions

Expense transactions, just like any other, call for journal entries. The timing of your entry depends on which accounting method your company uses. Under the cash method, you record expenses only when you actually pay them. Under the accrual method, you record expenses as they are incurred. For each method, the debit will always be to the particular expense account involved, but the credit account could be either cash or a current liability account (such as utilities payable).

The exceptions are depreciation and amortization, which never involve cash and are always made as adjusting entries. For depreciation expense, the credit account will be accumulated depreciation. For amortization expense, you can credit either accumulated amortization (a contra asset account) or the intangible asset account itself.

chapter 9

Managing the Payroll

There's no way around it: If you have employees, you have to pay them. Payroll is one of the most involved and time-consuming aspects of accounting, and it looks pretty complicated at first glance. Once you get through the initial setup and get the hang of it, though, payroll is really not so tough. Yes, there is a lot of paperwork, but much of it is fairly repetitive and will become routine before you know it.

A Big Pile of Forms

Having employees can be pretty time-consuming all around. Paying them is no different. You have to deal with state and federal taxes, multiple report filings, unemployment insurance, and a whole lot more. Even if you have only one employee, you have to fill out every form and meet every filing deadline.

Once you have the basics covered, you can use your accounting software to help you manage payroll. Most of them come with a payroll module, and the rest often provide an add-on program that interconnects with the standard software. This is by far the easiest and quickest way to do your own payroll. The setup is the most labor-intensive part, but even that takes less time than you would imagine. Once that's done, your part will be limited to telling the program everyone's gross pay—the software can do all the rest. It will calculate every deduction, figure out the take-home pay, keep track of the tax payments you (as the employer) have to make, even print out the paychecks. Before you get started cranking out the paychecks, though, there are several important steps you have to take.

Payroll Basics

You've probably gotten a paycheck at some point in your life and were as dismayed as everyone else when you first realized how much money is taken out. Now you will be the one taking the money out and sending it to the tax men. In addition, employers have to kick in more payroll taxes on top of the ones they deduct from employee paychecks.

ALERT!

Whether you use payroll software or process payroll manually, it's important to use the most recently published tax tables. Most accounting software will remind you to update them regularly, usually through an Internet download (though some will send you a CD if you ask). If you've taken the manual route, contact your tax agencies to find out whether there have been any changes, and request the latest set of tables.

As the employer, you have to account for two sets of taxes: withholding taxes and employer taxes. The withholding taxes are the employees' own income taxes, taken directly out of their paychecks and sent to the tax office (by you). The employer taxes are additional taxes that you have to pay on behalf of your employees, and they include Social Security and Medicare as well as any state and federal unemployment insurance.

The paycheck math is pretty simple. Start with the employee's gross pay, deduct all the withholding taxes, and make out a check for the rest (a.k.a. net pay). There could be other deductions (as you'll see later in this chapter), and applying the right tax rates can be tricky, because they change a lot. Once you get the hang of it, though, it will become as routine as recording a cash sale.

The First Forms

Before you can hire your first employee, you have to register as an employer with the IRS. You can do that by filing Form SS-4, which is simply an application for an employer identification number (EIN). This number will appear on every one of your federal filings that involves employees (and some other filings as well). The form is pretty easy to fill out—it mainly asks for basic information, including the name of your business, some contact information, entity type, and how many employees you expect to have in the upcoming year.

After you mail or e-mail that form to the IRS, you will receive your EIN, usually within a week or two. Your company's EIN will be a nine-digit number that looks like this: 11-1111111. Even if your company operates under different names (for example, JKS Company, dba John's Carpentry), you still need only the one EIN.

In addition to your federal EIN, you need to get identification numbers (sometimes called account numbers) from any applicable state and local tax authorities. These state and local numbers will be used for reporting and depositing payroll taxes, and possibly some other taxes as well, such as sales tax. A lot of states will have you use your federal EIN for state tax filings, giving you fewer numbers to keep track of.

To get your state ID number, contact your state department of revenue to find out which forms you have to complete and submit, and where to send them. Once the department accepts your request, it will send you the forms or coupons you need to start making tax deposits.

Don't wait! Get your EIN as soon as you can, even before you open your doors for business (if possible). That way, you will have your assigned number before you need it for your first filing. You can't make tax deposits without it, and late tax deposits can be subject to hefty fines.

What You Need from Employees

To start paying your employees, you need some information from them, all contained on IRS Form W-4. Every new employee must fill out one of these forms and sign it, preferably on the first day on the job.

The W-4 holds two key pieces of information: the employee's Social Security number and how many allowances she's claiming for tax purposes. Those allowances affect how much federal and state income tax will be deducted from her take-home pay.

If an employee wants to change her withholding, she has to complete a new W-4 form. Why would someone fill out a new form? There are lots of reasons, but the most common are marriage, divorce, and having a baby.

Still More Forms

The forms you have already dealt with have to do with setup: getting identification numbers and collecting employee information. From here on out, you will fill out and file after-the-fact forms that spell out the details of the prior period's payroll. These forms are usually sent along with payments.

On the federal front, you have to complete and submit Form 941 (usually quarterly) to report withholding taxes and your matching Social Security and Medicare contribution. Then there's Form 940 (also available in EZ form for smaller employers), used to report your federal unemployment tax responsibilities (usually filed annually). At year-end, you have to prepare a Form W-2 for each employee, just like the ones you would get at year-end if you were someone else's employee. The IRS also gets a Form W-3, which is a summary of all the W-2s you have handed out.

State and local forms tend to follow the federal model, for both the information you include and the timing. Of course, your state or local government may ask for specific items not included on federal forms, or have a different filing schedule. You can find out exactly what you have to do to satisfy these requirements by checking out your state's Web site (local tax information is usually posted there as well) or by calling your state tax collector's office.

FACT

Of the states that do have their own income taxes, there are only three that do not follow the federal wage-table model for figuring out withholding amounts. In North Dakota and Arizona, you withhold a straight percentage of each employee's federal withholding. In Pennsylvania, you simply multiply each employee's gross pay by the state's fixed percentage.

All about Payroll Taxes

As an employer, you are responsible for sending in two kinds of payroll taxes: the kind you deduct from paychecks, and the kind that you pay in addition to the payroll. There are three basic withholding taxes, two standard employer-side taxes, and unemployment insurance (also an employer-only tax).

The withholding taxes, which are deducted from your employees' gross paychecks, include income tax (always federal, usually state, and sometimes also local), Social Security, and Medicare. The two employer-side taxes are the "matching" contributions to Social Security and Medicare. Then, finally, come federal and state unemployment insurance obligations.

Yes, it's a lot of taxes, a lot of calculations, and a lot of paperwork. On the plus side, the grand total is deductible from your company's income, lowering the company's income tax burden.

Withholding Taxes

Any tax you deduct from an employee's paycheck is a withholding tax. The four most common withholding taxes are federal income tax, state income tax, Social Security, and Medicare. In some states, you may also have to withhold for unemployment or disability insurance.

In order to figure out how much to deduct for income taxes, you need to know some basic information about each employee. That includes his marital status and the number of allowances he's claiming, both of which you can get from the W-4. You also need his gross salary for the period and the amount of any pretax deductions.

FACT

Pretax deductions are subtracted from your employees' gross pay *before* you figure out how much income tax to withhold. Common examples include retirement plan contributions and health insurance premiums. For example, suppose Mary earns $250 per week. If she pays in $10 to her 401(k) and $20 toward health insurance, you would calculate her income tax withholding on $220 instead of $250.

Unemployment Taxes

If you've got payroll, chances are that you are required to deal with federal unemployment taxes (FUT), and the state version as well. At the federal level, these taxes are paid only by employers (no withholding here), and they're based directly on the total wages paid to employees. When it comes to state rules, though, there's a lot of variation.

Here are the general rules of state unemployment taxes:

- They are paid by employers only.
- They reduce your FUT burden.
- The tax rate is based on how many of your employees have filed unemployment claims.
- There's a cap on the maximum tax you'll owe for each employee.

As you'd expect, the specifics vary pretty widely, especially when it comes to crunching the numbers. Plus, in a couple of states, employees as well as employers do have to pay in to the system, and that means extra withholding responsibilities for employers. In regard to the FUT impact, if you pay any amount of state unemployment tax, you get a break on the federal; also, some states levy this tax even when your company is exempt at the federal level.

Employee Benefits and Bonuses

One way to attract and hold on to the best employees is to offer benefits, such as health insurance or a retirement plan. Another is to reward them for good work by bumping up their annual pay with a bonus. Most of the time, both of these extras run through the payroll.

Bonuses are simpler. They act just like regular paychecks, except for the amount. The only tricky part, as you'll soon learn, comes when you compute the withholding taxes for very big bonuses. Benefits are just plain more involved. They require more planning and paperwork, along with some special tax treatment.

Dealing with Benefits During Payroll

The two most common employee benefits are retirement plans and health insurance, both of which usually include contributions made by the employees themselves. When employees pay in to their retirement plans or for part of their health insurance premiums, you deduct their contributions directly from their paychecks; however, you deduct them on a pretax basis. That means when you're figuring out how much federal and (usually) state income tax to withhold, you don't base it on an employee's entire gross pay amount. Instead, you base it on gross pay minus any health insurance or retirement contributions the employee has made.

Special Considerations with Bonuses

At first glance, bonuses work just like regular paychecks. You start with a gross amount and take out taxes according to the tables. When the bonuses are in line with the employee's regular paycheck, such as when an employee earning $300 a week gets a $300 bonus, your payroll job stops right there.

Very large bonuses, though, take a little more thought. For example, if your company had an astronomically good year, you might hand out giant bonuses—say, $5,000 for an employee who normally earns $26,000 per year. Withholding the amount you normally would for his $500 weekly paycheck would leave him with a big tax bill next April. On the other hand, treating that one-time $5,000 bump as a regular weekly salary when you look in the tax tables would have you withhold far too much (though he may prefer that you do that, so ask him). To keep things simple, many employers just use a flat percentage, somewhere between 10 percent and 25 percent.

Calculating Take-Home Pay

The first step in figuring out take-home pay is calculating the gross pay, which is how much the employee has earned during the pay period. For salaried employees, getting to this number is a piece of cake—it's the same as last time (unless you've handed out raises). When you pay your employees in any other way, such as hourly or on a commission basis, you'll need to do a little math to come up with their current gross pay.

ESSENTIAL

When you start to pay employees, know what your state minimum wage is. The federal minimum wage rate is $5.15 per hour (or $206 for a forty-hour weekly salary). Some states have higher minimum wage rates. When the federal and state rates are different, you have to pay whichever is higher.

Let's take a brief look at what counts as taxable compensation, regardless of how you pay your employees. Most of the payroll laws refer to wages as an all-encompassing category. It includes what you think of as wages (hourly pay), fixed salaries, pay for piecework, overtime pay, bonuses, commissions—pretty much any label you could put on employee earnings, whatever scale they are based on. It doesn't matter if it's extra compensation above and beyond the normal salary; it doesn't even matter if you don't pay your employees in money (you could pay them in shoes, French fries, or legal services). Anything you give an employee in exchange for work they've done counts as taxable compensation.

On the flip side, there are plenty of things that seem like compensation that do not count as taxable when you're figuring out the payroll taxes. These include things such as:

- Loans to employees
- Expense reimbursements
- Nontaxable benefits (such as employer-paid health insurance)
- Gifts and awards

Then, as in most things that have to do with taxes, there are gray areas in which compensation being taxable or not depends on circumstances. These gray areas include things such as tips, advances against future earnings, and vacation pay.

Calculating Withholding Taxes

Every time you pay your employees, you have to take out taxes; you can't just give them gross pay for three weeks and take out a bigger lump of taxes in week four, for example. The tax amounts will be different for each employee, and maybe even for the same employee over different periods. The income tax you withhold for each employee throughout the year is supposed to come very close to what his full-year liability would be, and that depends on several unique factors. Your responsibility is limited to withholding taxes based on the information he gave you when he filled out his most recent W-4.

It sounds really tough, but isn't as bad as it seems. The IRS has detailed withholding tables you can use to look up how much income tax to deduct for each employee. You can get a free copy of the standard tables by calling the IRS (at 1-800-TAX-FORM) and requesting a copy of Publication 15. If you are using payroll software, it's even easier because the tables are built right in. All you have to do is enter each employee's wage and allowance information.

FICA taxes (the combined name for Social Security and Medicare), though, are two standard percentages multiplied by the gross pay, unchanging until an employee hits the $90,000 (as of 2005) Social Security tax limit. For the Social Security portion, the rate is 6.2 percent; you multiply that by the employee's gross pay. When his pay hits the $90,000 cap, you don't have to withhold Social Security taxes any more. The Medicare portion has no wage limit. You simply multiply employee wages by 1.45 percent and withhold that amount all year long.

FACT

There are several states that do not have a personal income tax on the books, so employers in those states don't have to withhold state income taxes. The no-withholding states are Alaska, Florida, Nevada, New Hampshire, South Dakota, Tennessee, Texas, Washington, and Wyoming.

As for state and local income taxes, the process is pretty much the same. You simply contact your state office of taxation to get a copy of its payroll tax rules. In those guidelines you will also find the rules for employees who live in one state and work in another. Sometimes you have to take out taxes for both states, sometimes only one, so check with your state tax office to find out which you have to do. Some states also impose an unemployment or a disability insurance tax on employees, usually a tiny fixed amount every pay period (such as $5, or 0.5 percent).

Dealing with Other Deductions

Once you are done with the withholding taxes, the next set of subtractions is considered voluntary deductions. These are items that the employee actually chooses to have taken directly out of his paycheck. It's up to you as the employer to decide whether you will offer these programs for the convenience of your employees. A large number of employers offer the two most common: retirement plan contributions and health insurance premiums.

Other work-related deductions, again done for the convenience of the employee, include things such as union dues, uniform purchases and cleaning, and parking. Deductions are not always limited to work-related items, though. Some employers will take out anything from charitable contributions to U.S. savings bond purchases. Again, it's your choice which of these voluntary deductions will be available to your employees. When you do offer them, you have to honor them, even if that becomes inconvenient.

An Example with Numbers

For this example, you have one employee, Joe Block. Joe is single and claimed no exemptions on his Form W-4. Your company is located in Ohio, where Joe lives. You pay Joe a steady salary of $300 per week. There are no voluntary deductions taken out of Joe's paycheck.

According to the standard federal income tax tables (for 2006), you withhold $31 from Joe's paycheck every week. Based on the 2006 withholding tax tables for Ohio, you take out $6.42 for state income taxes. His Social Security tax comes to $18.60, which is $300 times 6.2 percent. His Medicare tax is $4.35, calculated by multiplying $300 by 1.45 percent.

Once you subtract all the withholding taxes from Joe's gross weekly salary, you come up with his net take-home pay of $239.63. That will be the amount of his paycheck; on his pay stub, you will list every amount withheld from his gross pay.

The Journal Entries

Now that you have completed the actual paycheck portion of the payroll, you have to record the transactions in your payroll journal. The first transaction records the payroll itself. If you have only one employee, the journal entry will mirror his pay information. When you have more than one employee, your journal entry will be a summary of the totals for all employees. (Note: In the example below, the FICA Payable entry includes $18.60 for Social Security and $4.35 for Medicare.)

Payroll Journal Entry 1	
January 13, 2006	
Salary Expense	$300.00
Federal Income Tax Payable	$31.00
FICA Payable	$22.95
State Income Tax Payable	$6.42
Cash	$239.63

To record payroll for the week ending January 13, 2006.

A second transaction entry is also necessary so you can record the employer tax obligations for this payroll period. The taxes involved in this journal entry include the employer matching contributions to Social Security and Medicare, any employer-based state taxes (such as unemployment), and federal unemployment taxes. Continuing with the example from the previous section, the employer portion of FICA would equal exactly the amounts withheld from Joe's paycheck, which came to a total of $22.95 ($18.60 plus $4.35). Since the company does not have to pay state unemployment taxes, it has to pay the full amount of FUT, which comes to $18.60 ($300 times 6.2 percent).

Payroll Journal Entry 2	
January 13, 2006	
Payroll Tax Expense	$41.55
FICA Payable	$22.95
FUT Payable	$18.60

To record the employer portion of payroll taxes for the week ending January 13, 2006.

Those two journal entries take care of recording the payroll for the period. As you can see, only Joe's net pay is credited to the cash account. That's because it's the only amount actually paid at this time. Both the withholding taxes and employer taxes will be paid later on, when you file your payroll tax returns. At that time, you will debit the various tax payable accounts and credit your cash account, just like any other regular cash disbursement.

Payroll Tax Reporting and Filing

The rules for reporting, filing, and paying payroll taxes are written in a lengthy and somewhat convoluted way. Just thumbing through the various federal tax instruction guides, not to mention the state versions, could turn off even the most enthusiastic numbers cruncher. What they really say, though, when you cut through all the long-winded language, is basic: fill out this form by this date and mail a check to this address.

Because they are tax forms, there is some math to deal with, but most of it has been done throughout the year as you've been processing payroll. Some of these numbers will come straight out of your payroll journal, but you may have to perform simple calculations to arrive at others. The forms may look intimidating at first, but once you see what they are really asking for—a number you already know—you can relax and start filling in the blanks.

These are the two most important things to remember: file the forms on time, and make all your payments in full and on time. To make that even easier for you, you can now use credit cards to pay virtually all your payroll taxes (state and local payment requirements vary). Filing late, paying late, or paying the wrong amount can lead to fines, fees, and penalties that quickly add up. Sometimes, in fact, the penalties can add up to more than the original tax bill!

Report Withholding Taxes on Form 941

All the federal income, Social Security, and Medicare taxes you withhold from your employees' paychecks are reported together on IRS Form 941. In addition, the company portion of employment taxes shows up on this form. Form 941 is a quarterly tax return, so at the end of each three-month period you file it with the IRS. Payments, however, typically are due every month; if you pay a lot in wages, though, you may have to make tax deposits every other week.

The form itself is very straightforward. It starts with the total salaries and wages paid during the period, then moves on to the amount of federal income taxes withheld. Next comes the total Social Security and Medicare calculation; since you'll deposit both sides of this together, it's calculated in a lump sum. Add that total to the federal income tax total to get your total taxes due. Subtract all the payments you've already made to arrive at the remaining balance.

Federal Unemployment Tax

Right now, the FUT rate is 6.2 percent on the first $7,000 of gross wages for each employee you have; once each hits that $7,000 limit, you can stop paying in on his behalf. If your company also has to pay state unemployment taxes, you can use that to offset some of your FUT responsibility. This credit comes with a little hurdle to jump over: your state unemployment taxes must be paid in full, on time, and before the due date of your FUT return. Then you can take a credit that effectively knocks your FUT rate down to 0.8 percent, no matter what your state unemployment tax rate is.

ALERT!

If for some reason you can't pay your state unemployment taxes before your federal due date, don't worry. You can still grab the credit by simply filing for an extension for your FUT return. When that extension is granted (and it usually is), just make sure to pay the state amount by the new due date. That way, you'll still be entitled to the full federal credit.

Your FUT information is reported on IRS Form 940, and many small businesses can use the EZ version. This return has to be filed only annually (usually by January 31, with the prior year's information). Depending on how much you owe, though, you may have to make payments more frequently. If your FUT payable amount hits $500, you have to make a deposit right after that calendar quarter is done. For example, if your FUT has grown to $550 by June 30, you have to pay it by July 31. Otherwise, you can just pay when you file your Form 940.

Special Year-End Procedures

Even though you have to report, file, and pay payroll taxes throughout the year, there are a bunch of extra procedures to deal with at the end of the year. Some of these are additional informational returns to be filed with the IRS; some are special forms to be sent to employees and independent contractors who've worked for you during the year.

If you neglect to create or send Form W-2 to your employees, or if you purposely file incorrect forms, be prepared to face financial consequences. For each missing or erroneous W-2, your company is subject to a $50 fine. When you've got a whole bunch of employees, that fine can grow big very fast.

For each employee, you must complete and send out a Form W-2. That form reports his annual salary, taxes withheld, and other crucial information for his personal tax return (such as any retirement plan contributions he made). Form W-2 must be sent to your employees by January 31 of the following year. For each independent contractor you paid more than $600 during the year, you must send a Form 1099. These forms state the amount you paid and the reason; here the reason is usually nonemployee compensation.

To the federal government, you'll send a copy of each employee's W-2 along with a summary report, Form W-3. The procedure is similar for the 1099s you've sent out; a copy of each goes to the federal government along with a summary report, Form 1096. All of these reports are due on the last day of February.

Never Mess Around with Payroll Taxes

One common and potentially business-crushing mistake made by new employers is using withholding taxes as a business bank account. Rather than make payroll deposits in full and on time, they cover their other cash-flow gaps by borrowing from the payroll tax account. Doing that is 100 percent illegal, and the penalties are pretty stiff, often enough to put small businesses out of business.

Withholding taxes fall under a special set of laws, different from virtually all other kinds of taxes. That's because the money you withhold belongs to your employees, not to your company, and you hold that money in trust for them until you turn it over to the government on their behalf. When your company doesn't make the payments, both civil and criminal penalties may apply.

The biggest is the 100 percent penalty, and you can be held personally liable for paying it. If the IRS can prove that your company willfully didn't pay the taxes, you'll have to pay both the taxes and the penalty, which can be equal to the total taxes that were due. Willful nonpayment means that you chose not to pay the taxes, for whatever reason; not paying them because your company doesn't have enough money counts as willful nonpayment.

Still Want to Do It Yourself?

There is no question that you can do the payroll yourself if you want to. The main benefit to that is saving money; both bookkeepers and payroll services cost money. However, figuring out the payroll can suck up a lot of time, even using dedicated software.

Contrary to popular belief, payroll services are not ridiculously expensive. In fact, most of the ones that you have heard of are very competitively priced. Most also have special deals for small businesses with few employees. In addition, using a payroll service could end up saving you money in the long run, in a couple of crucial ways. First, payroll services are substantially less likely to file returns late or make calculation mistakes (using the wrong tax tables, for example); that saves you both interest and penalties. Second, many of these companies will process tax deposits for you, so those aren't skipped or late and subject to fines and penalties.

chapter 10

Always Know Your Cash

With a new or small business, cash is absolutely the most important asset you can have. Without it in plentiful supply, your business simply cannot survive. Unfortunately, many business owners confuse profits with cash, thinking that if they're earning income it means they have money. That's not always true. Learning how to effectively manage your cash flow, especially in the early struggle-filled days, can mean the difference between success and failure for your company. This chapter will teach you what you need to know to come out on the winning side.

10

The Importance of Having Cash

No business can survive without cash. Even with monumental profits on the books and the promise of growing future sales, a company without cash will not make it. If you don't have enough money to pay your bills, your vendors will stop supplying you with whatever it is your company needs to generate sales. More small companies go out of business because they're out of cash than for any other reason. In fact, the bankruptcy courts are full of small-business owners whose companies just couldn't pay the bills any more.

FACT

Product-based businesses usually have more money troubles than do service businesses. That's because any company that sells products has to first buy them (or the materials necessary to create them). That almost always means cash has to go out before it can possibly come in. Service companies may not need a lot of cash at first, but that doesn't mean they won't need it before it comes in.

Luckily, there are a lot of things you can do to prevent that dire situation. The most important one is to know how cash really flows in and out of your business. Then you can plan for shortfalls before they occur, nipping that problem in the bud. The easiest way to avoid cash crunches is to put enough money into the business at the start; absent that, you may have to contribute more capital or take out a loan to cover temporary crises. New businesses often use more cash than they bring in during the first six months to a year, depending on the type of business. Count on that in your planning stages.

Earning Profits but Out of Cash

One of the most baffling accounting occurrences for the newly initiated is when their company shows a clear profit, but their cash is running frighteningly low. New business owners often confuse making money (i.e., earning profits) with having money. However, profits don't always mean sufficient cash, any more than cash in the bank means clearing a healthy profit.

That sounds questionable, but it's true. Every time you make a sale on account, it adds to your revenues and your profitability, but it has absolutely no impact on your cash until the customer pays up. If you have a lot of slow-paying customers, that could put you into a big cash crunch. Even if they aren't paying you, you still have to pay your bills.

It's very common for new business owners to focus on sales, doing whatever they can to seal a deal. A lot of times that means extending credit to the customer, sometimes without making sure that the customer has a good payment record. Even customers with stellar credit history sometimes hit cash crunches of their own and make late payments to keep their own cash flowing more smoothly. Payments that are late or never made can wreak havoc on your cash flow Even though your sales numbers look great, and you're hitting all the sales goals you've set for the company, you could still run out of cash.

The Basics of Cash Flow

Cash flow describes the way money comes into and out of your business. As you might expect, when money comes in, it's called cash inflow; when money goes out, it's cash outflow. Keeping track of both sides of your cash equation is critical to the successful management of your company. For many new and small businesses, the outflow will (at least initially) exceed the inflow, and that's called negative cash flow. Much better, of course, is the opposite situation, with more cash coming in than going out. That's the goal to strive for: positive cash flow.

Just because you have more money going out than coming in right now doesn't necessarily mean that you are out of cash. If you have a sufficient cash cushion to get you through slow times, similar to a personal emergency savings account, a little imbalance won't cause a bankruptcy. However, you still need to work on establishing and maintaining a steady positive cash flow.

In order to successfully manage your cash flow, you need to know what's going on right now and what steps you could take to make the situation better. Start with a detailed cash-flow projection, a sort of budget that tracks the cash moving into and out of your business. That will help you see where cash is going and give you some ideas to stretch out the outflow. In addition, you'll learn how cash comes in and possibly find some ways to speed up that process. You have much more control over cash going out than you do over cash coming in, so that will be your initial cash management focus: minimizing cash shortfalls by keeping tighter reins on your cash outflow.

Creating Your Cash Projection

The first thing you need to create a cash projection is a sales projection. After all, most of your incoming cash will be a direct result of sales. Try to come up with a reasonable estimate for sales over the next six months. If your business is already off the ground, you can look at sales from the last few periods and base your forward estimates on that; if you are really just starting out, enlist your accountant to help you with some realistic sales projections. Once you have sales estimates worked out, figure out how much of those sales will be made for cash, and how much on credit. Cash sales trigger immediate cash inflows, but leave thirty to sixty days for collection on credit sales.

Next, figure out your expected cash outflows for the same six-month period. Include every check you plan to write to pay vendors and cover basic business expenses, along with any cash you plan to take out of the business (after all, you need positive cash flow in your personal life, too). Finally, put your projected outflows together with your estimated inflows and see how they stack up. Whatever the result is, combine it with the company's cash reserves (i.e., its already existing cash balance).

What the End Results Mean

For most new and small businesses, good cash management can mean the difference between an ongoing business and a business failure. The trick of good cash management is anticipation and action: knowing what's coming and dealing with it before it happens.

You may end up with negative cash flow in some periods, which isn't great, but it doesn't mean the end of your business; in fact, it's practically unheard of for a new business to completely avoid this issue. However, ending up with a negative cash balance in your projections is a big problem, and one you'll need to address immediately. That situation occurs when the negative cash flow uses up all of your cash reserves (or even more than that), and the company has no cash to draw from. If you anticipate a negative cash balance in the upcoming months, acting now to shore up your reserves will help you better weather the problem. At the end of this chapter, you'll find a section on what to do when cash starts running low.

If you expect to receive cash from other sources, include that in your incoming cash projection as well. Those other sources could include additional owner contributions or loan proceeds, for example. Even though these inflows won't be repetitive, they still belong on your cash budget.

Tracking Your Incoming Cash

When money comes into your company, it's called cash receipts. When you do your bookkeeping, you record that incoming money in your cash receipts journal. This special journal is set up to make your job as easy as possible and to keep you from writing the same things over and over. Although the transactions may vary throughout the day, one thing will always remain constant: the debit account will always be cash.

The most common sources of incoming cash will be sales and accounts receivable collections. These accounts, along with sales tax payable, get dedicated columns in your cash receipts journal. There also will be other circumstances, though they may be rare, in which cash will come into the company from other sources. Those sources could include things such as:

- Owner contributions
- Loan proceeds
- Rebates or refunds
- Interest or dividends (from investments)
- Return of security deposits

These transactions don't occur often enough to merit their own columns; instead, the credit side of the transaction falls into the miscellaneous column. When you get to the end of a page, foot each column. Next, add the debit totals together; then add the credit totals together. When total debits prove equal to total credits, you know your journal is in balance. Then you can proceed to posting the transactions to the general ledger accounts. In addition, accounts receivable collections need to be posted to the individual customer accounts in the customer ledger.

To make your bookkeeping job as simple as possible, make sure that every transaction in your cash receipts journal corresponds to a bank deposit slip. That does not mean you can't combine multiple transactions on a single deposit slip (though tracking is much easier when you do). If you want to use some of the cash from the daily receipts, write a check or get a withdrawal from the ATM rather than pinching it from your deposit. It may seem like a lot of bother at the time, but later on, when you're trying to figure out why your cash seems out of whack, you'll be happy you did it that way.

Recording Your Outgoing Cash

Whenever you pay out cash (even if you do it by writing a check), you record that transaction in your cash disbursements journal. This special journal helps you track your outgoing cash as simply as possible by including special columns for the accounts you use most. The primary credit column in your cash disbursements journal (sometimes also called the cash payments journal) is for cash. The debit columns here could be ridiculously numerous; if the journal pages included a column for every separate expense or payable account, they wouldn't fit on your desk. For that reason, limit the dedicated columns to the top five or six—the ones that are repeated the most—and stick everything else in a miscellaneous column.

The most common dedicated columns in the cash disbursements journal are accounts payable, merchandise purchases, gross payroll, and owner withdrawals. Typically, payroll has its own special subjournal to hold the details of each employee's paycheck, and the summary transaction is recorded in the cash disbursements journal. When a transaction involves a payment to accounts payable, make sure to record the name of the vendor you paid and the invoice numbers covered by your payment.

Every time you finish a page in the journal, foot each column. Then separately combine the total debits and the total credits, making sure they're equal; that proves your journal is in balance. Once you know the page is balanced, you can post the column totals to the appropriate general ledger accounts. Amounts in the miscellaneous column are posted individually to their general ledger accounts, and payments in the accounts payable column must be posted to the individual vendor pages in the vendor ledger.

FACT

Some companies use special expense journals in order to keep their cash disbursements journal looking cleaner. When they sit down to pay the monthly bills, they record the disbursements in the expense journal. Then they write up column totals as a single line entry in the cash disbursements journal, with a reference to the subjournal.

Reconcile Your Bank Statement

If you've ever had any kind of bank account for which you received periodic statements, you know that the balance you think you have doesn't always match up exactly to the balance the bank thinks you have. In fact, as explained in Chapter 4, it would be pretty surprising if they did match exactly. That's why you prepare bank reconciliations (a.k.a. bank recs) every month, to verify your cash balance.

Doing your bank rec manually is usually pretty simple; how long it takes depends largely on your transaction volume, with more transactions translating into more time-consuming bank recs. With accounting software, the process goes more quickly and is even easier to do. In fact, most programs contain dedicated software procedures strictly to deal with bank recs and to make them as painless as possible.

Timing Differences

Timing differences come into play mainly with outstanding checks and deposits in transit, events you've recorded that haven't made it into the bank records yet. As soon as you write a check, you record it in your check register; that can happen even before you put the check in an envelope, let alone before it clears the bank. For that reason, your checkbook balance may be lower than the statement balance. The same holds for deposits: you may record a deposit slip in your checkbook before you actually take it to the bank, giving you a higher balance than the bank says you have.

Once you account for all the entries you've recorded that haven't made it into the formal bank records yet, you can turn your attention to items on the bank statement that haven't made their way into your journal entries yet. This can include things such as:

- Bank charges
- ATM transactions
- Check order fees
- Interest

Anything that appears on the bank statement that you haven't recorded yet fits in this category.

Common Errors

When it comes to mistakes made by banks and businesses, most are really just variations on a common theme: mixing up the numbers. Transposition errors top the list and are often the simplest to detect (they always result in a difference that's divisible by nine). Transposition errors occur when two digits of a number are reversed, such as recording $127 as $172. Another common mistake, one that's much harder to find, is simply picking up the wrong number; for example, check number 1230 on 4/16 for $360 is recorded for $416 by either your bank or your bookkeeper.

The Basic Format for a Bank Rec

If you've ever reconciled your personal checking account, you have some idea what a bank rec looks like. The standard format is the one you'll see on the back page of your bank statement. This tried-and-true method is simple and straightforward, and no one has devised a better way to do it (except to do it by computer, which still uses the same format).

To get yourself set for this process, collect all your canceled checks and deposit slips for the period; these are your source documents. Put the checks in numerical order and the deposit slips in date order. Then compare your source documents to the bank statement to make sure they match.

A bank rec comes in two sections: bank to book, and book to bank. In the bank to book section, you'll start with the bank statement balance. Add to that any deposits you've recorded that didn't show up on the statement to get an updated balance. Then list and total all your outstanding checks, and subtract that total from the updated balance. If there are any errors on the bank statement, note them, and either add or subtract them from the latest total. (Remember to report these errors to the bank.) The new final result is called the adjusted bank statement balance.

Next, your attention will shift to your cash balance, which you'll pick up from the company checkbook. To that you will add any interest earned on the account that hasn't yet been recorded, and subtract any new bank charges. If there are any errors on the book side, add or subtract them (as appropriate) to come up with a final adjusted checkbook balance. That bottom-line balance has to equal your adjusted bank statement balance for your reconciliation to be complete.

Once you've finished the bank rec, you still have two more steps to take to finish the full process. First, make entries in the general journal for all the adjustments you had to make to the book balance in your reconciliation; then post those entries to the applicable general ledger accounts.

What to Do When Cash Runs Low

If your cash supplies seem to be dwindling, don't panic. There are plenty of steps you can take to improve your cash situation, both immediately and for the long haul. For quick infusions, you (and your co-owners) may have to dip into personal funds or tap family and friends for instant loans.

When the situation allows for somewhat longer short-term solutions, you have more options open to your company. One of those options is called factoring, which means selling your accounts receivable. Factoring gives you speedier cash flow than waiting for your customers to pay, but at a price: you can't sell those receivables for full face value, so you'll get less money than if you waited for the normal collection cycle to kick in. Along those lines, you can also sell fixed assets, such as machinery, equipment, and buildings, and then turn right around and lease them; this common business deal is called (unimaginatively) a sale and leaseback. You get a big hit of cash right away and deductible lease payments going forward.

Long-term strategies should be implemented as early as possible, because it can take a while for them to have any effect. The simplest is to talk to your vendors; if you aren't buying from them on credit, it may be time to start. Start these talks with some knowledge under your belt, including what really goes on in the industry and in your area, not just what shows up as standard payment terms. Your suppliers want you to buy from them—you're their customer, and they can't profit without you. It may take a little negotiation, but if extending credit is a crucial part of keeping your company as a steady customer, you'll probably get what you want. (For more information about dealing with vendors, see Chapter 12).

Other long-term strategies include things such as re-evaluating your inventory mix. Think about dropping (at least temporarily) any products that are tying up your cash flow. Look for items that represent a relatively large cash investment and don't move out the door very quickly; replace them with faster-moving, less cash-intensive (on your side) merchandise. You can still place special orders for customers who want the products you stop carrying regularly, but ask for an up-front deposit. Finally, the best thing you can do to improve your long-term cash flow is to employ a combined focus on growing sales and improving collections; you need to have both for sustained profit growth and a comfortable cash balance.

chapter 11

Handling Customer Credit

In today's highly competitive business market, you may have to take extra steps to attract and keep customers. One of those extras may be extending credit to some or all of them. By letting customers purchase goods and services on account, you can encourage them to buy more from you without impacting their immediate cash flow. The trick is to do that without letting it have a negative impact on your cash flow. All it takes to do this successfully is a little caution and a lot of information.

Why Sell on Credit?

Most small-business owners do not want to deal with all the expected hassles that come with offering credit to customers. Most of them also realize that in today's highly competitive markets, extending credit (at least to some customers) can be essential to success. Many drag their feet, thinking about setting up a credit system only when they absolutely have to, and often without much planning. Although it's very common for businesses that sell to other businesses to extend credit to their customers, you can offer this convenience to individuals as well.

To make credit work for you and your business, figure out what you want to do before you get stuck extending credit haphazardly. That way, you will be able to spend more of your time growing your business than chasing after customers for payments. Plus, having the right credit policies in place can give your business a huge sales boost.

FACT

Any time you let a customer pay with anything other than cash, you have extended credit. Even though sales that are paid with credit cards or checks on the spot are recorded on your books as cash sales, they technically are still forms of credit, as your business has not yet received any money.

Keep in mind that offering credit may not make sense for your business, or at least not right now. Your company does not have to extend credit just because many other companies do; the decision should be based on what works for your company's unique circumstances.

Whether to offer credit depends on four factors:

- Your customers
- Your industry
- Typical transaction size
- Your financial situation

None of these factors should be looked at in a vacuum. Rather, consider all of them in connection to your business circumstances. That will help you make the best decision for your company.

The Business Side

First, look at your customer relationships. When your business depends on repeat customers, extending credit is a simple way to keep them happy and loyal. Knowing your customers well (as happens with repeat customers) also lends itself to offering credit; the closer the relationship, the more likely you are to get paid regularly and on time. Then there are your customers themselves: when your customers are well-established and financially stable, you are more likely to let them buy now and pay later.

Next, find out what the industry practice is. If offering credit is the standard, you may have to follow along to attract customers. In industries where it's rare to offer credit, you may decide to do it anyway to give yourself a competitive edge. Sometimes the industry standard will be crystal clear: for example, ice cream shops don't normally offer credit for cone purchases, but car dealers almost always write up credit agreements. Other times, the answer may be fuzzy, and the other factors will play a bigger part in your decision.

The Money Side

The size of an average sale is next on the consideration list. When you have a lot of tiny transactions, credit may not come into play at all. Bigger transactions (in money terms) often lend themselves to credit terms, as in the ice cream cone versus car example.

Finally, your company's financial situation will play a role in your decision. Having ample cash reserves gives you a lot more flexibility when it comes to customer collections: when you've got money in the bank, you won't sweat it when someone pays late. When cash is tight, which is often the case for new and small businesses, you may not be able to carry customer credit balances, and that makes offering credit a less good idea. This is particularly true when you are selling products that you have to buy (and pay for) in advance; shelling out cash, and then struggling to collect from customers, can quickly put you out of business.

Establish Your Credit Policies

The first guideline for setting up your company's credit policies is to take a look at other businesses just like yours. If you work in an industry that has pretty standard customs, you have a solid starting point from which to build your own credit rules. For example, most accountants send out bills after they've performed services, and wait for their clients to send checks. Pretzel stands, on the other hand, expect instant cash payment before they'll hand over the snack. Retail stores often accept credit cards, checks, and cash. Car dealers take a down payment and let the customer pay the balance over time, with interest. Your credit policies will be based on the kind of business you run, as well as the kinds of customers you have.

ALERT!

Many professional service companies use cash basis accounting systems and bill their clients for services. Technically speaking, using the cash basis means there is no accounts receivable account, since you don't record transactions until money changes hands. Practically speaking, you need to keep track of who owes you money, and how much. In these cases, you record the sale and the receivable on your books, but the sale would not count for tax purposes until payment was received.

Once you decide to offer credit, you need to figure out what types of credit you want to extend to your customers. The first level of credit is accepting checks and credit cards from customers at the point of sale. This practice offers a convenience to customers without increasing your risk of loss to an unacceptable point. Will there be times when a check bounces or a credit card payment doesn't come through? Yes, but those are typically relatively uncommon occurrences, especially with electronic, on-the-spot approval available. On your books, these transactions are recorded as cash sales, because you receive payment at the time of sale.

Level two is typically used by businesses offering professional services, such as consultants. The norm for these types of firms is to bill clients once a service has been performed. The client then has thirty days to mail in payment. For transactions like these, make an entry to accounts receivable when you record the sale.

The next level of credit usually involves business-to-business product sales, and its terms are a little more involved. This is commonly called trade credit, and it is the version most strongly dictated by industry norms. Trade credit comes with its own lingo, which is fairly standard across industry lines; you need to familiarize yourself with the terms if you plan to offer this option.

Understanding Common Trade Credit Terms

When you see credit terms included on an invoice, they look like a secret code: 2/10, n30. That "code" has a simple translation; it means that the customer can take 2 percent off the balance if she pays within ten days of the invoice date, or she can pay the full balance within thirty days.

Here's the breakdown. The first number (the 2 from the example above) is the discount percentage. This discount is used to encourage customers to pay quickly, which is an advantage for your cash flow. You can set your early-pay discount at whatever level you like, but it should be along the same lines as industry standards.

The second number (the 10 in the example) refers to the time limit for the early payment discount. Again, you have some flexibility here. You can set the time frame, usually for anywhere from five to twenty days, based on your cash-flow needs. Why five to twenty? The bottom limit is five, because it will take time for your customer to get the invoice and cut a check, and a little more time for you to receive payment. The top limit of twenty goes with a normal payment turnaround time of thirty days; any closer to the end date and you'll end up in arguments with a lot of customers.

The "n" stands for "net." In this instance, net means the stated net amount due. Essentially, it's the bottom line of the printed invoice, however much that is. The final number (the 30) stands for the final acceptable payment date, measured by the number of days from the invoice date. So, for a $100 invoice dated June 1 with 2/10, n30 terms, the customer could either pay $98 by June 11 (ten days from June 1) or $100 by July 1 (thirty days from June 1).

Where Can You Find the Industry Standards?

It used to take quite a bit of legwork to learn the inside scoop on industry practices, but now a simple click of the mouse or quick trip to the library can get you plenty of information. Some of the best information sources include:

- Your industry's trade association
- The U.S. Small Business Administration
- SCORE (Service Corps of Retired Executives)
- Credit agencies

In addition to these more official channels, you can get the direct scoop from other small-business owners in your area. Even if they're not in the exact same industry (i.e., they aren't your direct competitors), you can get an idea from them about the way similar companies conduct business.

Don't Give Credit to Just Anyone

Sure, letting people or companies buy from you on credit will increase your sales. If they don't pay you, though, the sale will not count, and you'll be out whatever they got (whether it's a physical product or a service you provided).

New business and small-business owners often feel that they have to extend credit to everyone who asks for it, fearing that they will alienate both existing and potential customers if they say no. Saying yes all the time, though, can get you into a serious cash crunch. The truth is, there are people and companies that simply do not pay their bills, or only pay after you put extensive time and effort (and sometimes money) into collecting what you are owed.

How to Get Credit Information on Customers

Before you extend credit to a customer, whether it's a business or an individual, take some steps to help ensure that you'll actually get paid. At the very least, have every potential credit customer fill out a credit application. You can get a standard form at the stationery store or create your own (have your lawyer look at it before you start using it). These forms ask for some basic information, including name and address, but may also request bank account and credit card information and names of other business creditors.

The next step is to get a credit report that gives you a good idea of the customer's credit history. Use whichever credit agency you prefer; you'll get basically the same information from any of the big three (TRW, Equifax, and TransUnion). When you're checking on an individual before issuing credit, make sure that you have his permission to do so (a spoken agreement is okay); if he already owes you money, though, you don't need permission to run the check.

Getting credit information for a business is even easier, because businesses typically make more information public. Your credit research level should match the amount of credit you're planning to extend: you need to collect more data for a $5,000 credit line than a $500 line. If it's a company you've already been dealing with, one that's been around for a long time and has a good reputation, you may decide to just take your chances; for unfamiliar or questionable businesses, though, start a file. At the very least, ask for the company's most recent set of financial statements. Although it seems counterintuitive, balance sheets are the most valuable statements to use for evaluating payment potential: it shows you both the cash the company has and the amount it owes to other creditors.

Setting Limits

A key component of your credit policy is just how much credit to offer to your customers. Just as your credit cards come with limits, the credit you offer will have a preset limit as well. It can be a blanket limit for everyone, or you can tailor the limit to the particular client. Remember, these limits aren't set in stone, and you can adjust them to specific situations and change them when they aren't working well.

The results of the credit check can offer some guidance in setting limits, and so can your experience with each customer. Someone with a stellar credit rating who has a proven track record of paying your company's bills on time may merit a higher limit than does someone with a spotty credit history. Sometimes, though, regardless of the numbers, your relationship with a customer can have the biggest influence on your decision. You may decide to raise the credit limit for client who has always paid you in full and on time, no matter how mediocre his credit score was when you ran the initial check.

Make sure that the credit limit you set is high enough to cover at least one or two typical customer invoices. For example, if a customer usually buys $500 worth of merchandise in a single purchase, buying on credit will be convenient for him only if his limit is at least $500.

Creating Invoices and Account Statements

In order for customers to pay you, they have to know how much they owe. Before writing a check, your customers, especially if they are businesses, will want a lot more information than just the amount due. Your company also has its own bookkeeping to consider. An invoice is the source document that satisfies everyone's needs here: You need it to record the on-account sale, and the customer needs it in order to pay you properly. At the end of each month, you need to prepare account statements for all customers whose accounts have had transactions during that month. Several different transaction types may have taken place, such as:

- Sales
- Credits
- Payments
- Discounts
- Finance charges

Sales, as you learned in Chapter 6, are documented by invoices. Credit memos are essentially negative invoices; they reduce the customer's balance. Credits are usually granted when customers return merchandise or are unhappy with goods received, or to remove a disputed charge from an account. Payments are usually received monthly from credit customers, often (but not always) for the full amount of the previous month's statement. Customers may take early payment discounts that you offered in an effort to bring in cash faster; when they do that, the payment won't match the previous statement balance and you have to adjust the account accordingly. Finally, you may decide to add finance charges to the statements of late-paying customers. Any transactions that apply to a particular account will appear on that customer's monthly statement.

Creating Invoices

Accounting software comes prepacked with standard invoice forms. Some programs let you customize the invoice design; for others, you're stuck with the layout they supply. All of them, though, will print your company name, address, and phone number on the top of the invoice, and some even allow for artwork (such as company logos). Invoices created by accounting software are automatically numbered in sequence, unless you manually override the invoice number. They also automatically include all pertinent customer information, including the bill to and ship to addresses, contact name, and details of the sales transaction.

Manual invoices require a little more work on your part, whether you create them on your computer or use preprinted manual invoices (available from most stationery stores or print shops). You have to fill in all of the customer information, as well as the details of the sale. Be extra careful with your math, especially when it comes to calculating any applicable sales tax; if you don't charge the customer enough, your company will take the loss. In addition, make sure you have a copy of every invoice somewhere, whether you save it on your computer or make a photocopy before handing it over to the customer.

Preparing Monthly Statements

A basic customer statement looks like a numeric grocery list: it contains every invoice number, total sales amount, payment received—basically a quick review of the month's activity without all the cumbersome detail. At the top, your company name and mailing address must appear (even if you enclose a preprinted self-addressed envelope), as well as the name and billing address of your customer.

Customer statements are created automatically by most accounting programs; all you have to do is request them. You may have several print options, such as not printing any zero or credit balance accounts, or not printing any accounts without activity. While it can be much more efficient to skip over the accounts with no current activity, it's a good idea to print zero and credit balance accounts that have had activity during the period. Even though you probably won't mail them, you can still look at them to make sure they appear correct.

QUESTION?

Why should I include a self-addressed envelope?
Customers will pay you more quickly when their bills come with payment envelopes. It's a lot easier to stick a check in a ready envelope than to bother with a blank one. Also, you'll avoid address errors.

With a manual system, you create statements for each customer based on the current information in your accounts receivable subledger. Each ledger page contains at least summary information of every invoice, payment, and credit transaction that's occurred during the month. That summary information is all you need on the statement, which is really just a listing of the monthly activity culminating in a total balance due.

Dealing with Collections

Sometimes customers just do not pay their bills. Your business, however, has a legal right to collect any money that they owe you. That doesn't mean you show up on their doorstep the very day an invoice becomes past due. It does mean, though, that you have to enforce your credit policies in a way that gets cash in your door without making your customers run away.

After a while, you'll get the hang of how your customers work. Some will pay right away; others will send a check after a reminder phone call or two. Others will say they're sending checks, then won't do it. The fine line you have to walk is whether to continue extending credit to delinquent customers or to cut them off and risk alienating them.

The Aging Schedule

In a perfect world, every customer would pay every invoice right on time and no checks would ever bounce. There are customers like that, plenty of them, but certainly not all fit into that mold.

Fortunately, there is a single accounting report that can help you stay on top of your delinquent accounts, figure out which ones are still collectible, and show you which are lost causes. That report is called the aging schedule, and it will give you all the information you need to manage your accounts receivable more efficiently, which in turn will improve your cash flow.

An aging schedule includes all of your credit customers. It classifies each of their invoices in one of four time categories:

- Current
- Over thirty days
- Over sixty days
- Over ninety days

Aging schedules count from the invoice date, and compare it to the current date, which means that an invoice in the over-thirty category would be for a sale that took place at least thirty-one days ago, not for an invoice that was already more than thirty days late. In most cases, you don't have to worry about invoices until they hit the over-sixty-day mark; that does indicate the invoice is more than a month past due (if you offer thirty-day credit terms). Once an invoice hits the over-sixty column, send out a past-due notice; that often works to get the invoice paid. Invoices that are still outstanding after ninety days require a phone call from someone at your company. If the customer is not responsive, you may need to call in a collection agency.

What to Do about Bad Debts

Sometimes, no matter what you do, you just won't be able to collect from a customer. When that happens, all you can do (from an accounting standpoint) is write it off. As soon as you know for certain that a particular account is uncollectible, remove that account from the books and consider the bad debt a cost of doing business.

The accounting procedure differs depending on whether you use the cash or accrual method. Technically, there's no such thing as bad debt expense under the cash basis, because no sale is recorded until cash changes hands. If you haven't booked a sale, you can't book a corresponding loss. There is one exception: a bounced check. When a customer pays you with a check, you record that sale. If the check is no good, you can deduct the full amount as a bad debt.

With accrual accounting, you write a journal entry to recognize the bad debt. Since these are (hopefully) rare entries, they are recorded in the general journal. You do this with a debit to bad debt expense and a credit to accounts receivable. Remember to credit both the accounts receivable control account in the general ledger and the individual customer account in the subledger.

Accounting for Accounts Receivable Transactions

When it comes to accounts receivable, there are three basic transactions: two that you'll see a lot of, and one that (ideally) you won't. The two everyday transactions are recording credit sales and collecting on-account payments. The third involves writing off bad debts. Credit sales are originally recorded in the sales journal, on-account payments in the cash receipts journal, and bad debt write-offs in the general journal (as you learned in the previous section).

Every accounts receivable transaction hits the general ledger account, but it also hits the individual customer account in your subledger. In the customer ledgers, every single transaction is recorded individually. Invoices show up as debits, increasing the account balance; the usual credit side of the entry includes sales and possibly sales tax payable. Payments show up as credits, decreasing the account balance; the debit side of these entries is cash. In the general ledger, though, only summary entries from the sales or cash receipts journal are posted.

chapter 12

Controlling Purchase Costs

Product costs take up a large chunk of the resources of merchandising and manufacturing businesses. Learning how to manage your inventory and control your total product costs can help free up a lot of precious cash. In addition, as you develop solid relationships with your vendors, you can get them to let you make your purchases on account, which also improves your cash flow. Here you'll find ways to optimize your inventory (to keep your customers happy) as well as your cash flow (which keeps you and your vendors happy).

Know What You Want Before You Buy

Planning your purchases may not sound like as much fun as coming up with a splashy new ad campaign, but it can do an awful lot for your bottom line in the long run. In fact, cutting costs has a bigger impact on profitability than does increasing sales. Consider this: Lower product costs mean higher gross profits on every single sale, with no extra work on your part. The trick is to purchase wisely, but to do that you need to know exactly what you want.

ALERT!

When you're just starting out, you may not have a handy roster of vendors to choose from. Rather than simply pulling names out of the phone book, try to get recommendations from other business owners who make similar purchases. You can also check with your local chamber of commerce to gauge the reputation of a local supplier.

No matter what you purchase for your business, whether it's ongoing inventory or a one-time equipment buy, consider the product specifications that will best suit your company before you even start talking to vendors. Specifications don't have to include specific brands or model numbers (though if you know those details, write them in); you can start with things such as price range, size, and functionality. Once you know what you're looking for, start calling around to vendors to get price, availability, and service information.

One-time purchases, such as fax machines or computers, are easier to deal with because you have to consider only what you want; you're the end customer here. Trying to buy inventory can be trickier, especially before you open the doors to customers, because you have to figure out what other people will want to buy. There's no hard and fast rule here to getting it right the first time, but planning your purchases will get you closer. Stick with what you've chosen to stock according to your business plan; you can adapt from there.

Choose Your Vendors Wisely

Your vendors have as much interest in your company's success as you do. When you make a lot of sales, they make a lot of sales; when you get paid, they get paid. Having reliable and trustworthy vendors can help your business succeed, just as dealing with unreliable or shady firms can cause major setbacks.

Start by asking around; other business owners in your area can be a great source of information. Once you've got a list of names, call your local Better Business Bureau to find out whether any complaints have been filed against any of the vendors on your list. You can visit vendor Web sites and even tour their physical locations. You can ask for customer testimonials and for product samples as well. The key is to get as much information as possible before you make a large monetary commitment to a vendor you don't know.

As you begin to choose vendors, particularly those who will stock your inventory, try to think of them as business partners. You want to choose the ones with whom your company can develop a long-term, mutually profitable relationship, and that relationship starts with your first request for a price quote. Don't be afraid to ask vendors for quotes; they're used to it and they probably expect it. After all, this is a major purchase, and it's never wise to make a major purchase without shopping around—especially when you're going to a vendor you've never dealt with before.

When you're dealing with a new business and new vendors, make sure to get price quotes from at least two sources for any purchase over $150. If your order will be a lot more than that, consider getting at least three different quotes; more is even better.

If you're having a hard time finding vendors, and an even harder time finding information about them, you can run your own test by placing a very small order, under $100 in total value. If that process goes well, take it up a notch and place a slightly larger order the next time. Once you feel comfortable with the vendor, you can place your full-blown orders without worry.

Getting Quotes

When you want to make a big purchase for your business, you need to know the total cost upfront. To get that information, you need to ask the people who sell whatever it is you want to buy. In order for that information to be fixed (as opposed to changeable), it's best to get it in writing. When your company is buying a product, that information will come in the form of a quote; when it's services you're after, the quote is usually referred to as an estimate.

The best way to get a quote is to talk with a salesperson; quote requests that come by mail are often ignored. Phone contact is fine, especially after you've begun to build a relationship with that vendor or salesman. For your first time out, though, a face-to-face meeting could prove more fruitful, especially if you're spending a significant sum. Even though salesmen themselves are seldom involved in setting company pricing policy, they often have some leeway when it comes to closing a deal. When you establish a personal connection with a salesman, he'll work harder with you and for you; after all, making a sale to you is his bread and butter. Flexible areas often include lower unit pricing when you buy in bulk, and better credit terms.

Hitting it off with the salesman is a great start toward developing a good relationship with a vendor. However, don't stop after getting a single quote just because you like the first salesman you meet with. Another vendor may offer better pricing, better terms, better merchandise, and maybe a salesman that you'll like even better.

Avoid These Vendors

There are some vendors that you should avoid. If you run across a vendor with one (or more) of the following characteristics, run in another direction:

- Accepts cash only
- Asks for checks made out to cash
- Won't send a brochure or catalog
- Won't give you a price quote or estimate in writing

- Dirty, disorganized stockroom
- No warehouse or storage facility

If one (or more) of these factors is the norm in your industry, and the vendor in question has gotten high marks from a reliable source, it's probably safe to keep him on your list. However, if it's the vendor telling you this is normal practice, and you can't verify that with anyone else, look for a different vendor.

Getting Vendors to Extend Credit

It can be hard for new, small, unproven businesses to get credit terms from vendors. In fact, some vendors may insist on deposits or cash on delivery until they're comfortable with your company. Even though your brand-new business won't have a credit history, let alone a credit rating, there still are things you can do to help convince vendors to extend credit to your fledgling company.

FACT

When a vendor offers you an early payment discount, do whatever you can to take advantage of it. Although 1 percent or 2 percent doesn't seem like much at face value, it can add up. Every penny you save on your purchases translates into an extra penny of profit for your pocket.

From your company's perspective, you want to ask for as much credit as possible for as long as possible. Learn what the industry norms are, and what's standard in your local area before you start talking to vendors. If typical terms include a $5,000 credit line and a 60-day payment window, don't ask for $1,000 line for thirty days; if you ask for less, you'll probably get less.

Once you've gotten credit established with a vendor, make sure to pay promptly, especially in the beginning of your relationship. As your company develops a sterling credit reputation, you'll be able to ask for even better terms: a higher credit line, a longer payment window, early payment discounts. On top of that, vendors are more likely to go the extra mile for customers who make timely payment. That can come in handy when you need something unusual, like a last-minute special order.

It helps if you think of your vendors as potential financiers for your business. Every time they let you buy something now and pay for it thirty days from now, it's as if they've given you a short-term interest-free loan, something no smart entrepreneur would ever turn down.

Why You Want Vendor Credit

It's important to understand why it's crucial for your company's success to get those vendors to let you buy now and pay later. Inventory and other major purchases are among the biggest cash drains your company faces, and postponing the inevitable payout improves your cash-flow situation.

Here's how the cycle works without vendor credit. On Monday, you get ten inventory items and pay $500 for them. That inventory hits your shelves on Tuesday. By the end of the week, you've sold four units for $100 each, and two of those sales were on account; that means your company has brought in only $200 cash so far, after putting out $500, which gives you a $300 cash-flow deficit. If you have vendor credit, you put out no money up front but still would get $200 back, for $200 of positive cash flow. You would pay your vendor for the initial purchase after you started bringing in money because of it.

In a nutshell: Without credit from your vendors, you have to pay for your inventory before you sell even one item, creating a drain on your cash flow. With vendor credit, you can pay for your inventory after you've begun selling it and collecting from customers, giving a positive boost to your cash situation.

How to Get Vendor Credit

Just as your company shouldn't extend credit to a company it knows nothing about, so it is for your vendors. Until your company has a solid reputation and a sterling credit rating, it may take some creativity on your part to get vendors to let your company make purchases on account. Luckily, there are a few different tacks you can take to accomplish that. The first step, though, always involves asking for credit.

All the vendor really wants is to feel assured that he's going to get paid. It's your job to provide that assurance. If you already have a set of financial statements, no matter what time period they cover, you can show them to the vendor. Don't worry if they show a small loss or a little negative cash flow; as long as you have some cash in the bank, and ongoing revenues, you have a good weapon in your arsenal. If your financial statements aren't much to look at, or you don't have any yet, show the vendor a pared-down version of your business plan. Include your sales forecasts and prospective financial statements, but leave out any proprietary information.

Offer existing credit references, as well. If your company got a startup loan from the bank, let the vendor know. That tells him that the bank considers your company a worthwhile investment, and helps build his confidence in your company.

Another thing to try when your company is new and unproven (meaning a credit risk for the vendor) is asking for lower-than-usual credit terms for a trial period. If the vendor normally offers a $5,000 credit line but is hesitant with you, ask for $1,000 line to start with. He has less to lose, and you have a chance to prove your company is reliable.

Creating Purchase Orders

If your company sells products, it first needs to buy them. In order to avoid potential inventory snafus, most buying companies use purchase orders to confirm the details of the agreement.

When you deal with vendors, especially new or troublesome vendors, a purchase order is your safety net. These documents come from your company, and they specify exactly what is being purchased. Purchase orders typically include the following information:

- Quantity being purchased
- Item number and/or description
- Agreed-upon unit cost per item
- Extended total cost (quantity times unit cost)
- Applicable sales tax
- Expected delivery date
- Agreed-upon payment terms

In addition to product and payment specifications, the purchase order includes contact information for your company, the name and address of the vendor, and the person (on the vendor side) whom you dealt with when agreeing to the purchase. Purchase orders also come with unique identifying numbers, to make tracking easier for both you and your vendors.

Dealing with Purchase Problems

Like most areas of business, purchases aren't completely problem-free; in fact, there are lots of different ways that troubles can arise. Orders may be filled incorrectly or incompletely, merchandise may be damaged while it's being transported, products may be of lower quality than expected (particularly when dealing with a new, untested vendor), and some shipments do quite literally get lost in transit. These troubles call for some level of price reduction from the vendor; however, trying to work with your vendors to sort things out can make them more open to working with you should you need payment extensions.

The first rule of purchases is this: inspect before you accept. Once you accept and sign for a delivery, it's yours, as is. If you discover a problem after the fact, it's your problem. That doesn't mean your vendor won't work with you to fix the problem; it just means that the order is legally yours once you sign for it, and that makes you legally obligated to pay for it. Avoid this problem by inspecting every delivery before you accept it.

Make sure that the goods you've received are in fact the goods you have ordered. While the quickest way to do this is to match the packing slip (usually attached to the outside of the box) to your purchase order, that's not the best way. Open each box and look through it to make sure it contains everything that should be there, and that no items are broken or damaged. If that's not really feasible, at least check the outside of each carton or container to make sure it's not damaged; if any are, you can open them to make sure the goods inside are unharmed. Count the items (or cartons) to make sure the agreed-upon quantity has been delivered. When it all checks out, sign off on the order.

If there's something wrong with the order, get on the phone with the vendor before signing anything and before the delivery driver leaves. You have a few options here. First, you can refuse the entire order. Second, you can accept correct and intact items but refuse anything that's wrong or damaged; if you do this, indicate on the delivery sheet which items you're refusing and why, and make sure that the delivery person initials it. Third, you can work out a deal with the vendor to accept the entire order on the condition that he issue a credit allowance for any incorrect items on the shipment (don't do this for broken or damaged items, only wrong ones). Do this only if you think you can sell the items.

Review Their Invoices

When you receive an invoice from a vendor, verify it immediately. It's not uncommon to find mistakes on invoices. Typically, you'll have at least two other documents to compare with your invoice: your original purchase order and the product packing slip. Make sure every number on the source documents match the invoice, including quantity, unit price, extended price, sales tax (if applicable), and freight or delivery charges.

Once you're satisfied, you can file the invoice for payment. If the vendor offers early payment discounts, flag the invoices to make sure you remember to pay within the discount period. Lacking that price benefit, pay on time but don't pay early; if the terms ask for payment in thirty days, take thirty days to pay, as that maximizes your cash-flow capabilities.

Should there be any question about the accuracy of any invoice, contact the vendor immediately. Have any applicable purchase orders or packing slips readily available, and send over copies if needed. To keep things friendly, it's a good idea to pay any other open invoices while this one is being resolved. Also, if there are other items on the invoice that you don't dispute, you can offer the vendor a partial payment on the invoice.

Recording Accounts Payable Transactions

When you have accounts payable transactions, you have inventory purchases. Companies that have inventory use the accrual accounting method. So, if you have accounts payable, your company uses the accrual method. That makes things a little easier, because there's only one way to do things:

you record all transactions when they happen, whether or not money changes hands.

There are two basic accounts payable transactions: purchases and payments. Purchase entries, recorded in the purchase journal, always include at least a debit to purchases and a credit to accounts payable. As you record these entries, make sure to indicate the vendor, his invoice number, and your purchase order number.

Purchase returns and allowances are recorded in the general journal, usually upon receipt of a credit memo from the vendor. These entries include a debit to accounts payable, since the balance you owe will be reduced, and a credit to the purchase returns and allowances account (a contra account).

When you pay your vendors, record the entry in your cash payments journal. These entries always include a debit to accounts payable and a credit to cash, but they may also include an additional credit to purchase discounts. As you record these entries, include the vendor and the invoice number (or numbers, if you're paying for more than one invoice at a time) in the description box.

As you fill a page in either the purchases journal or the cash payments journal, foot all your columns; then verify that your total debits equal your total credits, making sure that your journal remains in balance. Once the numbers are verified, you can post dedicated column totals to the associated general ledger accounts. Each line item, though, must be posted individually to the specific vendor's account in the accounts payable subledger.

chapter 13

The End of Period Cleanup

You've done a lot of things during the accounting period, whether that period was a month or a year. Now it's time to wrap up all of that information, to give it a definite end point. To finalize this period, there are many steps you have to take and a lot of adjustments you have to make. When that's all done, you'll have some revealing reports to read and a fresh, clean slate for starting the next accounting period.

13

Accounting Periods

In accounting, financial results are measured by periods. Some periods are set by outside authorities, such as the bank that gave you your business loan, or the IRS. Some are set solely at your discretion, so you can have as many periods as you want as long as you meet legal requirements. Any period with a defined beginning and end can be used for an accounting period. Most of the time, though, it's just easier to go along with the periods you need to have for tax purposes—and that usually means quarters.

Some small businesses can get by with a single, annual accounting period. These companies have relatively few transactions, predictable income, and no outsiders (such as loan officers or investors) clamoring for reports throughout the year. If the only time you really need financial statements is to figure out your taxes at the end of the year, you can make the year your sole accounting period.

QUESTION?

Why use a fiscal year that's different from the calendar year?
The end of the fiscal year is a pretty busy time, with all the year-end responsibilities that need to be handled. For that reason, a lot of companies pick their slowest season for the fiscal year-end, even if that doesn't mesh with the calendar year.

When your business income is not very predictable, you need to run financial statements at least quarterly, at the end of every three-month period. That's really the only way to stay on top of your estimated income tax obligations, to avoid coming up too short at year-end. Also, in most cases, quarterly reports are frequent enough to satisfy any outside demands.

To keep things simple, most companies match their accounting periods to the calendar, which also tends to match up with a lot of tax filings. That means their business year (or *fiscal* year, to use the accounting term) follows the regular calendar, and runs from January 1 to December 31. It doesn't have to be that way, though. Your fiscal year can start and end whenever you want it to, based on what makes the most sense for your business.

No matter which periods you decide to use to measure your company's results, there are standard activities you have to do at the end of every period. The point of these procedures is to give you accurate numbers to look at. Yes, you can look at the numbers every day all year, but you'll be seeing rough numbers that may not reflect the exactly true picture of what's going on in your company. They may be pretty close, but they are almost never completely correct.

What's Wrong with Rough Numbers?

When you look at rough numbers, the problem isn't so much that they're incorrect as that they're incomplete. For example, as you learned in Chapter 10, you may not know your true cash balance until you've reconciled your account with your bank statement. You won't have your bank statement for December on December 31, though; you probably won't get that until the middle of January. That means your cash account will be a rough number until you get the bank statement and make any necessary adjustments, such as recording interest or fixing a mistake.

Some other accounts may also need tweaking. Which ones and how many depend somewhat on whether you use cash or accrual basis and how accurate your bookkeeping is. Accrual basis by its nature calls for account adjustments, and mistakes in your records call for formal correction before you can move ahead. Most of the time, though, you'll adjust the same accounts over and over. Here are the usual suspects:

- Accumulated depreciation and depreciation expense
- Prepaid assets and whichever expenses are linked to them
- Unearned revenues and their related revenue accounts
- Cash
- Accrued revenue and expense accounts

In addition to these old standards, you'll fix any account that has a mistake in it. Throughout the year, you can correct simple errors as you notice them; now, though, you will actually look for any mistakes that need to be fixed.

Working in Two Periods at Once

Since there's virtually no way you'll be able to close an accounting period until you are well into the next period, you have to work in two periods at the same time. The trick is to make sure you keep the information separated, by *changing* your accounting period without closing it.

When you are using a manual accounting system, the easiest way to change without closing is to simply start a new page for that account. If it's an account with very little activity (such as your capital account), you can skip down on the page and leave a big enough gap to record any adjustments or closing entries. Just make sure to clearly indicate the new period before you make any new entries so there's no confusion when you are ready to close the old period.

For software users, the steps you need to take may differ slightly based on the program you're using, so check your instruction manual. Most of the time, though, you can move to the next accounting period by just changing the dates. That will put you squarely into the new period for entering current transactions, but it won't bar you from going back to the prior period. The trick is to leave both periods open and switch back and forth between them as needed. Once you actively close a period—and that typically takes more than just changing a date—you won't be able to flip back to it any more.

The Working Trial Balance

A working trial balance is like a supercharged version of the regular report. It starts with the three-and-a-half standard columns that you find on your standard trial balance: account number (the half), account name, debit balance, credit balance. Then it adds on a couple of columns for mapping out the adjusting entries (more about those in the next section). Finally, it ends with a set of four columns—two sets of debit and credit columns, one for income statement accounts and one for balance sheet accounts. From this final group of columns, you'll be able to directly prepare your financial statements.

Unlike that final set of reports, though, the working trial balance is used as a work in progress. Since it's for your eyes (and maybe your accountant's eyes) only, it often ends up looking pretty messy. Whether the whole thing is done manually or you start with a printout from your accounting software, make your notes in pencil, and don't be afraid to cross out when you need to.

This is the place where your raw general ledger numbers will be polished to perfection, but the job it takes to transform them can get messy. Some numbers will need to be adjusted as a matter of course, such as recording periodic depreciation. Some entries will account for things that haven't actually happened yet but belong in this period anyway, such as accounting for half a week of salary expense when the period ends on a Wednesday and paychecks don't come out until Friday. Others will be used to correct mistakes that you've found in the ledger accounts, such as mispostings.

At the bottom of the page (or on an attached page if you run out of room), write a note for each adjustment you make, numbered in the order of the adjustments. For instance, for the first entry you include, write the number 1 next to all the numbers that go into that entry. Your first note will apply to that first adjustment. That way, when you go back and look at things later, you'll remember which numbers go together and why you made the adjustment. Once you feel sure all the numbers are in good shape, you can create financial statements with confidence.

Making Adjusting Entries

Sometimes transactions take place in one period but impact another. Other times, you know a transaction will be finalized in the future, but at least some part of it has ties to the current period. These two situations are the main reason for adjusting entries, which are entries that account for transactions that occur in one period but affect another. You have to record these out-of-time entries as you get ready to close one accounting cycle to make sure they have been included in the right period.

The two main types of adjusting entries are deferrals and accruals. These are mostly used in accrual basis accounting systems, but some entries can apply to people who use the cash basis as well; depreciation is the most common example. Accrual entries are used to record transactions that haven't actually happened yet, at least on the money side (these will be explained in more detail in the next section). Deferral entries are pretty much the opposite: they record expenses that you paid in advance but haven't incurred until now, or revenues that you've been paid for already but haven't yet earned.

Deferral entries are sort of like postponed transactions; the money part has already happened, but the income statement impact was put off until later. Remember those two balance sheet accounts, prepaid expenses and unearned revenues? Here is where these two accounts make a transformation from balance sheet to income statement. Prepaid expenses turn into current expenses, and unearned revenues turn into current revenues.

Insurance expense is a perfect example of a prepaid expense. You probably paid your business insurance premium in one lump at the beginning of the year, but that coverage isn't just for the month you sent the check; it's for the whole year. When you paid the bill, you made an entry in the prepaid insurance account. Now you have used up part of that premium, and you have to make an adjusting entry to reflect that. Depreciation is another major form of expense deferral, and it is recorded as part of the adjusting entries.

The flip side of prepaid expense is unearned revenue, meaning that a customer has paid you for something you didn't do yet. Any time a customer gives you a down payment, a deposit, an advance, or a retainer, they all hit the same unearned revenue account. When you got that advance money, you recorded a liability on your books; what you owed was goods or services instead of money. Now, when you have completed the work or delivered the product, that revenue has been earned. An adjusting entry is called for to show that.

Adjusting for Your Deferred Expenses

Two kinds of asset accounts are involved in the deferral adjusting entries: prepaid expenses and fixed assets. These are assets that are used up over time; these entries show just how much was used up during *this* period.

First, the prepaid expense account. In this example, your company paid a $1,200 premium in January to your insurance company for the whole year's worth of business coverage. That works out to $100 per month throughout the year ($1,200 divided by 12 months). This is what the adjusting entry looks like:

March 31, 2006	
Insurance Expense	$100.00	
Prepaid Insurance		$100.00

To recognize one month of insurance expense.

The adjusting entry for depreciation looks somewhat similar, but it has one big difference. Instead of posting a credit to the fixed-asset account, you use that contra account for accumulated depreciation instead. In this example, your company has one fixed asset that you bought for $6,000 and depreciate over five years (sixty months) using the straight-line method. Your monthly depreciation expense would be $100 ($6,000 over sixty months). This is what that entry looks like:

March 31, 2006	
Depreciation Expense	$100.00	
Accumulated Depreciation		$100.00

To record monthly depreciation.

Deferred Revenue Adjustment

Deferred revenue is a good kind to have: your company gains the positive cash flow from the customer's advance payment but doesn't have to record any taxable revenue at that time. Adjustments come when you begin earning that money, by delivering goods or services. When that happens you shift all or part of your liability account to your revenue account.

For this example, suppose a client paid you a $3,000 retainer to be used for legal fees. In this period, you performed three hours of legal work for him at your standard rate of $250 per hour, or a total of $750. Here's what the adjusting entry would look like:

March 31, 2006	
Unearned Revenue	$750.00	
Revenue		$750.00

To recognize legal fees earned in March 2006.

Don't Forget Inventory

At the end the accounting period, you also need to adjust the inventory you have recorded on the books to match the inventory you actually have. This includes the inventory you have for resale (even if it isn't in finished form yet), but it may also include some other kinds of inventory. For example, if you keep a large amount of office supplies on hand, you may have chosen to record that initially as an asset. When that's the case, at the end of the period you have to make an adjusting entry for the part that you've used up during the period.

As for merchandise inventory, you can't prepare an income statement without knowing how much inventory you have now (that's called your ending inventory). That's why you need to do the count and adjust the general ledger balance. Even if you use a perpetual inventory system, you may still need to adjust inventory to account for broken or spoiled items. At the end of the period, your inventory balance—the number that will show up on your financial statements—should reflect usable inventory only.

The journal entry here will look just like a prepaid expense entry. For regular inventory, you would debit cost of goods sold and credit your inventory asset account. For other kinds of inventory, such as office supplies, you would debit supplies expense and credit the office supplies asset account.

Accounting for Accruals

When you make an adjusting entry to account for something that hasn't happened yet, but will, that entry is called an accrual. Accruals, as you might guess, are critical parts of accrual basis accounting, the system that strives to record transactions in the period they most relate to regardless of when they are finalized.

It sounds odd, accounting for things that haven't happened yet but belong in a past period. That goes back to the matching principle, which requires that you record revenue when it's earned and expenses when they're incurred. It does not matter that no money has changed hands yet; only the circumstances of the transaction matter here. For example, even though your savings account only pays interest quarterly, you actually earn that interest every month.

So, accrual-type adjusting entries include both expenses that have been incurred but not yet paid and revenues that have been earned without any cash being received. Here are some very common examples of expenses and revenues that often need to be accrued:

- Payroll and payroll taxes
- Property taxes
- Interest expense
- Interest income
- Bad debts (a.k.a. uncollectible accounts)

Accruals for items such as payroll and payroll taxes are necessary because pay periods don't usually conveniently end on the last day of the accounting period. If the period ends on Tuesday, but you don't write paychecks until Friday, you have to accrue for the two payroll days that happened in this period. The same principle applies for accruing income, such as interest. If your books close on the last day of the month, but your bank pays out interest on the tenth day of every month, you have to accrue interest income for the last twenty (or so) days of this period. Other accruals, such as the one for bad debts, are based on estimates. Today, you don't know how many customers won't pay their bills, but you're pretty sure some of them won't. However you choose to estimate your bad debt expense (as explained in Chapter 11), this is the time to record that number.

ALERT!

When the transactions you accrued finally take place, it's common to accidentally double-count them. To make your life easier, make reversing entries for all your accruals in the very beginning of the new period. The backward entry is the exact opposite of the accrual, so your accounts will show the right net balance when you record the real transaction.

Accounting for Accrued Expenses

The journal entry to record an accrued expense always acts the same, no matter what expense you are working with. Each time, you debit an expense account and credit some kind of liability account. Here you don't use your standard accounts payable account (which is used for vendor invoices, and must match the vendor ledger), because that could get complicated going forward. Instead, you can create specific accounts for the expense accruals you will have most of the time (such as payroll payable) and use a catchall account for the rest (such as expenses payable).

For example, suppose you have a standard payroll of $1,000 per week paid out every Friday. The current period ended on Wednesday, meaning you need to accrue three days of payroll to account for everything in the right period. Three days of payroll comes to $600 ($1,000 divided by five days, then multiplied by three days).

March 31, 2006		
Payroll Expense	$600.00	
Payroll Payable		$600.00

To record three days of payroll expense.

One way to make sure you catch all the expenses you can accrue is to run through your checkbook for the first few weeks of the next period. Any payments you made for bills that affected the last period count as accruable expenses. This includes things such as your phone bill, utilities—pretty much anything that you use now but pay for later.

Accounting for Accrued Revenue

The most common revenue that needs accruing, at least when it comes to small businesses, is interest on bank accounts. The entry works the same way for any kind of revenue your company has earned for which payment has not yet been received, and no sale has already been recorded (as it would be with your normal accounts receivable activity).

Suppose your company has an interest-bearing bank account for which interest is posted on the fifteenth day of each month. Your April 15 bank statement shows $30 interest paid into the account. Fifteen days' worth of that interest belongs in April, but the rest really applies to the month before. In this example, you accrue $15 (half of the $30) in March to an interest receivable account (because as of March 31, you had not received the cash in your account).

March 31, 2006		
Interest Receivable	$15.00	
Interest Income		$15.00

To record interest earned.

Prelude to Financial Statements

Once you're sure that your numbers are good, it's time to create your financial statements for the period. You have to do this before you close out the books for the period, since that final step effectively erases your temporary accounts, all of which show up on at least one financial statement.

There are three major statements to prepare: a balance sheet, a statement of profit and loss, and a statement of cash flows. Each of these statements gives you part of your company's financial picture, and the three together can show you how your business is doing overall. You can create these statements directly from the end columns on your working trial balance.

As you'll learn in the next chapter, each statement has a standard format to follow, from the heading down to the bottom line. Once you have that format set up, you can simply fill in the numbers and make sure they balance properly. In most accounting software programs, these reports will be generated automatically, and all you have to do is print them out and make sure they look right.

If you need these financial statements for someone outside your company, such as the bank, have your accountant prepare them, or at least look them over for you before you send them out. Outside parties often look for specific values and certain relationships among your accounts. Your accountant will be well versed in these requirements and can tell whether your numbers will make the grade. If they don't, he can provide reasons and suggestions to help you explain any temporary shortfalls.

Closing the Books

At the end of every official accounting period (as determined by you), you will close out the books so you can start the new period with a clean slate. Every temporary account will be closed out into the equity account(s). The income statement accounts, both revenues and expenses, will all have zero balances until the new period kicks in. Any owner's drawing accounts, which track the cash you take out of your business for personal use, will follow that same path. As you'll see, this process (done manually) takes four journal entries.

For the purposes of closing entries, a single-use account is created. It's usually called the income summary account, but you may never actually see it if you use a computerized accounting system that closes the books automatically at a single click of the mouse. Income summary acts as a momentary holding account, to give a spot to park the balances you intend to close while you sum them up. There's a good reason why you don't just close them into the regular accounts: There are a lot of temporary accounts to close, and the entries take up a lot of space. Rather than fill up the pages for an account you may use throughout the period, this huge entry hits only the income summary account, and the summary numbers go to the regular accounts.

To close an account, you make a journal entry for the exact opposite of that account's balance. For example, if your revenue account has a credit balance of $5,000, you would close it by posting a debit entry for $5,000.

This is what the closing entries would be like for a sole proprietorship. You would write them up in the general journal. Once you post them, the temporary accounts will still exist; they simply will have no balances. After you post these entries, prepare a post-closing trial balance to prove that your general ledger is in balance before you begin the next period.

Closing Entries		
Service Revenue	$5,000.00	
Income Summary		$5,000.00
To close revenue into income summary.		
Income Summary	$3,500.00	
Advertising Expense		$500.00
Payroll Expense		$1,500.00
Office Expense		$200.00
Rent Expense		$800.00
Repairs and Maintenance		$300.00
Miscellaneous Expense		$200.00
To close expense accounts into income summary.		
Income Summary	$1,500.00	
Bob Smith, Equity		$1,500.00
To close income summary to owner's equity account.		
Bob Smith, Equity	$1,000.00	
Bob Smith, Drawing		$1,000.00
To close owner's draw account to owner's equity.		

Make sure to back up your computer files before you set off the closing-the-books process in your accounting software. Once that process starts, you will not be able to retrieve any of the account detail that was there just a minute before. Inevitably, if you don't have it, you will be sure to need it.

chapter 14

Preparing Financial Statements

As a business owner, you need to know how your company is doing financially. Financial statements are the reports that can show you just that. These reports spell out how well your company has performed, where it stands right now, and what it took to get there. Even though financial statements show past information, they hold the key information you need to be even more successful in the future.

Three Major Financial Statements

In accounting, there are dozens upon dozens of reports you can create to learn specific information. To get a clear, big-picture view of your company's financial position, though, you need three very special reports. These three reports are the balance sheet, the statement of profit and loss, and the statement of cash flows. Both on their own and working together, these three major financial statements let you know what's really going on for every aspect of your company.

At the end of every accounting period, you'll create these financial statements as part of your regular cleanup work. Virtually all small businesses prepare all three statements for every period, but a lot of these reports end up being filed away without so much as a glance—and that's a big mistake. Some business owners really look at only their year-end numbers, some don't bother printing them out at all, and some give them just a quick glance before moving on to the next project. The most successful business owners use these statements to nip potential problems in the bud, to capitalize on surprising successes, and to make sure that the numbers are in line with what they expected. The best time to deal with any of these issues, even the good ones, is right away, and you can only do that if you know what's going on.

In addition, creating these statements for yourself, you may have to put them together for someone else. For example, the statement of profit and loss will show up on your company's tax return. When you have a bank loan, the bank may want to monitor your balance sheet. The most important reader, though, is you. As you'll see in Chapter 17, these reports contain a gold mine of information that will help you successfully grow a thriving business.

How These Statements Interconnect

Even though they each contain very distinct information, the three main financial statements are completely connected. In fact, you can't produce a balance sheet without first creating a statement of profit and loss, and you can't prepare a statement of cash flows without having already produced the other two financial statements.

The statement of profit and loss contains the bottom-line earnings for the period, whether they're positive (for profits) or negative (for losses). Those earnings are folded into the owner's equity, on the balance sheet, at the end of the period. Without that step, the balance sheet could not balance; the equity accounts are not complete until they reflect the current period earnings.

No matter which statement you're working with, all the numbers will be pulled from the general ledger (except the ones the statements calculate). All the statements also speak to the past; they are reporting what happened during the prior period, rather than what's to come.

The balance sheet is sort of the financial statement middleman. It pulls information from the statement of profit and loss and offers information to the statement of cash flows. As you might guess, the statement of cash flows needs to know how much cash the company started the period with, and then works down to the ending cash balance. Sometimes, it needs additional balance sheet information as well, such as the changes in accounts receivable and accounts payable. The statement of cash flows also gives something back to the balance sheet: verification. If the ending cash on the balance sheet doesn't match the ending cash on the statement of cash flows, there's a mistake somewhere that you need to fix.

The statement of cash flows also pulls information off the statement of profit and loss. Revenues generate cash, even if it's not immediate (as in the case of credit sales). Costs and expenses eat up cash, though again, the impact may not be immediate.

The Statement of Profit and Loss

The statement of profit and loss is by far the favorite among business owners; after all, this is the one that shows the profits. This statement can show you much more than the bottom line, though. It can let you know if you've been setting your prices too low, paying too much for the merchandise that you resell, or spending much too much on postage. In addition to spelling out just how well your business has done over the past year (or month or quarter), it contains clues for improving profitability and beefing up that bottom line.

FACT

Statements of profit and loss for service businesses are shorter than those for product-based businesses. Service companies don't need a section for cost of goods sold or gross profit, because they don't sell any goods. Other than that missing section, the statements look pretty much the same.

First, though, you have to put it together. Three kinds of accounts appear on this financial statement: revenues, costs, and expenses. The statement is a kind of vertical equation that basically says "revenues minus costs minus expenses equals profit or loss." In the body of the report, revenues are listed right on top; costs (if you sell products) come next; and expenses are at the end. At the very bottom comes the bottom line, the company's overall net profit or loss for the period.

All statements of profit and loss are topped with a standard report heading, which contains three lines:

- The name of the company (ABC Company)
- The name of the statement (Statement of Profit and Loss)
- The period covered by the statement (For the year ended December 31, 2007)

You have some leeway with the name of the statement, as long as readers can tell what kind of report it is. Other common names for this financial report include "income statement," "profit and loss statement," and "report of earnings"; when your accountant is talking about the report, she'll probably call it your "p & l." The period line must reflect the actual time covered by the statement, whether it's a month, a quarter, or a year.

Getting to the Bottom Line

The statement of profit and loss is put together using compiled data from actual business transactions. It details how your company earned money, along with how much was spent in trying to create revenues. You can pull final numbers from your general ledger or from a completed working trial balance.

Once you have all the raw numbers you need, you can begin to put them together and start your calculations. Revenues always come first. Start with your gross revenues, which just means your total sales; if you have more than one sales account, you can list them individually and then total them, or just include the combined total figure. Then you subtract any contra sales accounts, such as sales discounts or sales returns. The result of that calculation is called your net sales. If you don't have any contra sales accounts, your gross sales and net sales will be the same, and you don't need to list both.

ALERT!

When your company uses the cash accounting method, include only sales for which the cash has already been received. If no cash has changed hands yet, don't include the sale. For accrual accounting, you have to include every sale transaction, regardless of whether your company has gotten any money.

For product-based businesses, the cost of goods sold section comes next. On your statement of profit and loss, you can either show the net cost of goods number or display the whole calculation. When you're doing the report for yourself, it's easier to have the calculation right there on the same page; when you're preparing the report for someone else, you may include just that final number in the financial statement along with a more detailed supporting schedule (just attach that to the back). The full-blown computation starts with your beginning inventory, then adds in all the purchases of the period to give you the total cost of goods available for sale. From that subtotal, subtract the ending inventory (what you have left in stock) to get the cost of goods sold. Next, subtract your cost of goods sold from your net sales to come up with your gross profit.

The next section of the statement is common for all businesses, and it includes all the company's expenses for the period. You can choose to group the expenses—into variable and fixed, or sales and general, for example—or you can just list them all in one big group. The most common division is between selling expenses and general and administrative expenses. If you don't have a lot of different expense accounts, though, it's easier for you to just keep them all together. (To refresh your memory about which expenses belong in which category, check out Chapter 8.) Regardless of how or whether you divide up your expenses on the report, you still need to come to a grand total for all the operating expenses.

Finally, you've reached the bottom line. To get to your company's profit or loss for the period, subtract the total operating expenses from the gross profit (for product-based businesses) or from the net sales (for service businesses). When the result is positive, your company has made a profit; when the result is negative, it has sustained a loss for the period.

What This Statement Really Looks Like

Now that you know what goes into a statement of profit and loss, here's one you can use as a guideline for creating your own. This example includes virtually everything, which means that some lines may not apply to your company. Remember, service businesses won't have the cost of goods sold section, so you can skip that part if your company doesn't sell any products.

If your business is a C corporation, you may include an extra section for income taxes, since C corporations do have to pay taxes on their own income. In that case, you'll rename that net profit line "net profit before income taxes." Then, add in a line for the amount of income taxes that will be due; remember to include federal, state, and local levies. Finally, subtract your tax figure from that preliminary profit to get your final bottom line, typically called "net profit after taxes."

XYZ Company

Statement of Profit and Loss for the Period Ended December 31, 2006

Revenues	
Sales Revenues	$130,000
Less: Sales Discounts	2,000
Net Sales Revenues	$128,000
Cost of Goods Sold	
Beginning Inventory	$ 30,000
Plus: Purchases	80,000
Cost of Goods Available for Sale	110,000
Less: Ending Inventory	50,000
Cost of Goods Sold	$60,000
Gross Profit	**$68,000**
Expenses	
Selling Expenses	
Advertising	$3,000
Delivery Charges	1,500
Packing Costs	2,500
Sales Salaries & Commissions	22,000
Total Selling Expenses	$29,000
Administrative Expenses	
Computer Expenses	$300
Depreciation	500
Insurance	800
Office Expense	250
Office Salaries	18,000
Rent	6,000
Utilities	450
Miscellaneous	100
Total Administrative Expenses	$26,400
Total Expenses	$55,400
Net Profit	**$12,600**

The Balance Sheet

A balance sheet provides a financial snapshot of your business at a frozen point in time. Also known as the statement of financial position, this report will give you a clear picture of where your business stands. The balance sheet contains current pictures of your assets, liabilities, and equity; looking at it lets you see what your company has and how much it owes, as well as your revised equity share.

FACT

Of all the financial statements, the balance sheet is the only one that comes with a specific date rather than an activity period. That's because it tells you the balance of your permanent accounts on a fixed day—the last day of the accounting period.

Balance sheets come with a standard format, although the layout has two options (vertical or side by side). The report always contains the three permanent account categories: assets, liabilities, and owner's equity. It also follows the rule of the accounting equation; assets must equal liabilities plus owner's equity. In the vertical format, the three categories are listed one after the other; assets come first, followed by liabilities, and finally equity. In the side-by-side format, assets appear on the left side of the statement, and liabilities and equity go on the right. How you decide to lay it out is really a matter of personal preference.

As you learned in Chapter 5, individual assets and liabilities fall into different categories. Those categories appear as sections on the balance sheet, and accounts are listed in the associated categories. This practice makes it easier to do a quick analysis of your balance sheet at a glance (as you'll see in Chapter 17).

Asset Categories

On your balance sheet, your company's assets will be broken out into four basic categories: current assets, long-term investments, fixed assets, and intangible (or other) assets. Most new and small businesses will find the bulk of their assets in the current or fixed categories.

Current assets include anything expected to be converted into cash within a year of the balance sheet date. On the report, they are listed in order of liquidity; the ones that can be turned into cash the fastest are listed first. Here's the typical listing of current assets (in order) for small businesses:

- Cash
- Accounts receivable
- Inventory
- Prepaid expenses

Your company may also have some short-term investments (such as a six-month CD). In addition, it may have multiple cash and prepaid expense accounts, but you can list these as combined totals on the formal balance sheet.

Most companies have some fixed assets; manufacturing companies usually have the most, and the most expensive. Common fixed assets owned by the majority of businesses include office furniture and equipment, computer systems, vehicles, and shop displays. Other examples include land, buildings, and heavy machinery. If your company has fixed assets on the balance sheet, it will also have accumulated depreciation, the fixed-asset contra account.

Assets fall only into the fixed-asset category if they're being used by your business. If your company sells trucks, for example, those trucks count as inventory and not as fixed assets. That doesn't mean you can't ever sell your assets, or that you have to reclassify them as inventory if you do. It just means that their main purpose is use, not being sold.

Long-term investments are just regular investments that your company owns as a way to generate a little extra income over the long haul. These investments can be stocks and mutual funds, or even land that the company is holding on to strictly for investment purposes. Your company may have these when you want to hold on to earnings for future plans but also want to earn more than you'll get as interest on a simple savings account. Intangible assets include things such as patents and trademarks, which are long-term assets with plenty of value but no real physical form. Their decline in value is measured over time as amortization expense, but there's usually no accumulated amortization account. Instead, you just decrease the asset account as it loses value over time.

Liability Categories

Liabilities come in two flavors: current and long-term. Current liabilities include any debts or obligations that will come due within one year of the balance sheet date. Long-term liabilities will be outstanding for more than one year; however, the part of long-term liabilities that is due in the upcoming twelve months is usually put in the current category.

Current liabilities include the day-to-day stuff, such as accounts payable and sales tax payable. It can also include accrued expenses for companies that use the accrual accounting method. Long-term liabilities are usually for loans, such as business startup loans or mortgages.

A Sample Balance Sheet

Now that you know what to put on your balance sheet, here's how it will look when it's all laid out. This sample balance sheet contains the accounts most commonly used by new and small businesses; your company may have different or additional accounts.

The owner's equity in this balance sheet is for a sole proprietorship or single-member LLC. To learn about the different equity sections for partnerships, multimember LLCs, and corporations, see Chapter 15.

Jill's Toy Shop

Balance Sheet: December 31, 2006

Assets	
Current Assets	
Cash	$1,000
Accounts Receivable	1,300
Inventory	3,800
Prepaid Expenses	2,200
Total Current Assets	$8,300
Fixed Assets	
Computer Equipment	$3,500
Office Equipment	2,100
Office Furniture	850
Store Displays	3,800
Vehicles	21,500
Less: Accumulated Depreciation	6,800
Total Fixed Assets	$24,950
Other Assets	
Start-Up Costs, Less Amortization	$850
Total Assets	**$34,100**
Liabilities	
Current Liabilities	
Accounts Payable	$1,950
Total Taxes Payable	2,750
Accrued Expenses	$1,200
Total Current Liabilities	$5,900
Long-Term Liabilities	
Loan Payable	$21,800
Total Liabilities	**$27,700**
Owner's Equity	
Jill Smith, Capital	$6,400
Total Liabilities	**$34,100**

The Statement of Cash Flows

Statements of cash flows are the most complicated reports you'll prepare. It's much easier when you have accounting software or an accountant to create the report for you. On the plus side, you can tell whether you've done it right based on the ending cash balance, which has to equal the current cash number on your balance sheet. Whether you decide to brave it and create this report manually or get some help, it's a very important report to understand. This statement tracks your cash movement, and it's the most critical report for keeping your new business afloat.

FACT

When you use the cash accounting method, you can just pull numbers from your general ledger, because every transaction originates with cash. It gets more complicated for accrual accounting; the cash itself may be harder to track because you record transactions even when no cash changes hands.

This statement will cover the same period as your statement of profit and loss. It starts with the beginning cash balance for the period (which is the same as the ending cash balance for the last period). Then, there are three categories (formatted on the report as separate sections) that track the cash flowing through your company: operating activities, investing activities, and financing activities.

Operating activities include all the day-to-day transactions that bring in or use up cash; mainly, revenues and expenses. Investing activities include buying and selling long-term assets to be used by the company; these may include things such as stocks and bonds, as well as fixed assets and property improvements (for example, paying to have a building renovated). Financing activities include the things you do to raise cash for your company, such as taking out loans or bringing in more equity contributions; they also include the payments you make as you pay down debt or pay out dividends.

Of the three sections, operating activities is the most important. This category speaks to how successfully your business maintains a positive cash position solely through its daily transactions. If your company is generating enough cash to survive from its operating activities, its chances of staying afloat and flourishing are very good.

Statement Styles

There are two different formats you can use to prepare your statement of cash flows, but one is far easier (and more commonly used) than the other. The two styles are direct and indirect; of the two, the indirect is simpler to prepare and much more popular for that reason. The format difference really appears only in the operating activities section; the other sections look the same either way.

The direct method focuses on grouping the major sources of cash receipts and causes of cash payments. For example, cash used to pay for inventory is listed separately from cash used to pay employees. The cash coming in and the cash going out are summed to come up with the total cash provided (or used, if it's negative) by operating activities.

The indirect method starts with your net income (loss) for the period and converts it into cash flow. For example, noncash expenses such as depreciation are added back to the bottom-line number, and accruals and deferrals (used in accrual basis accounting) are converted into their cash effect. Here's how a conversion works: A decrease in accounts receivable from the period prior to this one indicates more cash has come in, since accounts receivable decreases based on customer payments. That converts on-account sales information into the cash effect for this period. The basic conversion strategy is this: Increases in assets, such as accounts receivable, translate to decreases in cash, and vice versa. Increases in liabilities, such as accounts payable, translate to increases in cash, and vice versa.

A Sample Statement, Indirect Method

Since statements of cash flow can get pretty complicated, this example is a simplified version. To create one of your own, you'll need the balance sheets from both the current period and the prior period, as well as a current statement of profit and loss. (Note: numbers in parentheses indicate amounts that have to be subtracted.)

ABC Company

Statement of Cash Flows
for the Year Ended December 31, 2006

Cash flows from operating activities		
Net Profit		$10,000

Adjustments to convert net income into net cash provided by operations:		
Depreciation expense	$500	
Decrease in accounts receivable	650	
Increase in prepaid expenses	(300)	
Increase in accounts payable	450	$1,300
Net cash provided by operating activities		$11,300

Cash flows from investing activities		
Equipment purchase	$(6,500)	
Net cash used by investing activities		$(6,500)

Cash flows from financing activities		
Owner withdrawals	$(3,000)	
Net cash used by financing activities		$(3,000)
Net increase in cash		$1,800
Cash at beginning of period		$3,200
Cash at end of period		$5,000

Remember, the bottom line on the statement of cash flows—your cash at the end of the period—must equal the cash figure on your current balance sheet.

chapter 15

Different Entities Mean Different Equity

There are a lot of different ways to legally form your business. Each form, or entity, comes with good points and bad. No matter which one you choose, your everyday accounting will be pretty much the same. The big difference shows up in your capital accounts and on your income tax returns. If you're already in business, you already have an entity; if it turns out that the one you're using isn't the best for your company, you can always change it.

15

Meet the Business Entities

From the accounting standpoint, you have only to deal with three entities, or forms of business: sole proprietorships, partnerships, and corporations. That's because even though other forms exist, they share the same accounting structure as one of these three.

FACT

LLCs, the most common small-business entities, get to choose whether they want to be treated as partnerships or corporations for accounting and tax purposes. If they do nothing, they will automatically be treated as partnerships. To qualify for corporate treatment, they have to fill out a special IRS form.

Most transactions will be exactly the same, no matter which entity you use to create your company. A cash sale is still a cash sale; paying your phone bill works just the same. Others are unique to the entity type, mainly involving the equity accounts. The one you may be most concerned about is how you get to take money out of your business—and the entity you choose makes a pretty big difference there. The other major difference is the tax impact: some entities pay their own taxes; some leave that job to you, as the owner. Some entities have to file their own tax returns, even if you end up paying the taxes personally; some just get melded into your personal return.

Which One Is Best for Your Business?

Choosing the best entity for your business is a matter of sifting through your needs and plans. There really isn't one entity that's best for all businesses (though some people will tell you there is), and you don't have to be stuck forever with the choice you make now. For legal purposes, you have four main choices: sole proprietorships, partnerships, LLCs, and corporations. Both partnerships and corporations come in a few different varieties.

As you begin to consider the different entities, remember to take your personal situation into account. After all, it's your time and your money that will go into supporting this business venture, at least initially. Some structures are much more demanding than others, and require a lot of maintenance (meaning paperwork). If you don't have the time to dedicate to that extra business task, at least not without kissing every minute of your personal life goodbye, consider one of the less challenging entities. On the other hand, if you have a lot to lose, both personally and professionally, you may want to use the safest possible entity no matter how much time and money it costs.

Overall, your decision will be based on a variety of factors, including:

- Number of owners
- Optimal taxation
- Liability concerns
- Costs
- Ongoing maintenance procedures

In some cases, the number of owners will limit your entity choices. Only single-owner companies can be sole proprietorships; only multiowner companies can be partnerships. Both LLCs and corporations (all varieties) allow for any number of owners.

Setup costs may be a factor in your decision-making. It costs nothing to launch a sole proprietorship. Partnerships range widely in price, depending on the complexity of the partnership arrangement, but a simple general partnership costs next to nothing to form and maintain. The biggest cost is your partnership agreement, which is legally optional but practically a must-have. LLCs come next in the price scale. They require state creation and registration fees and may require a lawyer's assistance to be set up properly. Corporations are typically the most expensive entities to create and maintain. They also require by far the most comprehensive ongoing maintenance—and skipping any required procedures can strip your company of corporate status. If you don't think you can keep up with all the paperwork, don't form a corporation.

When it comes to liability and tax issues, every situation is unique. To help you with this part of your decision, talk your accountant or attorney. If the professional you use for personal matters isn't experienced in business matters, get a second attorney to use for your company.

Accounting for Sole Proprietorships

A sole proprietorship has a single owner, making his equity the easiest of all to calculate. For this entity, the basic accounting equation says it all: the assets minus the liabilities equals the owner's equity (a rearrangement of the classic assets equal liabilities plus equity version). Since you are the only owner, you do not have to split up the equity any further, as you would for other business structures.

Sole proprietorships have one permanent equity account, called either owner's equity or owner's capital. You can have any number of temporary accounts to handle your withdrawals, as long as you have at least one. Technically, revenues, costs, and expenses fall under the equity umbrella, because they all eventually are folded into the equity account; practically, though, they aren't included as equity accounts. Withdrawals also are closed into the permanent account at the end of the period, but they still keep a place in the capital section during the period.

FACT

Some entrepreneurs like to split out their withdrawals to make their personal finances easier. For example, they may have one withdrawal account for general cash, one for estimated tax payments, and one for health insurance premiums. This can help when it's time to do your personal tax return, as deductible items are already added up in a single spot.

On your balance sheet, only the single permanent owner's equity account appears, after closing entries. If you want (or need) to demonstrate how the capital has changed, you can prepare the optional statement of changes to owner's equity. This simple statement contains just a few lines: the opening account balance, a list of changes to it (which can include income, losses, contributions, and withdrawals), and the resulting ending account balance.

Entries That Increase Equity

Any time you post a credit to your permanent equity account, you increase your stake in the business. There are essentially two ways to do that: by earning profits, or by making capital contributions.

Profits are posted to your capital account during the closing entries (as you learned in Chapter 13). Contributions are posted as you make them, whether they take the form of cash or other assets. Any time you put any asset of your own into the business, it counts as a capital contribution. For the journal entry, you debit the applicable asset account and credit your capital account.

Entries That Decrease Equity

The two big equity depleters, marked by debits to the permanent account, are withdrawals and losses. Losses are posted to your equity account during closing entries, if costs and expenses have exceeded revenues for the period.

Withdrawals, initially recorded in dedicated contra equity accounts, all eventually hit the capital account as debits. However, you must record a withdrawal every time you take something out of the business. Most of the time this will be cash, but it's also very common for product-based business owners to raid their inventory. That, too, counts as a withdrawal and must be recorded in the same manner; in this case, your debit would still be the withdrawals account, but the credit would be to inventory.

Accounting for Partnership Equity

The accounting for partnership equity is quite similar to that for a sole proprietorship, but taken one step further. Now you have more than one owner, so you have more than one capital account. All profits and losses must be divided among you and your partners in whatever proportion you've all agreed upon. The division doesn't have to be equal among the partners, and it also doesn't have to match up with respective ownership shares. In fact, a single partner can have different percentages for his profit and loss shares; for example, a partner could get a 30 percent profit allocation and a 40 percent loss allocation. Whatever you all agree on and put in writing will control how profits and losses are divvied up.

Once you and your partners have settled on share percentages, the accounting part is pretty easy. As soon as you have the final profit or loss figures for the period, you simply apply each partner's percentage to that bottom-line number to figure out her share in dollars. Then, during your closing entries, instead of making one big entry into a single capital account, you allocate each partner's share to her individual equity account. For example, if the company's total profit comes to $6,000, to be divided evenly among three partners, each partner's capital account gets a $2,000 credit entry.

ALERT!

In the absence of a formal partnership agreement, partnership profits and losses must be divided in proportion to each partner's current capital stake. For example, if you own 50 percent of the company, you get 50 percent of all profits or losses. With a formal agreement, though, you can split up the earnings any way you want.

When it comes to withdrawals and contributions, there's no math to do. Each partner gets an equity credit for her contributions and a debit for any withdrawals. Your contributions and withdrawals won't hit your partner's equity accounts directly in any way. However, if either contributions or withdrawals throw your equity proportions out of whack, you may need to address that when it comes time to divide profits.

Distributing Partnership Profits and Losses

Since partnerships don't pay their own income taxes, being pass-through entities (structures where only the owners pay taxes on the business income, which you'll learn more about in Chapter 16), any profits or losses have to be divided among the partners. The partners then include their shares of those profits or losses on their personal income tax returns. Each partner's portion is called a distributive share, and it's 100 percent taxable even if the partner doesn't get any actual money. In other words, as a partner you have to pay income taxes on your share of profits even if you don't withdraw a dime, and even if no cash is available for you to withdraw.

FACT

The phenomenon that occurs when a partner has taxable income from the company but doesn't receive any money is called "phantom profits." That's because the actual profits to the partner are invisible, except for their tax effect. This can occur because of a decision among the partners to leave all the cash in the business to finance growth, or because there's just not enough cash to go around.

In most cases, distributions are based on how much equity each partner has in the company now, or when the company was first started. However, if you and your partners want to divide earnings in some other way, you can. Many small partnerships don't like to use fixed distribution percentages, carved in stone, because equity shares can change over the life of the partnership depending on individual contributions and withdrawals.

The Most Flexibility

Partnerships offer the most flexibility when it comes to splitting up profits and losses for businesses that have more than one owner. Unlike corporations, in which earnings have to be divided based on each owner's respective equity percentage, partnerships allow owners to figure the split however they want as long as they all agree to it in writing. So, for example, a partner who has a 50 percent equity stake in the business could get 25 percent of the profits and 60 percent of the losses.

If you and your partners do choose to divide profits and losses in any proportion that's different from your equity shares, you have to put that decision in writing, and all of you have to sign off on it. This is usually incorporated into the partnership agreement.

Good Reasons for Uneven Splits

While it's perfectly legal to split profits and losses however you and your partners want to, there has to be some reasonable basis for the numbers you come up with (at least a reason that will satisfy the IRS if it starts asking questions). Good reasons include things such as one partner working more hours for the company, which means she deserves a bigger share of profits or losses; or one partner bringing in more new clients than any of the others.

While technically you aren't required to have a partnership agreement to have a partnership, it's in the best interest of you and your partners to take the time to draw one up. It will cost you some money up front (definitely have a lawyer do this), but it will save you a lot of money and heartache down the line.

Although the IRS may look at uneven profit distributions, it's usually more interested in uneven loss distributions. That's because partnerships are pass-through entities, and losses sustained by the partnership are directly deductible from other forms of income on the partners' personal tax returns. Make sure that you and your partners have a solid explanation for any seemingly uneven distributions, especially if one partner gets a disproportionate share of losses only.

The Corporate Equity Section

Corporations have the most complex equity sections of any business entity, and for C corporations it can get much trickier than for S corporations. Owner's equity for corporations has more components than other business forms. It starts with the two basic divisions that all companies have: contributed capital and earnings. That's where the first difference occurs; rather than folding earnings into contributed capital accounts, they get their own permanent account, called retained earnings.

The next big difference comes with the two different contributed capital categories; other entities have only one. With corporations, the amount you put into the company will be split up into two separate accounts, one for stock at par value and one for any excess over that par value. Par value simply means the dollar value assigned to a single share of stock in the corporation, which may have absolutely no relationship to its actual value; it's just a number you pick so the stock has a dollar value on the books. You can't pay in less than that amount for a share of stock, which is why small corporations often set their par value very low, sometimes even at zero (in states that allow that). If you gave your corporation's stock a par value of $2 per share, but you paid in $10 per share for 100 shares (a total of $1,000), your journal entry would look like this:

General Journal Entry		
Cash	$1,000.00	
Capital Stock		$200.00
Additional Paid-in-capital		$800.00

To record $1,000 capital contribution for 100 shares of $2 par value stock.

Even the stock category can be subdivided, but only for C corporations. S corporations are allowed to have only one class of stock, but C corporations are under no such restrictions and can have as many different classes of stock as they like. Every share within a certain class of stock has the exact same rights, such as those for voting and dividends. Different classes can have different rights; for example, you can have one class with no voting rights but a higher dividend payout, or two classes with the same voting rights but different dividend payouts.

Retained earnings are self-explanatory: earnings that you keep in the business instead of paying them out to the owners. Every time your corporation has profits, they initially increase that retained earnings account. These retained earnings can be used to expand your business or to purchase major assets, among other things, or to pay out dividends to the shareholders. When you do decide to pay dividends to the shareholders, those dividends decrease retained earnings rather than any contributed capital accounts. Should the corporation sustain losses (instead of profits), the balance of retained earnings would decrease, and might even go negative. For many new and small corporations, it's not unusual for the retained earnings account to be negative for the first year or two.

Why Have Different Classes of Stock?

It may seem cumbersome to have more than one class of stock for a small corporation, but there are times when this strategy makes a lot of sense. For example, if you've raised money from friends and family to build your corporation, you may want to pay them regular dividends without letting them have voting rights (which can equate to control over business decisions). You may also want to pay dividends to shareholders who don't work for the company without paying dividends to those of you who are drawing a salary. You can also pay different dividends to different shareholder classes; for example, Class A could get $0.25 for each share, and Class B could get $2.00 per share. When there's only one class of stock, each share counts exactly the same, has the same voting rights, and gets the same dividend.

ALERT!

S corporations cannot have more than one class of stock; it's strictly forbidden by the IRS. However, they can split that one class into two pools of voting and nonvoting shares. If you want the flexibility to make different dividend payouts to different shareholders, though, use a C corporation for your entity instead.

Retained Earnings Is Not an Asset

Retained earnings is an equity account, a separate spot to keep track of any profits not paid out as dividends. Like all other equity accounts, retained earnings has a claim against assets, because it represents ownership interests. However, retained earnings is not linked to a specific asset account—not even the cash account. You can have retained earnings without having any cash, which is one reason why some corporations do not pay out cash dividends. For example, your corporate balance sheet could show $25,000 in retained earnings when the company has only $2,000 in cash.

Dealing with Dividends

One of the reasons you started your business was to make some money. When you formed that business as a corporation, it became more formal. Instead of just bringing home some extra cash (a.k.a. taking owner withdrawals), you have to deal with dividends. Every single time you take cash (or inventory items) out of the business, except for your regular paycheck, you have paid yourself a dividend. With an S corporation, there's no direct tax impact, since you've already paid personal income taxes on all the profits anyway. With a C corporation, though, you've just increased your personal income for tax purposes.

For any kind of corporation, taking money out when you haven't officially declared a dividend can bring other sorts of consequences (as you'll see in Chapter 21.) Also, most states keep a tight rein on how much you can pay yourself in dividends, though these laws vary a lot from state to state. Essentially, the aim is to make sure you aren't draining money out of the corporation that rightfully belongs to the company's creditors.

Here's the generally accepted, official way to handle dividends:

1. Your company has positive retained earnings.
2. Your corporation has enough cash on hand to pay the dividend.
3. The board of directors declares that dividends will be paid, specifying the amount.
4. The corporation pays out dividends to all eligible shareholders.

There are two basic journal entries that go along with dividends. As soon as dividends are declared, the corporation has a legal obligation to pay them, and that means a new liability has to be recorded. The general journal entry is a debit to retained earnings and a credit to dividends payable. Then, when the dividend is actually paid, another journal entry is needed.

This second entry is a debit to dividends payable (to wipe out the liability) and a credit to cash.

That's the official version; the small-business reality is usually pretty different. Many small-corporation owners, especially if they are the sole owners, just write themselves checks whenever they need extra cash. From an accounting perspective, this transaction skips the dividends payable middleman and results directly in a debit to retained earnings and a credit to cash. Use caution when you pay yourself like this, though. Not only can you bring on some extra, unexpected personal income taxes, but you can also jeopardize your corporation's existence. Before you make unofficial dividends a habit, talk to your accountant about better ways to get money out of the corporation.

chapter 16

The Income Tax Impact

One of the biggest uses for all the accounting work you've done throughout the year is the company's tax return. No matter what industry your business is in, its tax return depends mainly on the business structure. You have to file a business tax return every year, whether your business earned profits or sustained a loss. Only profits lead to income taxes, and that's a pretty good problem to have.

Financial Statements Flow into Tax Returns

The first time you look at any business tax return form, you'll see that it resembles your financial statements, without the numbers filled in yet. That's really all the tax return is, after all: a standard form on which to report your company's revenues, costs, expenses, and bottom line. Some business tax returns also ask for balance sheet information; again, the form looks just like an empty balance sheet, waiting for you to fill in the blanks.

The biggest difference between your financial statements and your tax return is the layout. For tax purposes, you combine different numbers than you would for your own review or planning purposes. For example, there's a single line for tax expenses on some business tax returns. There you would lump together payroll taxes, property taxes, and any other non-income-based taxes. On your own statement of profit and loss, though, you list those very different taxes separately. The order of items on the tax return probably won't match your financial statements to a T, either. But every revenue, cost, and expense you've recorded throughout the year will show up on the tax return, in one form or another.

The same goes for tax returns that include pared-down balance sheets (for some corporations and partnerships). All of your asset, liability, and equity account balances must be included (or the report won't balance), but not necessarily in the same way they appear on your balance sheet.

Different Income Taxation for Different Entities

The way to determine your company's income taxes depends wholly on its entity. Each entity comes with its own tax forms, not to mention unique tax benefits and drawbacks. Overall, though, there are really only two basic categories that your company's income taxes could fall into: pass-through and regular.

It seems that regular taxation would be the norm; in fact, it covers only one business structure, the C corporation. Here, regular taxation means that the company pays its own taxes on its own income. Every other entity deals with pass-through taxation. There, the company pays no income taxes on its profits; instead, all the profits pass through to the owners of the business and show up on their personal income tax returns.

ALERT!

LLCs come with the option of being taxed like C corporations, sole proprietorships (for single members), or partnerships (for multiple members). That gives the LLC members a chance to weigh which method is more advantageous, and then choose how their company will be taxed.

Each type of taxation comes with distinct features; which will be more beneficial for you depends on a wide combination of factors. For example, your personal financial situation plays a role in how you shift income between yourself and the company. Current tax rates also make a difference; for example, for several years corporate dividends were taxed at lower rates than were some other forms of personal income.

With a corporation (particularly a C corporation), you have the most income-shifting capabilities. Partnerships, however, allow you the most flexibility in dividing up income among multiple owners. Sole proprietorships are the most limited when it comes to tax planning, but the simplest when it comes to tax returns; they're the only entity for which only a single income tax return must be prepared, rather than at least two (the company's and yours). Even with the simplest business tax return, though, there's still room for tax planning. This is one area where you get a lot of bang for your accounting fees buck: Experienced business tax return preparers know their way around deductions and loopholes, minimizing your tax bill.

Introducing Business Tax Forms

For every business entity, there's a separate income tax form. Even those entities that don't have to pay any income taxes on their own still have tax returns to fill out; these are referred to as informational returns. Plus, no matter what type of business structure you've chosen for your company, some form of income from that company will show up on your personal tax return.

Most of the forms look pretty complicated, and the tax law behind them can be even more so. This is not a task for amateurs; get a professional involved. However, you still need to know the basics of how your company gets taxed so you can understand what the accountant is talking about, and to make sure the way he handles things makes sense. Don't be afraid to ask questions when something seems off to you; even the most qualified tax preparer can make a mistake or overlook an uncommon deduction.

Sole Proprietorships Use Schedule C

In the eyes of the IRS, a sole proprietorship is the same tax entity as its sole proprietor. There's no separate tax return to be filed for these companies. Instead, you simply add an extra form, called Schedule C, into your personal tax return. Very small businesses can use a simplified version of the form called Schedule C-EZ. Both versions of Schedule C look like statements of profit and loss, with the EZ containing only summary information and the regular Schedule C including expense breakdown details.

FACT

Single-member LLCs are treated like sole proprietorships for tax purposes, unless they opt to be taxed like C corporations. If you are the only owner of an LLC, you'll report your company's income on Schedule C, just like a regular sole proprietorship.

In addition, as you will learn later in this chapter, sole proprietorships use Form SE to calculate self-employment taxes.

Partnerships Use Form 1065

Even though partnerships don't pay any income taxes as an entity, they still must file an annual tax return on IRS Form 1065. On this form, you report all the profits and losses of the company and spell out the share that goes to each individual partner. Each partner's share of profit and loss goes on a separate form called a Schedule K-1, and those schedules are sent to the partners at tax time so they can prepare their own tax returns.

In addition to the year's financial data, Form 1065 asks for a lot of information about the partnership, including things such as:

- Its tax ID number
- Name and address of the business
- The type of business
- The names and contact information for all partners
- The name and contact information for the Tax Matters Partner (TMP)

The TMP is chosen by the partners to represent the company to the IRS. This is really only so the IRS has a single person to deal with all the time, rather than just whoever is around. The TMP doesn't have to be a tax specialist, but it helps if he knows his way around Form 1065 and has a basic understanding of the company finances. Should the IRS ever call for something the TMP can't handle, he can bring the partnership's tax accountant into the conversation.

S Corporations Use Form 1120S

Although S corporations themselves don't have to pay any federal income taxes, they still have to file an informational tax return annually. The company's profits and losses for the year are reported on IRS Form 1120S. The form looks like a specialized statement of profit and loss, basically because you have to report all the details of the company's revenues, costs, and expenses to get down to the taxable bottom line. Some S corporations also have to include balance sheet information on a separate schedule in the return.

Since the S corporation is a pass-through entity, Schedule K-1 forms have to be prepared to let each shareholder know how much of the income (or loss) he has to report on his own tax return. These forms are included in the corporation's 1120S as well as sent out to each shareholder.

C Corporations Use Form 1120

C corporations are the only business entities that always have to pay income taxes on their own income. That income is reported annually on Form 1120. The first page of the form is essentially a statement of profit and loss, though it may not look very much like the one you're copying the numbers from. Unlike the other business tax forms, Form 1120 includes lines for the total corporate income tax, estimated tax payments made throughout the year, and any balance of tax due.

Corporations come with their own graduated tax rate schedule, similar in nature but different from the rates for individuals. Sometimes the corporate rates are higher, and sometimes the personal rates are higher; it really depends on that year's tax tables. It can also differ for different income levels. For example, in 2005 corporations paid a 15 percent rate on income from $29,701 to $50,000, while single individuals paid 25 percent on that same income level. The rates switched places when income hit between $100,001 and $150,150; corporations paid 39 percent versus 28 percent for single individuals.

FACT

Some types of corporations, called personal service or professional corporations, are taxed at a single rate of 35 percent on all of their profits. Certain professionals (architects and consultants, for instance) have to use professional corporations if they want to incorporate, and they are stuck with that flat tax.

Since C corporations have to pay taxes on their profits, they also have to make quarterly estimated tax payments throughout the year. If you underpay the tax, meaning your estimates fall short of the eventual actual tax bill, your corporation could be subject to tax penalties. You can avoid this issue by making sure your payments each equal at least 25 percent of last year's final tax bill.

Different Ways to Pay Yourself

One of the reasons you started a business was to make some money. Once your business is profitable, you have to decide whether, when, and how you want to transfer some of that money into your personal accounts. The different ways you can do that, and the potential tax implications, depend largely on your business entity.

Sole proprietorships offer the least flexibility here: your only option is withdrawals, and they have absolutely no impact on your tax situation. That's because you've already paid tax on all of the company profits through your Schedule C. Taking money out of a sole proprietorship is strictly a balance sheet transaction. The same goes for benefits: technically, it's as if you bought your own health insurance or set up your own retirement plan, and any contributions made on your behalf count as withdrawals on the books.

QUESTION?

What about payments to LLC owners?
Payments to LLC owners (also known as members) depend on how the company is taxed. When taxed like a sole proprietorship, payments are withdrawals; taxed like a partnership, they can be withdrawals or guaranteed payments. When the LLC is taxed like a C corporation, all payment options available to shareholder-employees are available to members.

Partnerships work in much the same way as sole proprietorships, at least when it comes to owners taking cash out of the company. In most cases, payments made to partners will count as withdrawals and have no tax impact. There is, however, something called a guaranteed payment to a partner; these payments get slightly different treatment than do standard distributions. Guaranteed payments are made to partners for roles other than simple ownership, such as employee or lender; as the name implies, these payments are guaranteed, unlike regular distributions. Also, regular distributions come out of capital and are usually based on a percentage of profits; guaranteed payments are considered deductions for the partnership and cannot be measured as a percentage of profits.

If you set up a corporation, you have more options available for paying yourself. The two most common are salaries (which are required of owner-employees) and dividends. Salaries are taxable to you as the employee and tax-deductible to the corporation as the employer. Dividends, though, offer no tax benefit to the corporation, even though they're taxable to the recipients.

Your Payment Strategy Impacts Your Personal Taxes

Like most of the other tax issues surrounding your business, the impact on your personal tax return depends on the entity you've chosen for your company. No matter which business structure you've used, though, if your company has earned profits (and even sometimes when it hasn't), you will pay some kind of tax on business-related income.

One of the main differences among the entities, when it comes to your personal taxes, is *where* the business income shows up. Other twists are based on how you've chosen to take money out of the company. Those decisions affect how much tax you'll pay on that income.

One thing most business owners have in common (the exception being C corporation shareholders) is the obligation to make quarterly personal estimated tax payments throughout the year. Since your business income isn't subject to withholding taxes, you have to make periodic payments to the IRS, which really are prepayments against your final tax bill. To do this, you have to estimate your share of business income for the whole year, figure out the tax that would be due on that estimate, divide it by four, and file Form 1040-ES along with a check for the estimated taxes. This is another area where your accountant can be very helpful.

For Sole Proprietors

All of the profits (or losses) for your sole proprietorship are reported on Schedule C, as part of your overall Form 1040. Profits are added to your total income for income tax purposes; losses are deducted directly from your other income (and directly reduce your total taxable income). That profit or loss information is reported in detail on Schedule C and as one lump-sum line item on your 1040.

In addition to income taxes, sole proprietorship profits are subject to self-employment taxes. Self-employment taxes cover Social Security and

Medicare in one chunk, which includes the amount you would have had withheld as an employee plus the additional expense you would have had to pay as an employer. These taxes are calculated on Schedule SE, based on the lion's share of the bottom-line profits you've reported on Schedule C. One-half of the total self-employment tax you have to pay is deductible from your income (right on the front of your 1040) for income tax purposes, similar to the deduction you'd get as an employer paying the tax on behalf of an employee.

FACT

As a sole proprietor, you also get to deduct all health insurance premiums you've paid for yourself (and your family) as well as any contributions you have made into a retirement plan on your own behalf. These deductions show up on the first page of your 1040 and go toward reducing your taxable income.

For Partners

In partnerships, every penny of profit (or loss) flows through to the partners, whether they take cash distributions for the year or not. The K-1s dictate how those profits are shown on the personal tax returns. For example, interest income on the K-1 turns up as interest income on the partner's personal return. Even if you've been doing your own personal income tax returns for years with no problem, the year you get your first Schedule K-1 could be the time to pay a professional. These forms are intricate and a little tricky, and it will help to at least have someone walk you through it the first time.

Like sole proprietors, partners have to pay self-employment tax on their share of the company's profits. This goes for both your share of the year's profits and any guaranteed payments you've received. Your self-employment taxes are calculated on Schedule SE and added to the total tax bill on your 1040. Half of these taxes can be deducted from your total taxable income; there's a special line for that deduction on the front page of your 1040. There you will also find the lines you can use to deduct health insurance premiums and retirement plan contributions made on your behalf.

For Small-Corporation Owners

When you own and work for a corporation, at least part of the money you get out of the company will be in the form of salary. That shows up on your tax return just as it would from any job. You just copy the information from the W-2 you got from the corporation onto your Form 1040. That's the same whether you have an S or a C corporation. After salary, though, the two corporation types head in different directions on your tax return.

ALERT!

The question of whether your S corporation losses are fully deductible on your personal tax return is pretty tricky. It depends on how much basis (a special measurement of equity) you hold in the company. To avoid any reporting snafus, have a professional help you with your personal tax preparation along with that of the business.

Each shareholder in an S corporation gets a Form K-1 reporting her share of the company's income. The specific kinds of income pass through the corporation directly onto your tax return. For example, if the S corporation had some capital gains, you have some capital gains. Your share of the regular business profits also show up on your personal tax return, but they aren't subject to self-employment taxes; you can also (sometimes) get a dollar-for-dollar taxable income reduction for losses suffered by your S corporation. You'll pay tax on your full share of the profits whether or not you take a single dollar in dividends. Benefits paid on your behalf by the company also are added to your income, but the biggest one is also 100 percent personally deductible: health insurance premiums. Other common (but not wholly deductible) add-backs include life and disability insurance and many traditional fringe benefits, such as parking and transportation.

Dividend income from your C corporation is reported on Schedule B of your personal tax return, along with any other interest and dividend income you've earned throughout the year. It gets treated no differently from dividends you received from your investments. Any money you take out of the corporation that isn't specifically considered salary (or loans or leases, as you'll learn in the next section of this chapter), is considered a taxable dividend by the IRS.

If you use your corporate checkbook to pay your personal cable bill, you've just paid yourself a personal dividend—even if you pay the money right back. Use caution here, or you could end up with a very high amount of dividend income, which is subject to double taxation.

Tax Planning Strategies

Tax planning strategies range from the very simple to the excruciatingly complex, but they all have one thing in common: they seek to minimize your overall tax bill. There are dozens of means available to help you accomplish this goal, from gray areas to loopholes to income shifting to tax deferral. Most sound strategies use a combination of methods to keep income taxes to a bare minimum.

There are two major ways to cut down your tax bill: reduce your taxable income, or reduce your tax rate. You can lower your taxable income by taking full advantage of allowable deductions, especially those that are deductible to businesses but not to individual taxpayers (company cars, for instance). While you can't literally reduce your tax rate, you can do things that have the same effect, such as shifting income to the entity that will pay the lowest tax rate, or taking steps to minimize income that would be subject to self-employment tax in addition to income tax.

Loans and Leases

Some of the neatest tricks for getting money out of your business without incurring either double taxation or self-employment tax include loans and leases. While these two items may seem to have nothing in common, they do share one important factor: you need a legally binding contract to really make them work and to keep them from being reclassified by the IRS.

Loans are a great way to get money out of the company, whichever way the money goes initially. When you want to put money into the company without changing your equity standing, you can give it a loan and take back payments. This is especially beneficial with C corporations, where you can't get equity contributions back without invoking taxable dividends. If you need a lump sum of cash from the company coffers, treating it as a loan won't set off any tax liability. The key is to have a written legal loan agreement in place, and that has to include:

- Date of the loan
- Original loan amount
- Interest
- Payment schedule

Yes, your loan has to include interest, at the current going rate. When you don't charge interest, the IRS will, and in that case you'll have to pay tax on that interest income even if you never actually got it.

ALERT!

Don't confuse tax avoidance with tax evasion. Tax avoidance involves using 100 percent legal means to reduce your tax bill, which is something you have every right to do. Tax evasion, on the other hand, employs illegal methods to get out of paying taxes.

Leases allow you to rent property to your company. That rental income will be taxable but won't be subject to double taxation or self-employment tax. Any form of rent expense is deductible to the company. However, you cannot use this in connection with a home office.

Get the Family Involved

When it comes to income shifting, paying family members in the lower tax brackets can be an excellent way to go. Get your kids involved in the business, and give them paychecks. This gives a beneficial twist to just doling out allowances: your kids have some job responsibility, and your company gets an expense deduction.

In order for this plan to work, your kids have to actually work for the business in an age-appropriate capacity. You can hire your five-year-old to sweep up, your ten-year-old to do the filing, and your fifteen-year-old to work the register. Once they're employees, you can even include them in your company's retirement plan.

chapter 17

The Best Use of Your Financial Statements

Financial statements contain a wealth of information; you just need to know where to look. More than just a yardstick for past performance, your financial statements can provide significant clues for maximizing profitability, improving cash flow, and successfully growing your business. They'll help you make decisions, large and small, and maybe even point your company in directions you never dreamed of. Whether your business is brand new or several years old, there's a lot to be learned from your financial statements. Now is the time to get started.

What Can Your Statements Tell You?

At face value, your financial statements tell you a lot about your company's performance. The statement of profit and loss lets you know how much the company sold, and whether those sales resulted in overall profitability. The balance sheet tells you where the company stands right now, and gives you a look at the overall financial position. The statement of cash flows informs you how cash moves through your business and whether operations are supplying or draining cash. All this data is critical to your future plans, but it's really just a small part of the total knowledge you can gain from these exceptionally enlightening reports.

When you delve deeper into these statements, and add a little math to the mix, it will open up a whole new world of information that you can use to make your business a better one. With critical analysis, the relationships among the accounts become clearer, as does the impact they can have on one another. Different ways of measuring the same numbers offer new perspectives and insights, and can spark innovative and profitable ideas.

Your financial statements can tell you things such as:

- Whether your company has sufficient liquidity
- Whether the company is holding too much inventory
- Whether you need to revisit customer payment terms
- Whether you're charging enough for your products and services
- How to put your assets to better use
- Whether serious financial problems are on the horizon
- How well your company stacks up to competitors
- How well the company fares according to industry standards

The more you know about your business, the better its chances of success. Noticing potential problem areas before they blossom into full-grown crises can save a business from ultimate failure. Planning and allowing for growth before it kicks in helps your company expand in the most profitable ways. Your financial statements contain all this information; all you have to do is analyze it.

Vertical and Horizontal Analysis

The two simplest ways to analyze your financial statements are vertically and horizontally. A vertical analysis shows you the relationships among components of one financial statement, measured as percentages. On your balance sheet, each asset is shown as a percentage of total assets; each liability or equity item is shown as a percentage of total liabilities and equity. On your statement of profit and loss, each line item is shown as a percentage of net sales.

FACT

Some companies use a sort of combination vertical and horizontal analysis in one. These reports contain financial data from more than one period, with a vertical analysis applied to each one. This way you can tell at a glance how statement components have changed in their proportions from one period to the next, without any extra math.

A horizontal analysis provides you with a way to compare your numbers from one period to the next, using financial statements from at least two distinct periods. Each line item has an entry in a current period column and a prior period column. Those two entries are compared to show both the dollar difference and percentage change between the two periods.

Performing a Vertical Analysis

For a fledgling business, vertical analysis of the statement of profit and loss can be particularly enlightening. Looking at every item on the statement as a percentage of sales tells you exactly where each penny of your revenues is going. Once you know that, it's easy to see which items are eating up too much of your profits. Those are the areas where you can try to cut back. In the two-year version of this analysis, you can see how components have changed, which may not be apparent until you see them expressed in this manner.

The following example shows you what a vertical analysis looks like for both a statement of profit and loss and a balance sheet.

Vertical Analysis

Joan's Colorful Kites

Statement of Profit and Loss for the Year Ended December 31, 2005

	Amount	Percent
Sales	$18,000	100.00%
Cost of Goods Sold	7,000	38.89%
Gross Profit	$11,000	61.11 %
Selling Expenses		
Advertising	$ 500	2.78 %
Commissions	750	4.17 %
Delivery Fees	1,200	6.67 %
Salaries	5,000	27.78 %
Total Selling Expenses	$ 7,450	41.39 %
General & Administrative Expenses		
Insurance	$ 800	4.44 %
Rent	1,200	6.67 %
Depreciation	200	1.11 %
Utilities	400	2.22 %
Total General & Administrative Expenses	$2,600	14.44 %
Net Profit	**$ 950**	**5.28 %**

Vertical Analysis

Joan's Colorful Kites

Balance Sheet

December 31, 2005

Assets		
Current Assets:	**Amount**	**Percent**
Cash	$ 600	14.12 %
Inventory	2,000	47.06 %
Prepaid Insurance	250	5.88 %
Total Current Assets	$ 2,850	67.06 %
Fixed Assets:		
Office Equipment	$ 1,800	42.35 %
Less: Accumulated Depreciation	-400	-9.41 %
Total Fixed Assets	$ 1,400	32.94 %
Total Assets	$ 4,250	100.00 %
Liabilities & Owner's Equity		
Current Liabilities:		
Accounts Payable	$ 1,800	42.35 %
Taxes Payable	500	11.76 %
Total Liabilities	$ 2,300	54.12 %
Owner's Equity	$ 1,950	45.88 %
Total Liabilities & Owner's Equity	$ 4,250	100.00 %

As you can see in the statement of profit and loss, Joan's gross profit is sizable, at 61 percent. The selling expenses, though, are eating up a huge chunk of the revenues, even more than product costs; that could be an area in which to cut back. General operating expenses take up a reasonable percentage of sales, leaving Joan with about a 5 percent bottom-line profit. As for the company's balance sheet, inventory makes up the lion's share of her current assets, which could translate into cash-flow problems down the line. Also, her company is financed with more debt than equity. That's not uncommon for new businesses, but all of this debt is current, which could suck up all the current assets of the company.

Horizontal Analysis

The main point of performing a horizontal analysis on your financial statements is to see how things have changed from one period to the next. These changes are called trends in accounting lingo, and you can tell a lot about your company by the trends in its financial statements. In addition to that, it will help shine a light on numbers that should have changed by a certain amount but didn't. For example, if your sales increased by 20 percent you would expect your gross profit to change by a similar amount.

The following example uses a two-year comparative statement of profit and loss. Look for the important trends and potential trouble spots.

Horizontal Analysis

Joan's Colorful Kites

Statement of Profit and Loss
for the Years Ended 12/31/2004 and 12/31/2005

	2005 Amount	2004 Amount	Change in Dollars	Percent Change
Sales	$ 18,000	$ 15,000	$ 3,000	16.67 %
Cost of Goods Sold	7,000	6,000	$ 1,000	14.29 %
Gross Profit	$ 11,000	$ 9,000	$ 2,000	18.18 %
Selling Expenses				
Advertising	$ 500	$ 200	$ 300	60.00 %
Commissions	750	400	$ 350	46.67 %
Delivery Fees	1200	720	$ 480	40.00 %
Salaries	5000	5000	$ -	0.00 %
Total Selling Expenses	$ 7,450	$ 6,320	$ 1,130	15.17 %
General & Administrative Expenses				
Insurance	$ 800	$ 800	$ -	0.00 %
Rent	1200	1200	$ -	0.00 %
Depreciation	200	200	$ -	0.00 %
Utilities	400	280	$ 120	30.00 %
Total General & Administrative Expenses	$ 2,600	$ 2,480	$ 120	4.62 %
Net Profit	**$ 950**	**$ 200**	**$ 750**	**78.95%**

First, Joan's sales went up by about 17 percent, while her product costs went up by only around 14 percent. That helps add to her profitability on both sides—increased revenues and decreased costs. Most of her selling expenses increased as well, but that seems to have contributed to additional sales without increasing as much as sales did. Joan was also able to keep most of her general operating expenses under control, leading to much greater profits in 2005 than the company saw the prior year.

Calculating Crucial Financial Ratios

The idea of calculating financial ratios can seem intimidating, but it's really much easier than it sounds. A ratio is really just a fraction, expressed in a slightly different way to let you see how two numbers compare to one another. You actually use ratios every day. For instance, if it takes you two hours to drive 120 miles, you know that you've driven 60 miles per hour, a ratio you calculated by dividing 120 miles by two hours. If that drive uses up ten gallons of gas, you know that your car gets twelve miles per gallon, a ratio computed by dividing 120 miles by ten gallons.

QUESTION?

Are financial ratios required to make a complete set of financial statements?
No, a full set of financial statements doesn't have to include ratio analysis. However, there are times when you need to know particular ratios. For example, if you have a business loan, the bank may require your company to meet specific ratio minimums.

Financial statement ratios really aren't much different: they take some figures off the financial statements and compare them. The meaningful analysis comes with the particular numbers you use to compute these ratios and with what the results indicate. The three main categories of analysis are profitability, liquidity, and debt and investment.

A full ratio analysis can tell you a lot about the financial health of your company. Some ratios will let you know how well you're managing cash.

Others tell you if your company is in a position to take on more debt. Still others provide an objective measure of your profitability. By looking at the ratio results, both individually and collectively, you'll understand your company's finances in a completely different (and more comprehensive) way.

Profitability Ratios

Business owners want to know about profits, which makes this group of ratios the most commonly used (at least voluntarily) among entrepreneurs. As the name indicates, profitability ratios measure how profitable your company is at different stages. You calculate gross profit margin, operating profit margin, and net profit margin (whenever applicable). By taking this measure from different points on your statement of profit and loss, you can see clearly where your revenues are going and whether any expense types are eating up a disproportionate share of the income.

FACT

Interest and income taxes are held out separately from operating expenses because they aren't really part of your operations. Interest expense is typically temporary, linked to a particular business loan, and therefore doesn't count as an ongoing operating expense. Income tax expense (only an issue for corporations) comes after the fact and exists only when there are profits to tax.

Your company's gross profit lets you know how much of your company's sales dollars are left over after you've paid for the goods you sold. The operating profit tells you how much is left after cost of goods and operating expenses are deducted from your revenues (those expenses don't include income taxes and interest). For service businesses, the gross profit and operating profit are the same, for they don't have any cost of goods to deal with. Finally, the net profit shows how much is left of your sales dollars after you deduct absolutely everything: costs, expenses, interest, and income taxes.

To calculate these ratios, you simply pull the applicable profit from your statement and divide it by your net sales. Gross profit margin equals your gross profit divided by total net sales. Operating profit margin equals your income from operations divided by total net sales. Net profit margin equals your bottom-line net profit divided by total net sales. When your company doesn't have any interest or income tax expense, the net profit margin is the same as the operating profit margin.

With all profitability ratios, higher numbers are better numbers. Remember, though, that what's considered good or normal for one industry could be considered paltry for another. Service businesses, for example, will naturally have much higher operating margins than do product businesses. Product industries with high markup (such as clothing) will have higher gross margins than those with lower markup (such as hardware). Don't look at your margins without some kind of industry reference to put them in perspective.

Liquidity Ratios

Liquidity ratios measure your company's ability to pay its bills—in accounting terms, to meet financial obligations. While it's important to be able to pay all the bills, the current liabilities are more critical, especially for a new small business. Your current liabilities cover the things you need to run your business every day: inventory, supplies, power. If you can't pay these vendors, they may stop providing goods and services, and your company wouldn't be able to function.

ALERT!

Your quick ratio can never be greater than your current ratio; if it comes out that way, recalculate both. Your total current assets can't be less than your total current assets minus inventory; that's why the current ratio has to be greater.

The two most important liquidity measures are the current ratio and the quick ratio. The current ratio spells out in no uncertain terms whether your company will be able to meet its immediate financial obligations. It literally calculates how many dollars of current assets you have on hand to pay down your current liabilities. To compute the current ratio, divide your total current assets by your total current liabilities (you can find these numbers on your balance sheet).

The quick ratio takes the current ratio up one more notch. Here you don't include inventory in the numerator, even though it's a current asset. The logic behind this acknowledges that inventory is the toughest current asset to get rid of fast; it's the one that will take the longest to convert into cash. Since you can't pay your bills with inventory, product-based companies can get a better liquidity picture using the quick ratio. To compute the quick ratio, first subtract the inventory from the total current liabilities; then divide that result by the total current liabilities to get the quick ratio. If your company doesn't sell any products, compute only the current ratio.

Debt and Investment Ratios

Most new businesses need to borrow money to get started. One very common problem is taking on too much debt too soon, as they try to grow at lightning pace; the more in debt a company is, the harder it is for that company to succeed. Also, when debt is disproportionately high, it cuts too deeply into the company's profits, and that means you're getting a smaller return on your investment in the company. By looking at debt and investment ratios, you can better gauge your company's debt position and learn whether you're earning a reasonable return on your investment.

ALERT!

You can find out what is an acceptable debt ratio for your company from your banker or your main creditors. Although their numbers may not be exactly the same, they will be in the same ballpark. That will give you a reasonable frame of reference for your debt ratio, letting you know whether it's too high or right on target.

One critical financial ratio often used by creditors is the debt ratio, but it's an important piece of information for you as well, especially if you plan to take on more debt. The debt ratio is calculated by dividing total liabilities by total assets (both of these numbers come right off your balance sheet). When this ratio runs high, meaning close to 1.0, that indicates a bigger risk of failure for the company. Debt ratios between 0.5 and 1.0 show that your business is financed mainly by debt. That debt consumes both your cash and your profits, making it harder for your equity to grow and for your company to add more debt when necessary.

Investment ratios let you know how much you're earning on your investment in the business. After all, one of the reasons you started your own business was to make some money, and it's important to know just how much that is. Even if you're getting a salary from your company, you should also be earning profits from your investment. The quickest way to measure that is to calculate the return on investment (ROI) ratio, which measures how well the company is using its assets to generate profits. You calculate this ratio by dividing your net profits by your total assets (net profits comes from the statement of profit and loss; total assets from the balance sheet). As you'd expect, a higher ROI is better, because that means you're earning more on your investment. At the very least, a healthy ROI should provide more return than you'd get if you put your money into a standard savings account.

Using Ratio Analysis

The numbers used in this ratio analysis come from the 2005 financial statements for Joan's Colorful Kites, used for the vertical and horizontal analyses performed earlier in this chapter.

First, a look at the profitability ratios, which actually appear on the vertical analysis. The gross profit margin came to 61.11 percent, calculated by dividing the $11,000 gross profit by the $18,000 in sales. The operating profit margin, in this case equal to the net profit margin (since there are no income taxes or interest expenses), came to 5.28 percent. That margin was calculated by dividing the bottom-line profit of $950 by the total sales of $18,000.

Next come the liquidity ratios. The current ratio for Joan's Colorful Kites equals 1.24, computed by dividing total current assets ($2,850) by total current liabilities ($2,300). This result indicates that Joan has sufficient current assets to cover her current liabilities. The quick ratio, however, paints a different picture. This ratio comes to only 0.37, which means that when you take inventory out of the equation, the company has only $0.37 to pay down each $1.00 of current debt.

Now take a look at the company's debt and investment ratios. The debt ratio is on the high side, but not so high that Joan would have a hard time getting a business loan. When you divide the total liabilities of $2,300 by the total assets of $4,250, the result is a debt ratio of 54.12 percent. Last, but not least, comes Joan's ROI. The net profits of $950 divided by the total assets of $4,250 provides Joan a 22 percent return, much higher than she'd receive if she turned those assets into a savings account.

Nipping Problems in the Bud

New businesses are usually fraught with financial problems: margins too low, debt too high, not enough cash, not enough profits. That's normal and to be expected. How you deal with these initial setbacks, though, can mean the difference between success and failure for your business.

Even seemingly unrelated financial problems go together. A lack of sufficient cash can cause lower profits, for example, and too much debt can lead to too little cash. As you analyze your financial statements, look at the big picture instead of focusing on just one area. New business and small-business owners often focus only on boosting net profits rather than the overall financial health of their companies. Profitability is very important—without it your company can't stay afloat—but it's not the only puzzle piece that matters.

Look into using your assets more efficiently, to get as much as possible out of them. Every asset on your books, from your desk to your inventory to your equipment, plays a part in your company's profit potential. Using the same old assets in different ways can spark productivity and profitability. Find ways to pump up your cash inflow at the same time that you decrease the outflow; this will help you pay down debt sooner and avoid the need to take on more debt before you really want to. By combining your ratio, vertical, and horizontal analyses, you can spot trends in the making and possible trouble spots, and take corrective action before it's too late.

Profitability Problems

You can increase your profitability with either a top-down or bottom-up approach. A top-down approach focuses on increasing sales and gross profits, while a bottom-up approach directs attention to trimming expenses. The quick way to increase sales and the gross profit margin is to increase your markup (a.k.a. raise prices). Use this method with caution, though, as you don't want to raise prices so high that customers stop buying from you. You can also try to increase your gross margin by paying less for inventory purchases; look into new suppliers, or try renegotiating with your existing vendors to keep your product costs as low as possible.

FACT

You can give your bottom line a double boost by both increasing your gross margin and cutting back on expenses. If you find a way to lower product costs, don't stop there. Try to minimize some of your operating expenses as well.

On the bottom-up front, take a good look at your interest and operating expenses, and cut back anywhere you can. There will be some expenses your company is stuck with, at least for now, such as rent and loan interest. Others, though, can be tweaked; for example, you can cut back on your advertising spending and look for ways to get free publicity, or shop around for a less expensive insurance policy.

Manage Your Company's Debt

Having liabilities isn't good or bad; it's just a normal business practice. Be careful to not let debt spiral out of control, though. As soon as you notice that your company is starting to owe more than it can pay, you need to take steps to bring your liabilities back into the reasonable range. To do this, try to make sure that your current liabilities aren't greater than your current assets. When that balance shifts toward the negative, it means you don't have enough current assets to meet your immediate obligations, a sign of coming money troubles.

One good first step: stop using credit cards to pay for business expenses. Credit card interest is among the highest you'll pay, eating up a disproportionate share of profits and giving very little in return. If your company needs to borrow money (and using credit cards counts as borrowing) just to pay the monthly bills, sit down with your accountant and take a good look at your budget. Until your debt is back under control, slash any absolutely unnecessary expenses and take positive steps to boost your cash flow.

A Basis for Decision-Making

Whether your company is struggling to get by or ready to expand, you'll need to make some decisions about what to do next. The best place to gather what you need to inform your decisions is your financial statements. As you analyze your financial statements, the best ways to keep your company going and growing become apparent.

Some of the biggest decisions new business and small-business owners face are:

- When to put more of their own money into the company
- If and when to take on additional debt
- Whether new debt should be long- or short-term
- How and when to expand
- Whether it pays to keep the company going

These choices are hard to make, especially the one about deciding if it's time to let the company go and try something else. A lot of new business and small-business owners avoid these decisions, letting events just unfold until decisions are made for them. Planning ahead and making careful, informed decisions helps you preserve more of your capital.

Most of all, though, a complete analysis of your financial statements will help you manage your business more efficiently every day. Those daily, seemingly small decisions can have as much impact on your company as the major ones. Take direction from your analysis; if numbers fall below your plans and expectations, take steps now to correct the problem and keep your company from failing. When the numbers are as good or better than expected, you can start thinking about expansion. Growing your business in small, manageable chunks will serve you better than will an overnight expansion.

Boosting Profitability and Positive Cash Flow

For most small companies, the important points to come out of financial statement analysis are ways to boost profits and improve cash flow. Since the two usually go hand in hand, a positive change in one can bring the same in the other; however, there are times when focusing solely on one of these issues can bring about a negative change in the other. A prime example of profits and cash flow moving in opposite directions is when a business suddenly begins offering credit terms to customers; this often triggers an immediate increase in sales and therefore profits, but it leads to a decrease in cash inflow.

As a business owner, you have more control over your cash outflows and your expenses than you do over your inflows and revenues. The easiest way to minimize cash outflow and expenditures is to cut operating expenses wherever possible. The more you can do that, the more cash you'll have to work with. That "extra" cash can be used to pay down high-interest debt (such as credit card bills with ongoing balances) more quickly; that, in turn, cuts down both your interest expense and cash outflow going forward, which will eventually improve both your profitability and cash situation.

If your company doesn't have outstanding credit card debt to deal with, make extra payments on your highest-interest loans when you find yourself with cash on hand. The sooner those loans are paid off, the less interest you'll pay overall, improving both your cash flow and your bottom line.

Other steps you can take to improve cash flow include extending accounts payable as far as possible while tightening the reins on accounts receivable. Talk to your vendors about adding some time to your credit terms, and use every day they give you. At the same time, get tough with your customers about paying on time. To boost your incoming cash, you can offer small early payment discounts to your customers. Although that may seem counterproductive when you're trying to increase profits, it may actually have the effect you're going for. Early payment discounts encourage customers to pay you more quickly, and for them it has the effect of cutting costs, which can encourage them to buy more from you.

When You Need Outside Funding

Sometimes your company will need a cash infusion from the outside to keep things going. When that happens, you have two options for bringing in money: equity or debt. The financial statement analysis can shine a light on which option makes more sense for your company right now. A number of factors can play into this decision, including the current debt ratio and the existing equity structure.

When your company has a favorable debt situation and an existing relationship with a bank, getting a loan can be as simple as filling out a couple of forms. If your company already has as much debt as it can handle, or a debt ratio too high to allow for a bank loan, consider other sources for a business loan. When your company does borrow from your friends or family, treat it like any other business loan, complete with comprehensive loan terms and binding paperwork.

Equity financing may be tougher for a small business, especially one that's not incorporated. When you and your existing partners are already tapped out, inviting new investors dilutes your equity. Even if the investors won't act as co-owners, and won't take active roles in the daily business management, they'll want to see a piece of the profits. In fact, before they'll invest a dime, they'll want to see a clear picture of your company's growth and profit potential, and just how much return they can expect to get on their investment.

chapter 18

More Ways Accounting Helps Your Business

As a business owner, you're called upon every day to make decisions that could ultimately impact the life of your company. To make good decisions, you have to understand your company's financial position completely, and use that knowledge to strengthen the business finances. As you gain more experience, and more confidence, decisions that once seemed challenging will become intuitive. The one thing that won't change, though, is the fact that you'll need accounting information to make virtually every business decision.

18

Know Your Costs to Set Your Prices

It seems like a simple fact: to earn profits, your prices have to be higher than your costs. It stands to reason that if you just add some percentage to your costs, your company will profit. With product-based businesses, setting prices starts with a markup on the product costs; service businesses can start with a markup of an hourly rate (either for employees or owners). Those costs should be starting points, but many new business owners use these alone as a basis to set prices. For many new small-business owners, figuring out the complete costs of what they're selling can be difficult. However, not knowing the true costs can result in underpricing products and services.

FACT

The price floor is the absolute minimum at which you can set your prices without sustaining losses on each sale. The price ceiling is the absolute maximum price the market will bear. The price you charge for your products or services will fall somewhere in the middle.

Here's what your price needs to cover: the immediate cost of what you're selling, a portion of your selling and general expenses, and a reasonable profit left over for you. Include every component of cost of goods sold as you work the numbers for a product-based business. For a service business, use a reasonable hourly rate as your starting point; for yourself (if you're not counted as an employee), remember to add on the costs of benefits and employment taxes. Pull the selling and general expenses right off your statement of profit and loss; if you have figures from two or three periods to work with, take an average. As for your desired net profits, add on a reasonable percentage for your industry. For example, someone selling original artwork could expect to see a higher profit percentage on each individual sale than could someone selling one-size-fits-all rain boots.

The Break-Even Analysis

The break-even analysis provides you with a crucial piece of data: your company's break-even point. The break-even point occurs when your company's revenues exactly equal its costs and expenses, resulting in neither a profit nor loss. When sales fall below the break-even point, your business incurs a loss; when sales climb higher, you see profits.

To come up with your break-even point, you need three pieces of information: the total expected fixed costs, projected variable costs, and projected sales. Fixed costs include both administrative expenses (a.k.a. overhead) and interest, all of which must be paid whether or not you make a single sale. Variable costs include cost of goods sold and selling expenses; total variable costs naturally go up as sales volume increases. Your projected sales volume should be based on how much you realistically expect to sell at a particular price. Keep in mind, those projected sales are what you expect to sell, not your break-even point.

To calculate a break-even point for your service business, use service salaries as your cost of goods sold. When employees perform services on behalf of the company, divide up their salaries into units that match your revenue units (whatever basis you use to determine customer prices, such as hours). Don't forget to include a rate for yourself when you perform services.

If your break-even analysis doesn't pan out, which indicates loss potential, you may be inclined to keep working the numbers until you get a favorable outcome. Your energy may be better spent on rethinking this plan or considering a different direction for your company. When you start pulling numbers out of the air to make an analysis come out the way you want, you could be setting yourself up for losses.

Break Down the Break-Even Equation

Once you have those pieces, you have to do some math (you may even have to do a little algebra here). Here's the basic break-even equation:

$$BE = FC + (VC / S \times BE)$$

BE stands for break-even sales, FC stands for fixed costs, VC stands for your total projected variable costs, and S stands for your total projected sales.

It's easier to look at with numbers. In this example, the fixed costs are $30,000. Total projected variable costs came to $50,000, and total projected sales are $100,000. Here's how to work the break-even equation with these numbers.

$$BE = \$30,000 + (\$50,000 / \$100,000 \times BE)$$

$$BE = \$30,000 + (0.50 \times BE)$$

$$BE - (0.50 \times BE) = \$30,000$$

$$BE = \$60,000$$

In this example, the break-even point came to $60,000, which is less than the projected sales figure of $100,000. That means this analysis is favorable, and implementing this decision is likely to result in profits.

When to Prepare a Break-Even Analysis

Use this analysis every time you plan to make a major change in the business. Major changes include:

- Adding a new product
- Expanding the business
- Taking on significant debt
- Entering a long-term contract (with either a supplier or customer)
- Setting or changing prices

Prepare a break-even before you definitively decide to make such a major change. This will let you know whether that change can be profitable; if it can't, reconsider your plans.

Developing Pro Forma Statements

The financial statements you learned about in earlier chapters provide historical information. To keep your business on track, though, you must consider the future. Future-oriented financial statements are called pro formas, and they are based solely on your expectations of what is likely to happen over the upcoming period. Pro formas can help you predict cash flows and profitability in future periods, so you can plan ahead for any anticipated crunches.

FACT

If you prepared a complete business plan before starting your company, you've probably already worked with pro forma financial statements. Once your company has been around for a while, you'll have a better feel for the numbers and can develop prospective statements that will come very close to what will really happen.

To develop your pro formas, start with your existing financial statements, for as many periods as you have them. These historical reports provide a jumping-off point for future performance. Horizontal analyses can also be especially helpful in creating pro formas, since they show you trends already in progress. For example, if sales have grown by an average of 2 percent over the past few periods, you can reasonably project that same growth rate over the next few periods.

Some items are even more predictable. For example, if you have an outstanding business loan, you know how much of that will be paid down in the upcoming months and how much interest expense will be generated. Fixed expenses can be laid out in a similar manner; if you expect any increases (for instance, if your landlord has told you that the rent will go up by $100 per month), account for them in your pro forma statements. Remember to figure in any planned asset purchases and new loans that may arise as a result of those purchases.

Once you've gotten the numbers started, you can start filling in the pro formas, which look just like your regular financial statements. The only true exception is in the heading: you must label prospective financial statements clearly, especially when someone outside the business will be looking at them. Just as with the standard historical variety, a complete set of pro forma financial statements includes a statement of profit and loss, a balance sheet, and a statement of cash flows.

Sticking to a Budget

Although it's not included among the standard financial statements, one of the most useful reports you can prepare for your own use is a budget. A budget gives you something to measure your actual results against, so you can see right away in a concrete manner how your business is doing in comparison to your original expectations. In the beginning, preparing a monthly budget analysis helps you keep on top of the numbers so you can make adjustments immediately when actual figures move far away from what you have budgeted. As your budgeting skills improve, you can do the analysis quarterly.

ALERT!

Budgets tend to measure mainly revenue and expense items, as those impact cash more immediately than do balance sheet items. However, balance sheet items that affect cash should show up on your budget analysis. Examples include owner draws, impending asset purchases, and paying down loan principal.

A budget analysis is a report in which you compare budget projections to actual results. When this analysis shows deviations between expected and actual, whether the number is over or under budget, determine the underlying cause of the variance. Once you know that, you can begin to make changes to get the numbers back on track. Even though individual items on your budget are important, it's also important to look at the total net effect before you take any drastic measures; a couple of off items may not throw your whole budget out of whack.

In general, you want revenues to meet or exceed budget, and costs and expenses to come in under budget. Unfortunately, the opposite is usually what happens: revenues come in below expectations, and costs and expenses run higher. All this really means is that you need to revise your budget, and your plans, accordingly.

Financing Major Purchases

When your company is in need of substantial assets, cash on hand typically won't cover the bill. Luckily, many big assets come with seller financing attached, and since the asset itself will be used for collateral, your company's credit position may be less of an issue. Even with other lenders, asset-backed financing can be easier to obtain than a general business loan that comes with no collateral, since the focus is on the value of the asset itself and the security it provides to the lender. In fact, as long as it doesn't violate any covenants of your existing business loan from the bank, it can be better for your company to use a source of financing other than your bank for asset purchases.

The Pitfalls of Asset-Backed Financing

Even though it can seem like a simple solution to credit problems, asset-backed financing comes with some potential drawbacks of its own:

- Commerical financing companies often charge very high interest rates on their loans.
- You may need to come up with a sizable down payment as part of the asset purchase, which can be a problem when cash is tight.
- Even though it's with a different lender, the loan shows up on your balance sheet and in your debt ratio, which can make it harder to get additional business loans.
- Nonbank asset financing companies are much more likely to seize the collateral asset if your company misses a few payments.

When your company already has a good credit standing, these issues can be minor or even nonexistent. It's companies that are already struggling that get socked with higher interest rates and the worry of missing payments.

Consider Leasing Assets Instead of Owning Them

If your current debt ratio is cause for concern, look into leasing the assets you need rather than purchasing them. Leasing is very similar to standard asset-backed financing with one very big exception: no new debt shows up on your balance sheet. Of course, the assets don't go on your balance sheet, either, but that won't make as big a difference to your perceived financial position. Overall, leasing will be kinder to your cash flow than will purchasing.

The financing will still be based mainly on the value of the asset, and interest (usually still in the high zone) will be figured into your monthly payments. While you may still need to put some money down, it usually won't be as much as it would have been if you were purchasing the asset. Plus, it can be much easier for a new company without credit history to get an equipment lease than an equipment loan.

Management Accounting

The biggest difference between financial accounting and management accounting is the intended user: financial accounting is used to inform people outside your company; management accounting is used only by insiders, to make critical business decisions. Where financial accounting looks at the big picture, management accounting concentrates on the details. Unlike financial accounting, management accounting isn't subject to external rules and regulations; reports don't have to be in a prescribed format, and they can contain information relevant only to the particular issue at hand.

While the basic information is the same, the way it's used is very different. For example, rather than looking at the total cost of goods manufactured (for a manufacturing company), a management accounting report might focus on getting to the unit cost of manufacturing each product. Detailed information like that is critical to your business plans, including seeking ways to control costs.

FACT

Management accounting isn't solely concerned with cutting costs, though that's the picture most people get when they think about this branch of accounting. Other areas of importance to management accounting include things such as quality control, optimal inventory management, improving efficiency and productivity, and scheduling major purchases.

Management accounting reports often contain multiple scenarios, allowing you to see the impact of different decision alternatives. Since the information is all geared to a specific purpose, these reports can be more useful than the standard financial fare in helping you move forward with new ideas. For example, if you are trying to cut costs, you can create pro formas to show the impact of different cost changes on your bottom line.

The Importance of Internal Controls

Internal controls for a business are similar to checks and balances in the government; they are processes put in place to make sure things stay on the right track. Internal controls are useful for every business but are critical for companies with employees, especially employees who handle valuable assets. Retail businesses in which customers have direct access to small products can also benefit enormously from internal control procedures. While internal controls are crucial for helping you detect dishonesty, they can also help you reduce the risk that simple mistakes will keep you from seeing your company's true financial picture.

As much as you want to think the best of the people working with you and for you, the sad fact is that a lot of people are dishonest. Whether the scale is small or large, that dishonesty can cost your business—and you— a lot of money over time. Any employee can steal from your company, whether a bookkeeper or warehouse manager or the kid sitting behind the cash register. It's not just money that can be stolen (although that does happen a lot); many employees consider it perfectly normal to take home office supplies or small inventory items. That may not seem like a big deal compared to someone embezzling hundreds of thousands of dollars from the bank accounts, but it still can add up to quite a lot in the long run.

ESSENTIAL

Although internal controls can uncover wrongdoing, they're usually set up with the assumption of honesty in the background. To that end, most standard internal control procedures concentrate on preventing and detecting inadvertent errors. Also, when employees know these controls exist, they're less likely to act dishonestly.

Setting up a system of internal controls can keep such problems from getting out of hand. When you have internal controls in place, you're protecting your assets as well as the accuracy of your accounting records. The types of controls to put in place depend largely on the size and nature of your business; for example, a cash-intensive company with thirty employees would require more control measures than would a three-man operation where virtually no cash changes hands in the normal course of business.

Basic Internal Control Principles

The idea behind internal controls is to create an environment where mistakes are less likely and dishonesty is easily caught. Most of these principles will seem like plain old common sense, but you might be surprised at how many small-business owners neglect to use them.

At the most basic level, put some simple physical controls in place. Store cash in a safe; keep your warehouse locked and limit access to the key; make any sensitive computer files password-protected. If you have a lot of employees who work different shifts, get a time clock to track hours worked. If you have a retail shop, you can tag items with anti-theft sensors. Any company with valuable assets should consider an alarm system to deter break-ins.

Internal controls geared specifically toward employees include assigning specific responsibilities, making sure all transactions are immediately documented, and separating related duties. Documents are the evidence that a transaction has occurred, in addition to being necessary for accurate recordkeeping. Typical internal control documents include cash register tapes, signed delivery slips, and prenumbered invoices (so you will know if any are missing). Along those lines, assigning specific tasks to specific employees lets you know whom to question when something unexpected turns up. For example, having only one employee use the cash register at a time lets you know who's handling the cash.

The Importance of Separating Duties

Separating related duties involves making more than one person responsible for related activities, especially those activities that involve an easily pilfered asset. For example, having one person handle all the cash, make all the deposits, do the bookkeeping, and reconcile the bank statement gives that person almost a free hand with your company's cash.

Especially in small companies, it can be tough to separate tasks, and that's how many small companies get raked over the coals. There are two main ways to separate important duties:

- Assign different people to related tasks
- Don't have the person in charge of an asset be the same person who keeps the records for that asset

Related tasks include things such as ordering goods and paying vendor invoices. Someone could, for example, order things for personal use and then pay the vendor invoice with company funds. Separating accountability—meaning one employee is in charge of an asset but someone else keeps the records for it—is another way to protect your company. The person in charge of maintaining the inventory, for example, shouldn't also be in charge of counting the inventory.

Using Internal Audits to Your Advantage

As soon as the word "audit" comes up, most people think IRS and start to sweat. Internal audits, though, are good things that can help you manage your company more efficiently and profitably. These are really just systematic ways you can verify that your internal controls are working.

ALERT!

Although a lot of internal audit procedures are performed on a regular schedule, such as bank statement reconciliations, others are best done at unexpected times. For example, performing an impromptu inventory count can tell you more than a count you've scheduled months in advance.

Big companies often have dedicated internal audit staff. Small companies usually don't need full-time staff in this area but can still benefit from the types of procedures they would use. Basically, an internal audit involves independent verification to make sure things are really the way they seem. The verification comes by comparing documents to make sure they mesh; for example, making sure a cash register tape matches the corresponding cash deposit slip. The independent factor just means that someone not directly involved with the task in question (this can be you) makes that comparison. For example, you wouldn't have the cash register clerk do that verification himself and report the results to you.

chapter 19

Unique Issues for Specific Businesses

Most companies, whether they're large or small, new or established, have the same accounting transactions over and over again. The majority of transactions are common to every kind of business, as they all have the same basic accounts to deal with. Every once in a while, though, a particular business comes with a twist that calls for special transactions.

Common and Not-So-Common Transactions

Most of the time, for most companies, the everyday transactions look pretty much the same as everyone else's. Revenues are earned, bills are paid, assets depreciate. The journal entries to record those basic transactions are the same for a one-man law firm as for a giant manufacturing company.

Some businesses do things just a little bit differently, and that can trigger unique transactions that occur only within that type of company. Retail companies will have some transactions that aren't found in service businesses, and even some that aren't found in other product-based companies, such as manufacturers. To account for these uncommon transactions, a little individualized accounting is in order, and that may involve special accounts treated in unexpected ways.

Those unique transactions are often repetitive for the companies that use them. However, there are also events that take place across all different industries but happen rarely. Examples include fixed-asset sales (covered in Chapter 5) and capital contributions (in Chapter 15). With transactions specific to certain businesses, and unusual transactions common to most businesses, accounting manages to stay interesting. Some of the distinctions involved in these special transactions can be tricky, so ask your accountant for guidance whenever you're unsure about the accounting treatment.

Retail Is More Than Buying and Selling

Retail businesses have a specific focus: they buy products from suppliers and resell them to customers. In addition to the standard journal entries used by service companies, retailers also deal with inventory and cost of goods sold. Like most product-based businesses, retailers must often account for sales returns and discounts.

Retailers have a few unique transactions on top of the usual entries. One common example is layaway sales, as detailed in Chapter 6, in which customers make small payments toward buying a particular product. Another example is consignment shops, unique among retailers; rather than recording merchandise sales and cost of goods sold, the journal entry for a sale is more like a sales commission.

Another issue retailers may face involves exactly when to count merchandise in their inventory, meaning at which point ownership of the goods transfers from the supplier to the retailer. To figure that out, you have to know a bit about goods in transit, meaning items that are actually somewhere in between the seller and the buyer. Whichever company has the legal responsibility for those goods is the company that owns them, and that depends on the shipping terms. Shipping terms come in two basic flavors: FOB shipping point and FOB destination (the FOB just means free on board). FOB shipping point means that ownership changes hands from the supplier to the retailer the minute the goods leave the warehouse. FOB destination means that ownership changes hands only when the goods actually reach their final destination, with the retailer.

FACT

Sales returns and sales discounts are recorded in special contra accounts rather than in the general sales account. The reason for these extra accounts is to give you better information. If everything got lumped into one account, you wouldn't know how much came back as returns, or whether discounts were causing an increase in overall sales.

Manufacturers Produce Special Transactions

As you learned in Chapter 7, manufacturers have a lot more going on in the accounting department than do any other kinds of businesses. There are three different stages of inventory to deal with, and all sorts of extra things that go into figuring out product costs; in addition, the statement of profit and loss has a whole extra section to contend with. Although the rest of the transactions follow the standard flow, creating inventory triggers special accounting procedures.

Unlike companies that deal only with finished goods, manufacturers don't always know exactly what their product costs are. Instead of just pulling costs off a vendor invoice, manufacturers have to combine a variety of expenses to come up with their product costs: direct materials, direct labor, and overhead. How they combine those expenses and apply them to the three phases of inventory is the entire point of cost accounting.

Since figuring out product costs is such a big part of manufacturing companies, it has a whole special system of accounting, aptly named cost accounting. This extra system combines all the inventory-related information to come up with both total and individual unit product costs.

Two Distinct Cost Accounting Systems

Cost accounting, as the name suggests, deals with figuring out product costs. There are two different ways to do this, and each has its own system. In a job order cost system, product costs are computed based on a specific job, such as creating 250 wedding invitations or producing a complete set of kitchen cabinets. The other option, a process cost system, is used when you produce a high volume of products that are all the same, such as bagels or napkin rings; here the focus is on different steps in the production process. Which system you use depends on what you're manufacturing. Custom-made products call for a job order system; products that are all the same call for process costing.

How to Allocate Overhead

When you make your own products, part of that product cost comes from overhead expenses. Unlike direct product costs, which you can easily link to a specific product, overhead is like a big cost pool that you have to split up among your inventory. That cost-splitting process is called allocation. With it, you figure out exactly how much of your total manufacturing overhead goes into each product.

Manufacturing overhead includes expenses necessary to the production process but not directly linked to any particular product. Examples of these expenses include things such as electricity in the production area and oil that keeps the machines running. You couldn't make your products without these expenses, so they are included in your product costs rather than with your general expenses.

To figure out the right allocations, you first have to come up with a basis for dividing up your overhead. Then you'll have an allocation rate that you can apply to products. Your allocation basis could be:

- Direct labor hours
- Direct labor dollars
- Machine hours

Essentially, anything that's common to all your products and is also easy to measure can be used for your allocation basis. To compute the allocation rate, divide your total estimated overhead for the period by the total allocation basis. For example, assume that your total estimated overhead was $30,000. You decide to make your allocations based on labor dollars, and estimate $60,000 total labor costs for the period. To get your allocation rate, divide that $30,000 of overhead by $60,000 in labor costs; here, the allocation rate would be 50 percent, or fifty cents of overhead allocated for each direct labor dollar. If the direct labor for Product A costs $10, the overhead allocation for that product would be $5.

Accounting for Your Home-Based Business

Virtually every new business and small-business owner out there conducts at least some business from home. Among these are true home-based businesses, meaning there is no other office or shop to work out of. When you work solely from home, it's easy to forget that a lot of your household bills are really business expenses—or at least some portion of them are. You'll find that your business expenses will fall into one of two categories: completely business, or part business, part personal. Either way, you have to record the expenses as part of your ongoing bookkeeping.

Expenses that can be traced directly to the business can be recorded on your books as is. For example, if you repaint your office, that's a pure business expense. If you get a rider on your homeowner's insurance policy covering your home office and business equipment, the full cost of that rider is recorded by the company. When an expense crosses the line between business and personal, such as a security system that covers the whole house, you'll have to figure out what portion of that expense belongs to the business (see the next section for how to do that).

ALERT!

The IRS often pays close attention to the home-related expenses of home-based businesses. It's an area that a lot of people have trouble calculating correctly, making it a prime target for tax return revision. Because of this, it's doubly important that you document business-only expenses that could be mistaken for household expenses, and make sure combined expense allocations make sense.

The IRS has special rules concerning the deductibility of home work spaces. When your home is your only work space, though, it's easier to justify deductions should the need arise. The main rule that trips people up is this: The space has to be used regularly and exclusively for business. It's the "exclusively" that causes the most problems; that means you can't use the space for anything but business.

Accounting for Shared Expenses

When you work from home, some of your regular household expenses turn into business expenses as well. Any expenditure that benefits both your living space and your workspace is considered an indirect expense; these include things such as electricity and real estate taxes.

To figure out the portion that's deductible for business purposes, you can use a simple ratio. Measure the space you use for your work area, either in square feet or number of rooms (whatever makes sense), and divide that by the space in your whole house. For example, if you have a four-room apartment and use one room exclusively for business, you would use one-fourth as your ratio. Then apply that ratio to each shared expense to come up with the business portion. If the electric bill for that four-room apartment came to $100, you can record $25 as a business expense.

The journal entry here depends on how you paid the expense. If you paid the entire bill with a personal check, your journal entry includes a debit to the applicable expense account and a credit to owner's equity; paying business expenses with a personal check counts as a capital contribution. If you used two separate checks to pay the bill (a personal check for the personal portion, and a company check for the business portion), you record your journal entry just like any other cash disbursement: debit expense and credit cash.

Phone bills are the exception to the shared expense rules. If you have only one phone line in the house, it's considered 100 percent personal. You can still deduct specific business calls, but not any of the general phone line expenses.

The Depreciation Deduction

When you own your home and have a home-based business, you have to record depreciation for the business portion of your home. That's right: When you use your home for business, you are required to take depreciation. When you eventually sell that home, the portion used for business will count as the sale of business property. Even if you've never deducted depreciation, the IRS will act as if you did when recomputing any possible gain on the sale of your "business property." Since you'll have to pay that tax at some point (real estate values tend to go up), you may as well benefit from the tax deduction now.

To calculate the depreciation, you have to know both the fair market value of your home and how much you paid for it plus the cost of any improvements you've made over the years. The smaller of those two values will be the basis of your depreciation calculation. From that number, deduct the value of land included in the value of your home to get just the building portion (land never gets depreciated, so you have to subtract it). The next step is to multiply that building basis by the IRS depreciation percentage (you can find that at *www.irs.gov*).

When you have calculated your current depreciation expense, record a regular depreciation journal entry. That includes a debit to depreciation expense and a credit to accumulated depreciation.

Small High-Tech Companies

The technology industry lives by constant innovation. To the people on the outside, these advances seem instantaneous. The entrepreneurs and developers working within the highly competitive high-tech industry know the real story: what seems instant to the rest of us can take years and years of development.

That poses an interesting accounting problem: how to account properly for expenses that are incurred years before any revenues can possibly be earned, if ever. The answer comes in some special accounting rules specifically created to deal with research and development. Although business expenses are supposed to connect with the revenues they help create, that matching principle just doesn't make much sense in the case of research and development. For that reason, no matter what accounting method your company uses, research and development costs are usually recorded as expenses as soon as they are actually incurred, whether or not they eventually result in revenues.

The Technology Industry Responds

The research and development accounting rules come with a lot of controversy, mainly from the technology industry itself. The industry's argument is that the research and development can lead to a patent (in the case of hardware) or copyright (in the case of software), so the expenses should be capitalized (which means treated like an asset). That would help both their balance sheets and statements of profit and loss look better during the research and development phases.

The accounting industry, though, always takes the path of conservatism. Whenever there's any doubt, it takes the path that leads to lower profits and fewer assets rather than the opposite. Since research and development costs are not guaranteed to turn into patents or copyrights, they must be recorded as immediate expenses. In addition, it can be tough to figure out which costs go with which projects, as many technology companies have more than one development in the works at a time.

FACT

Different countries use different guidelines when it comes to research and development costs. Japan, for example, lets those expenses be capitalized as incurred, then amortized over time. That means if a Japanese company and an American company spent the exact same amount on research and development, the Japanese company would show higher profits on its current financial statements.

Software Development

Many small businesses create computer programs that will eventually be sold to companies and individuals. During the research and development phase, all the expenses are booked right away. However, as soon as that product is proven to be viable, and a complete working program exists, you have an asset on your hands; after that point, all the money spent to produce the software will be debits to an asset account instead of an expense account. That asset then is amortized over its estimated life, which is how long you reasonably believe it will be a salable product.

The accounting works differently when your company has been contracted to develop software for someone else, according to their specifications. Any costs that will be covered under your contract (which usually include direct costs, some overhead, and a profit) and will be paid by the hiring firm can be recorded as an account receivable on your books. Since those expenses will be reimbursed, they're not really expenses of your company, and you don't have to record them that way.

Building-Construction Transactions

As anyone who's ever been a contractor or hired one knows, construction jobs take some time to complete. Since these jobs can run so long (months, even years), they sometimes call for some special accounting procedures.

When a project won't be completed during the accounting year in which it was started, it's considered to be a long-term contract for accounting purposes; even if the actual contract covers only a two- month project, it counts as long-term if it straddles two accounting years.

Contractors and construction companies that deal with smaller jobs and residential real estate have more flexibility in their accounting choices than do very big commercial companies. Big firms have to use something called the percentage-of-completion method to account for their construction contracts, which makes them recognize profits every step along the way. Small real-estate construction contractors don't have to use this method if they don't want to. Instead, they have a choice; they can go with the long-term contract methods or they can use their regular accounting method (cost or accrual) to deal with revenues and expenses.

What Counts as Small

Your company can choose its preferred accounting method for a contract when:

- That contract is expected to be completed within two years of the start date.
- Your company's average annual gross revenues for the past three years aren't greater than $10 million.
- It's a home construction contract.

If you think it's ridiculous that a small construction company could bring in gross revenues of more than $10 million, consider this: in some areas, a single home can cost millions of dollars, and building just two or three such homes can put you over the limit.

The Basics of Percentage of Completion

The point of using the percentage-of-completion method for long-term contracts is to attempt to match up revenues and expenses with the actual work being done. As the job progresses, you record the revenues and expenses that go with that part of the process, and spread everything out over the entire length of the contract.

To figure out how much to account for at a particular point, you first decide how to measure the percentage of completion. There are two main choices: one based on performance and one based on costs. Using performance, your percentage will be based the amount of work done so far compared to the estimated total work; for example, if you're half done, you'd use 50 percent for your percentage of completion. The cost method is a little more concrete and is more commonly used. There you divide the construction costs that have come up so far by the total expected construction costs. For example, if you've spent $50,000 on this job so far and expect to spend $200,000 total, your percentage of completion would be 25 percent.

Once you know your current percentage of completion, you multiply it by the total revenue for the project (usually the contract price) to get the total revenue that should be recorded so far. If you've already recorded some revenue for this contract, subtract that from the new total to get the amount that goes with this period. For example, suppose your total contract is for $500,000 and you've already accounted for $100,000. Your new percentage of completion is 30 percent, for a total revenue of $150,000. Since you already recorded $100,000, your new journal entry will include a $50,000 credit to revenue.

chapter 20

Retirement Plans

Everyone dreams of a luxurious retirement. Whether your dream is to sail around the world or enjoy a lavish lifestyle right at home, you'll need a sizable nest egg to make that dream come true. One of the best ways to accomplish that is through consistent contributions to a tax-advantaged retirement plan. Now that you're the one calling the shots, you can also tailor that plan to your personal goals. In this chapter, you'll learn how to choose the best retirement plan for you and your business.

20

The Best Tax Shelter

If you want to minimize your income taxes while maximizing your wealth, consider starting a company retirement plan. Not only will you be able to attract and keep better employees; you'll also be able to use the plan for your own tax-sheltered retirement savings. Even better, there are several different plan types to choose from, each offering distinct benefits. One of them will surely suit your current financial situation and your long-term goals.

ALERT!

Pension rules are among the most complicated, even within the confusing world of tax laws. The different tax aspects of retirement plans can be daunting, and small missteps can bump your plan into the nonqualified category. Before you set up any retirement plan, call in an experienced professional to guide the way.

All retirement plans fall into one of two basic categories: qualified and nonqualified. The biggest difference between the two comes down to taxes; qualified plans get preferential tax treatment, and nonqualified plans don't. After that breakdown, retirement plans can be separated into defined benefit, defined contribution, or hybrid. Defined benefit plans focus on the eventual payouts and base your current contribution on the payments you want to get in retirement. Defined contribution plans set aside a fixed dollar amount or percentage of salary now, with no thought to how much will be available for distributions later on. Hybrid plans, as you might guess, offer some combination of defined contributions and defined benefits.

As with most things, retirement plans come with both advantages and drawbacks. On the downside, retirement plans take a lot of time to set up and manage. Also, there are fees, including those for a professional adviser, and account fees for the company that houses the plan, to name just two. On the plus side, you can score some substantial tax benefits for your company—a sort of reward offered by the government to encourage employers to offer retirement plans. When your plan is based on profits (such as a profit-sharing plan), it helps motivate you and your employees. Speaking of employees, this benefit can help you seal the deal with the people you want to hire. Finally, you get to save for your retirement as well.

Nonqualified Plans

Nonqualified retirement plans don't meet all the ERISA (Employee Retirement Income Security Act of 1974) and IRS guidelines, so they lose out on some important tax benefits. They can, however, offer substantial deferred compensation to upper-level employees. That's the main reason they don't qualify; their aim is to give extra pay to a few elite executives, not everyone at the company. You would use one of these plans as an incentive for a truly valuable employee; by shifting some of his pay into the future (that's deferred compensation), there's a better chance he'll stick around. On top of that, you can use deferred compensation for yourself and your co-owners as well; that strategy can help ease your tax burden now, since income taxes won't kick in until you get the payments. The downside, and there is a big one, is that your company doesn't get a tax deduction now; it has to wait until payment is actually made.

FACT

Nonqualified plans come with some pretty unusual names. For instance, "golden handcuffs" describes a plan that encourages long-term employment by promising payments if the employee sticks around. Other common nonqualified plans come with equally colorful names: rabbi trusts, golden parachutes, and top-hat plans, for example.

Qualified Plans

If you're looking for a current tax deduction for your company, a qualified plan is the only way to go. Qualified retirement plans have to meet all the requirements set out by the IRS and ERISA in order to be eligible for four substantial tax benefits:

- As the employer, you get an immediate tax deduction for the company's contributions into the plan.

- The income earned inside the retirement plan (such as interest, dividends, and capital gains) isn't taxable to the company at all.
- Employees—which includes you if you have a corporation—don't have to pay income taxes on any of the money contributed to the plan for them (either their own contributions or the company's).
- Distributions from the plan (such as retirement payouts) receive special tax treatment, except under some specific circumstances.

The most basic rule of qualified plans is that the benefits have to be similar for everyone, and not weighted heavily in favor of the top dogs at the company (that includes you). When tax advantages are a priority, as they often are for young companies, stick with a qualified plan.

Individual Retirement Accounts (IRAs)

For decades, IRAs have been among the most popular ways to put away money for retirement while getting a current tax deduction. You also don't have to pay any current income taxes on any money the account earns—until you start taking distributions, that is, and then you get taxed on every dollar you take out. A new twist was added with the arrival of the Roth IRA; this version gives you no tax deduction on contributions now in exchange for no taxes at all on the earnings (when you wait at least five years to take a qualified distribution). Both traditional and Roth IRAs continue to grow in popularity as more people get cracking on their retirement savings.

FACT

Many of the most popular small-business retirement plans are based on the IRA. In fact, some of them (such as the SEP and some SIMPLEs) are really just a collection of IRAs brought together under the umbrella of the company's general retirement plan.

As a business owner, you do have other options when it comes to putting away money for the future, but none is as simple as an IRA—regardless of their catchy acronyms (you'll read more about these later in this chapter).

If you want to save money for yourself without the hassle of a formal retirement plan and without having to make contributions for your employees, you can just open a personal IRA.

All you have to do to open an IRA is fill out a single form and send in a check. You can do it at your bank, do it with your broker, or even do it online with an electronic bank transfer. It can be a standard interest-bearing savings account, or you can fill it with stocks, bonds, and mutual funds. Multiple IRAs are also possible; for example, you might do that when you want to invest directly in mutual funds (as opposed to going through a broker and paying his fees) but want funds from different fund families.

The Common Rules

Here are the basic rules for both kinds of IRAs. You can't contribute more than your taxable income; for example, if your sole proprietorship earns $2,000 this year, that's the most you can put into an IRA (unless you have other income, such as a salary). For 2006 and 2007, the maximum contribution is $4,000 per *person* (no matter how many IRAs you have), but if you're 50 or older, you can bump that up by another $1,000. In 2008, that max jumps to $5,000 for everyone, and the $1,000 add-on can still be used for anyone who's at least 50 years old. Contributions have to be made with money; you can do it by credit card, but you can't do it with a diamond necklace. You have to make the contribution by the time you file your tax return in order for it to count in that tax year; for example, if you make a $4,000 contribution on April 15, 2007, when you file your 2006 tax return, the IRA deduction counts for 2006. Other than these rules, the two types of IRAs don't have much in common.

More Rules for Traditional IRAs

In addition to the tax differences mentioned earlier, the two IRA types veer onto different paths in other ways:

- You have to start taking distributions from a traditional IRA the year after you hit age 70½ or the year you retire, whichever comes last; there are no mandatory distribution requirements with Roth IRAs.

- Once you hit age 70½, you can't make any more contributions, even during that year; there's no age limit on contributions into a Roth IRA.
- There are many restrictions on when and how you can take money out of your traditional IRA, and restricted distributions can be subject to hefty penalties; with Roth IRAs, once the cash has been sitting there for five years and you hit age 59½, you can do whatever you want with it.

For the specific rules that apply to your unique situation, talk to your accountant or IRA plan manager before you take out any money, especially if you have a traditional IRA. Mistakes can lead to IRS penalties, and those can be pretty big.

SIMPLE Plans

The name says it all (or at least the acronym does): The Savings Incentive Match Plan for Employees, a.k.a. SIMPLE, is usually easier to manage and easier on the bank account than are many other types of retirement plans. Their drawback is that contributions are limited, and you may not be able to put away as much money each year as you could with other plans.

If you decide on a SIMPLE plan, you have to offer it to all your eligible employees, but even if none of them bites, you still can set it up and be the only participant. This loophole doesn't exist for other plan types. As long as you give your employees the *option* of participating, you can start saving for your own retirement with this vehicle, even if no one else does.

The simplicity comes with some strings attached. You can't have more than 100 employees, you can't offer any other retirement plans, and you have to offer this benefit to all eligible employees (more on that in a moment).

Plus, you have to make specific contributions into employees' accounts every year, no matter what.

Don't let those strings tie you down, though. SIMPLE plans can be great savings vehicles for small-business employers who want to offer a retirement plan benefit but can't afford the more expensive bells and whistles. Also, while your contributions are limited, the limits aren't ridiculously low; you, as the business owner, can contribute up to $10,000 for 2006, and if you're 50 or older, that max gets bumped up to $12,500 (also for 2006). Those caps go for employees, too. Finally, you have the choice of setting up your plan like either an IRA or a 401(k).

How the Company's Contributions Work

When you offer a SIMPLE plan to your employees, you are locked in to making contributions on their behalf (in addition to those they make for themselves) every year. To do that, you basically have two choices. You can make matching contributions for participating employees, up to 3 percent of their pay, or you can contribute a flat 2 percent for all eligible employees who make at least $5,000 a year, even if they don't participate. Whether or not your company has profits in a given year, you have to make these contributions.

The mechanics of contributions are pretty simple. For participating employees, you withhold their contributions from their paychecks and hold them in trust until you make a deposit into the retirement fund. On the company side, that contribution counts as a fully deductible expense as soon as you write the check. As for that math, you multiply the applicable percentage by the total employees' salaries to get the lump sum for the check, but you have make sure to allocate the right amount to each employee's account. Once contributions are made, whether by them or by you, that amount is considered 100 percent vested right away (i.e., it belongs completely to the employee, even if he quits the next day).

Eligible Employees

While you are required to offer the SIMPLE plan to all your eligible employees, you may have some who don't fit the description. The rules are slightly different, depending on whether you use the IRA or 401(k) base for the investments.

To count as eligible under the IRA form, an employee has to have earned at least $5,000 over the past two years and be expected to earn as much this calendar year. With the 401(k) structure, employees have to have earned at least $5,000 last year and be expected to earn at least that much this year.

Simplified Employee Pensions (SEPs)

When it comes to simple plans, SEPs also fill the bill. These plans were especially designed for small-business owners, with the goal of making it as pain-free as possible for them to offer retirement benefits. In fact, the only IRS form you have to fill out is Form 5305-SEP, which you can download directly from the IRS Web site at *www.irs.gov*. Essentially, a SEP is a collection of IRAs, one for each employee and one for you, that together act as a pension plan.

Although part of the selling point of SEPs is that they're "simplified," they can be a little tricky to set up when you have employees (but they are very easy to deal with if the plan is only for you). They're not as simple as SIMPLE plans, but that's balanced by a much higher contribution limit. If you're a sole proprietor with no employees, this could be the best fit for you.

Here are some of the key points you need to know if you're considering a SEP:

- When it's just for you, you set up an IRA and say that you want it to be a SEP.
- For 2006, employees can put away 25 percent of compensation (up to $220,000) or $44,000, whichever is less.
- The maximums are a little lower for you as a self-employed individual and involve more math.
- SEPs come with low costs and minimal administrative responsibilities.
- These are the only plans that can be first set up after year-end and for which you can figure out contributions after you know how the year's profits look.

- SEPs are not very flexible.
- You have to make contributions for all eligible employees, whether they want it or not, even if they leave during the year.
- If an eligible employee doesn't have an IRA, you have to establish one on his behalf and notify him, even if he doesn't want one.
- An eligible employee who won't participate can mess up the tax benefits for everyone else.

You can see why these plans can be great when you have no employees, but sticky when you do. If you are thinking about using a SEP and you have (or plan to have) employees, consider making participation a condition of employment. If a potential hiree doesn't want to participate, you may be better off not hiring him.

When You Have Employees

You have to provide all your eligible employees with a bunch of information when you establish a SEP. Each needs a copy of Form 5305-SEP, a statement that says these SEP-IRAs are different from the usual and that also provides an explanation of things, such as how withdrawals work. Plus, you'll have to provide written notification to employees when contributions are made. If it sounds too complicated for you to handle, don't worry; you can hire a plan administrator who does it all the time and can easily do it all for you.

ALERT!

Although the minimum eligibility requirements are written in stone, you are allowed to use easier requirements if you want to, such as letting employees participate when they reach age 17 instead of 21. You might want to do this if you have your own kids as employees and want to start putting away money for them, but remember—that rule applies to all your employees.

As for eligibility, there are some pretty strict rules. You have to offer the SEP to any employee who's at least 21, has worked for you for at least three of the past five years, and has gotten paid by you at least $450 for the year (that amount is for 2006 and may change going forward). If you have an employee who turns 21 during the year, he counts as eligible. If you have a part-time seasonal employee who's been working only three weeks each year for the past few years but has switched to full-time now, he's eligible.

The minute an employee becomes eligible, he stays that way for the whole year. It doesn't matter if he quits the next day. It doesn't even matter if you have no idea where he is. For that year, you have to make a contribution for him.

Calculating Your Contribution

As a self-employed person, you have to do some quick calculations before you can get to your contribution. This math effectively makes your maximum allowable contribution lower than it would be if you were an employee. To figure out your total compensation for these purposes, start with the total business profits. From that amount, subtract half of your self-employment tax, as well as the deduction for contributions into your own SEP-IRA. If it sounds as though you have to deduct your contribution to figure out what that contribution is, you're right. However, the IRS provides easy-to-use worksheets and tables that give you the correct rate for your contributions, which will be somewhat less than the rate you give your employees. Check out IRS Publication 590; it has everything you need.

Keogh Plans

As long as your business isn't incorporated, you can establish a Keogh plan for retirement savings. These plans let you put away more money than either SEPs or SIMPLEs, and they're also much more flexible; for example, these give the option of either defined benefit or defined contribution, while the others offer only defined contributions. On the downside, they're more complicated to set up and to manage, and that usually makes them more costly. If you're considering a Keogh, head straight to a pension professional for help with the details.

In addition to a lot of administrative burdens, Keogh plans also come with prohibited transactions rules and some fiduciary requirements—more reasons why you should have a professional set up and manage the plan. These rules, especially the prohibited transactions, are stricter for Keoghs than for any other small-business retirement plan. The one that's often a major sticking point has to do with the money itself: you (and any of your co-owners) can't borrow any money from the plan for any reason. As for fiduciary responsibilities, whoever manages the plan is held to the highest possible standards of conduct and must always act in the best interests of the plan. If the plan suffers losses, that manager (no matter who it is, even if it's you) could be held liable by the participants; that means he (or you) could have to pay them back.

FACT

Keogh plans mirror the style of corporate retirement plans but aren't available for corporations. If you have a corporation, you can use the corporate version of the Keogh through a standard profit-sharing or defined benefit plan. You'll have virtually the same pension plan; it just has a different name.

It seems like a lot of trouble, but the amount you're allowed to contribute could make up for all of that, especially if you have a lot of profits to put away. The maximums depend on whether your Keogh is set up as a defined contribution or defined benefit plan. For defined benefit, your contribution is limited to the lesser of 100 percent of your average compensation for the three highest years or $175,000. For defined contribution, it's the lesser of 100 percent of your share of the company's profit or $44,000. Both of those maximums follow the 2006 law and may increase in the future.

Choosing the Right Plan for You

The first thing to consider when you are trying to choose a retirement plan for your business is yourself—your financial situation, your goals, your age. After all, this is your company, and you deserve to reap financial benefits. Ask yourself why (despite the administrative and fee-oriented drawbacks) you want to start a company retirement plan. Think about the following reasons, and rank them in order of importance to you:

- To save for your retirement
- For the tax advantages, which let you save more money than you could without the plan
- To attract the best candidates with a competitive employment package

Even if all these reasons are important to you, try to figure out which takes priority. Different priorities will steer you toward different plans; after all, that is precisely why there are so many choices. Once you've settled on your goals, there are still a few other factors that will influence your choice. The first is your entity; some plans are only allowed for certain business structures. Then come simplicity and cost; as you might expect, some plans are easier to deal with than others, and some are cheaper to implement and administer.

Although your particular situation is unique, there are some general rules you can use to guide you in making your decision (and consulting a qualified professional couldn't hurt). If your goal is to save as much for your retirement as possible, look at Keogh (for noncorporations) or profit-sharing (for corporations) plans. If simplicity and cost are key factors, consider SEPs and SIMPLEs. For companies with variable profits, profit-sharing types of plans allow the most contribution flexibility. And if it's just you, and you want to sock away some cash for retirement without the hassle of a full-fledged pension plan, open an IRA.

Accounting for Contributions

Regardless of which type of retirement plan you have, the accounting looks the same. The main difference in your journal entries is between contributions made for you (as the owner, not as an employee of a corporation) or for your employees. Here's what the entries for company contributions look like under the accrual method of accounting. If you use cash accounting, your credit will be to cash and you won't use the final paying entry.

Journal Entry: Contributions for Employees

Date	Account & Explanation	Post Ref	Debit	Credit
01/30/06	Retirement Plan Contribution Expense		500.00	
	Retirement Plan Contributions Payable			500.00

To record retirement plan benefits expense for the pay period.

Journal Entry: Contributions for Owners

Date	Account & Explanation	Post Ref	Debit	Credit
01/30/06	Janine Smith, Withdrawals		500.00	
	Retirement Plan Contributions Payable			500.00

To record owner's retirement plan benefits for the period.

Journal Entry: Making the Contribution

Date	Account & Explanation	Post Ref	Debit	Credit
02/15/06	Retirement Plan Contributions Payable		1,000.00	
	Cash			1,000.00

To record payment made to retirement plan, check #154.

When the company makes contributions on your behalf, it doesn't usually get an expense deduction. Instead, you take the deduction on your personal tax return (there's a special line for this). When you're an owner-employee in a corporation, contributions made for you count the same as for any other employee. These are the general rules; however, your personal financial situation is unique, and your accountant will know the best way to handle your pension contributions and tax deductions. Contributions made by employees will be part of the regular payroll entry, since you withhold those contributions from their paychecks.

chapter 21

Common Small-Business Tax Snafus

Most new business and small-business owners are not intimately familiar with the Internal Revenue Code (IRC)—and for good reason. The IRC is complicated, long, convoluted, and changes frequently. It's very easy to make mistakes, even when you think you're doing the right thing. It's so easy, in fact, that there are some mistakes made by the overwhelming majority of new business and small-business owners. Once you know where the traps are, though, they're easy to avoid.

Don't Be Afraid of the IRS

Most people, upon getting any kind of notice from the IRS, immediately feel fear and panic. The horror stories are out there: individuals and companies that were audited and left bankrupt after a grueling investigation that ended with a giant tax, interest, and penalty bill. That does happen, but very rarely. Most IRS notices can be handled through the mail, with copies of requested documents.

Even if you are called in for a full-blown IRS audit, don't worry. As long as you've acted in good faith and kept decent records, everything is likely to work out just fine. Sure, you may have to pay a little more tax than you originally thought, and that may have some interest and penalties attached to it. More often than not, though, the settlement won't even come close to putting you out of business.

There are some simple things you can do to prepare for the possibility of having to deal with the IRS:

- Fill out the right tax forms completely, attach everything that needs to be attached, and mail them in on time.
- Check all your numbers two or three times before sending any forms.
- Make all the tax deposits you're required to make, on time.
- Let a qualified tax preparer do all or most of the tax work.

A lot of the time, IRS notices come because a form is incomplete or filled out wrong. In fact, one of the most common reasons is a missing signature. Sometimes, random individuals or businesses are flagged for audit, just to see if there's any extra revenue the IRS can collect; after all, that is its job. Even then, since you haven't done anything intentionally wrong, you don't have much to worry about (though you probably still will worry). To avoid as much stress as possible, the easiest way to deal with the IRS is to have your accountant deal with it for you.

Employees Versus Contractors

One the biggest trouble issues facing new and small businesses is that of employees and independent contractors. It's cheaper and easier to deal with contractors: you can hire them only as needed, they don't get benefits, you don't have to report or pay their payroll taxes, and you don't have to go through the exhaustive regulatory procedures that come with employees. Many new and small businesses choose to go the contractor route instead of hiring employees for those reasons, and several more. But the distinction can get tricky, especially when a contractor works only for your company or works out of your business location.

ALERT!

Some workers, called statutory employees, always count as employees no matter what. These employees include corporate officers who provide services for that corporation, food or laundry drivers, at-home workers given materials and requirements for performing work, full-time traveling salespeople who sell goods for resale, and full-time life insurance agents who work primarily for a single company.

The IRS watches this category pretty closely and reacts strongly to employees being misclassified as independent contractors (they don't care so much if it goes the other way). State law gets into the act, too, with its own distinction between the two categories. The state laws and IRS rules are fairly clear here, making it easier to put everyone who works for you into the right categories. When you don't, though, the consequences can be expensive.

Is Your Contractor an Employee?

When it comes to classifying the people who work for you, here's the basic rule: unless you can *prove* otherwise, everyone's an employee. It doesn't matter if you have an oral agreement or a written contract; those don't count as proof here. The combination of your state laws and the IRS rules for contractors has to be met, and you have to be able to show it.

Although there are dozens of rules that govern this issue, they boil down a few basic ideas. First, you don't treat contractors like employees: they get no training, no supervision, no instructions on how to do the job; they set their own hours; they could get someone else to do the work for them (a.k.a. a subcontractor); and they can do the work wherever they want to as long as they meet your deadlines. Second, true contractors tend to work for multiple clients, and work for each sporadically; in most cases, they offer services to the general public. That doesn't mean you can't use the same contractor over and over, but it has to be on an as-needed or on-call basis. Third, contractors are paid by the job, not by the hours they put in (although they are allowed to bill based on their hourly rate), and you don't have to pay them if they don't finish the job. They pay their own business expenses, file their own business tax returns, and can end up with either a profit or loss for their efforts. Finally, you can't fire them; as long as they comply with your contract specifications, you're stuck with them until the job is done.

The bottom line: the relationship has to be truly separate in order to prove that someone who works for you is a contractor rather than an employee.

Potential Consequences of Hiring Contractors

There are a lot of benefits to using contractors instead of hiring employees, but there are also some inherent risks:

- **Lawsuits:** Employees file workmen's compensation claims when they get injured on the job, but contractors may sue your company.
- **No control:** You have no control over the contractor's work, including missed deadlines or work quality; if you exert control, you have an employee.
- **Harder to sever:** You can't fire contractors; you can only breach your contract with them or sever the relationship after they hand you unacceptable work.
- **Government fines:** If the government reclassifies your contractor as an employee, you'll have a lot of taxes and fines to pay.

Big Benefits with Contractors

With the potential risks you run when using contractors, it's easy to forget the substantial benefits they can bring to new and small businesses. At the very least, there's no long-term commitment; he comes in for one job, and you never have to use him again. There's also no investment on your part: no employee search, no paperwork, no training—all things that take up your time and your company's cash.

Then there's the matter of payroll and everything that goes along with it. With employees, you have reports and tax returns to fill out and file, and tax payments to deposit. On top of that, you have to pay the employees regularly, and you also have to pay the corresponding employment taxes (an extra 7.65 percent of salary), unemployment taxes, and disability insurance. With contractors, you avoid all the filing except one tiny form at the end of the year (IRS Form 1099), and you don't pay anything but the agreed-upon price. Also, contractors don't get benefits, such as health insurance and retirement plans, but you may have to offer those to employees to attract and keep the ones you want.

Finally, your company won't be held liable for things the contractor does; it can, however, be held liable for things your employees do while at work. For example, if an employee drives your delivery van into someone's living room, your company legally is financially responsible; if a contractor does the same thing with his delivery van, you may lose a customer, but you won't lose anything else.

Salaries, Dividends, or Loans?

With sole proprietorships and partnerships, it makes no difference when or how much money you take out of the company, at least for tax purposes. After all, you personally pay tax on your full share of the company's income every year. These business structures don't allow for owner salaries, just withdrawals, which have absolutely no tax impact.

Corporation owners, on the other hand, can get money out of their companies in a few different ways. Each way has a different tax implication. Here, you and the IRS are at cross purposes: you want to minimize your tax bill, and it wants to maximize it. To do that, the IRS created some basic guidelines that reduce a little of the income-shifting capabilities available to corporations. With a little flexibility and planning, though, you can abide by the rules and still use them to your own tax advantage.

ALERT!

Some of the tax rules for corporations are quite complicated, and getting them wrong can land you in hot water with the IRS. To avoid unnecessary consequences (such as tax penalties), hire a qualified tax preparer with plenty of small-business experience.

The three main ways to get cash out of your corporation are salary, dividends, and loans. The type of corporation is a factor in the final mixture, as the tax implications for S corporation shareholders are quite different than those for C corporation shareholders. Since the name of the game is cutting the income tax bill to the bone, you want to shift as much income as possible into whichever category comes with the lowest tax rate. When you consider that you and your company are a single tax-paying unit, anything that cuts back any form of taxes leads to extra money in your hands.

The Salary Category

When it comes to managing the taxes for your business, salary can include more than a regular paycheck. This category also may encompass things such as bonuses and deferred payments, and fringe benefits as well; essentially, it's your total pay package. When you have a C corporation, you want to make that pay package as large and comprehensive as possible. S corporation owners, on the other hand, may fare better taxwise by keeping their actual salaries at a bare-bones level.

Unlike C corporation owners, S corporation shareholders don't have to deal with double taxation on dividends; they personally pay taxes on the total income of the business whether or not they take the dividends. Salary, on the other hand, is taxed at a higher rate than dividend income because it's subject to employment taxes. Looking at the S corporation and the shareholder together, more taxes will be paid all together on salary than on dividends. That makes it more beneficial for S corporation shareholders to shift the balance toward higher dividends and lower salaries.

Small C corporation owners want to do the exact opposite: put as much money into salary as possible and avoid paying themselves dividends. Here, the double taxation on dividends does come into play, with both the corporation itself paying taxes on profits and the shareholders paying taxes again on any profit distributions. Salaries, on the other hand, are completely deductible to the corporation, reducing its taxable income; only the shareholder-employee pays income tax on that money.

The Dividend Difference

Dividends are distributions of company profits, only available to corporate shareholders. The type of corporation you have, though, completely determines how these payouts are treated. With a C corporation, dividends spell double taxation, leading small-business owners to avoid using this method to get money out of the company. S corporation owners have to pay the same tax on profits whether or not they take the money out, and it can be to their advantage to maximize their dividend payouts.

If your business is set up as a C corporation, pumping as much money as possible into your salary can make the most sense taxwise when you think of you and your corporation as a couple. You want to minimize the total tax bill, including the corporate component; after all, it's your company and your money no matter what the name on the tax return says. For every dollar you take in salary and related items, the corporation gets a tax deduction. It pays taxes only on its remaining profits—the very profits used to pay dividends. When you receive dividends as a shareholder, even if you're the only shareholder, you have to pay personal income taxes on those dividends, which are already taxed to the corporation as profits. For that reason, C corporation owners (as opposed to pure investment-level shareholders) want to take as little as possible in dividends.

The situation is almost exactly the opposite for S corporation shareholders. There, salaries are a bigger tax drain than are dividends. Here's the main reason why: salaries are subject to employment taxes; dividends are not. Both forms of income show up on the owner's tax return; the only variable factor is the proportion. Yes, your salary and the related employment taxes are deductible to the business, but the business still has to pay them in the first place. A $10,000 salary can cost you and your corporation more than $1,500 in employment taxes on top of regular income taxes; dividends are subject only to income taxes, sometimes at better rates than other forms of income. By switching that $10,000 from salary to dividends, you kept that $1,500 in your pocket instead of sending it in to the IRS.

ALERT!

The IRS knows that C corporation owners want to avoid the dividend double taxation issue, so it put rules in place that, under certain circumstances, penalize owners for keeping profits in the company rather than distributing them and paying the extra tax. Talk to your tax adviser to make sure your corporation doesn't inadvertently fall into this tax trap.

The IRS knows all this, and it knows the strategies that owners of small corporations put into play to reduce their tax bills. For that reason, it keeps an eye on corporate shareholder-employee salaries. For S corporation shareholder-employees, the IRS looks to see that the salary isn't too low; for C corporation shareholder-employees, it checks to see that the salary isn't too high. Your best protection is paying yourself a salary that you can justify as reasonable. For example, in an S corporation, it's reasonable to keep your salary low enough to show profits. With a C corporation, it's reasonable to pay yourself the going rate for corporate CEOs.

Loans Between You and Your Corporation

While it may seem odd to lump loans in with salaries and dividends, think of them in terms of getting money out of the company without creating a big tax situation. Although there will be some taxes attached to your loan, whichever way it goes (from you to the company or vice versa), they'll be less costly than employment taxes or double taxation.

If you're wondering what part of a loan would be taxable, it's the interest; and, yes, it absolutely must be paid. Without a reasonable rate of interest attached to the loan, the IRS can choose to treat it as a dividend (particularly if you own a C corporation) or a capital contribution, neither of which would benefit your strategy.

Treat any loans between you and your corporation just as you would any other business loan. Draw up official loan documents that specify payment amounts and due dates as well as the interest rate of the loan.

Tracking Travel Expenses

Travel expenses are among the most common small-business tax deductions. They're also one of the biggest audit areas, for businesses big and small, in any structure. For that reason, it's critical that you keep good records of your expenditures; even better, maintain a log to keep track of all business travel costs. The most important fact to document in your log is the business purpose of the expense.

The rules for these deductions can seem confusing, because there are all sorts of gray areas. As long as you keep the basic IRS guidelines in mind, planning these business expenditures will be a snap. Here's the most important rule to remember: the expense has to be ordinary and necessary to your business in order to qualify for deductibility. A freelance writer who works out of her basement and deals with clients only by phone and e-mail will have a hard time justifying a deduction for a three-week trip to Honolulu; on the other hand, that same trip may make total business sense for a sales rep whose territory covers the Hawaiian Islands. The second most important rule is documentation: if an expense is more than $75, you have to have receipts to back it up.

Business Travel Expenses

Travel can be one of the biggest expenses for new and small businesses. From trade shows to conventions to visiting client sites, entrepreneurs spend a lot of time on the road. As long as you follow the ground rules (and they're pretty vague), most of the expenses associated with your business travel will be deductible.

Here's a list of commonly deductible travel expenses (full deductibility depends on the actual circumstances):

- Plane, train, cab, and bus fares
- Half of the cost of your meals (when the trip is long enough to warrant eating out)
- Baggage handling fees
- Hotel charges
- Laundry expenses
- Phone and fax charges
- Reasonable tips

If you're going to be away from home for a while, you may want to consider using the standard meal allowance (SMA) instead of collecting a huge pile of receipts. The average SMA is $39 a day, half of which counts as a deductible expense. In more expensive cities, the SMA is higher, up to a maximum rate of $64 per day. You can find out the per diem rate for the cities you'll be traveling in by checking out IRS Publication 1542.

When your trip combines both business and personal expenses, it isn't fully deductible. If the trip is mainly for business purposes, you can still deduct the cost of getting to and from the destination. If it's mostly personal, none of that expense can be booked to the business; however, dedicated business expenses (such as a convention entrance fee) can still qualify.

Using Your Car for Business

When you use your own vehicle for company business, you can deduct some related expenses in your company books. To figure out the business portion of use, you have to keep track of your mileage in three separate ways: total, business use, and personal use. Business use includes driving between two business locations, even if one of them is your own main place of business. Those locations can be job sites, client offices, or task destinations (such as the post office). To track those miles, keep a log right in the car. For each trip, record the date, the business destination, the total mileage for that drive, and its business purpose.

Driving from home to your main business location doesn't count; that's considered commuting and it's not a business expense. However, if you make a legitimate business stop along the way, you can turn that nondeductible commute into a regular business expense.

Once you know your three mileage totals, you can easily calculate the business portion of your vehicle expenses. Simply divide your total dedicated business miles by your total mileage, then multiply that result by your total vehicle expenses. Those include everything from gas to repairs to insurance. Parking and tolls, though, don't get lumped in here; they count as stand-alone fully deductible business expenses. If you don't want to bother tracking expenses, you can just multiply your business miles by the current standard mileage rate.

FACT

When your home qualifies as your primary place of business, every time you leave the house for a business-related task counts as deductible travel expense. Whether you're heading out to make a bank deposit or going to visit a customer, you've got a business expense.

About Fringe Benefits

For employees, fringe benefits are all good. For business owners, though, they have both good points and some slightly less good points. The good and the less good depend largely on the business entity: owners of C corporations get the biggest benefit from their fringe benefits than do owners of any other entity.

On the plus side, the value of fringe benefits can increase your overall compensation. Even better, some can do that without adding to your personal income tax bill, while remaining deductible expenses for the business. Consider health insurance premiums, for example: for C corporations, they're fully deductible by the company; for all other entities, they're fully deductible on the personal income tax returns of the business owner. Retirement plan contributions typically follow the same path. Plus, any of these expenses that you pay on behalf of employees are completely deductible business expenses.

Other fringe benefits, such as life insurance premiums, are only tax-free to C corporation owners. For any other business owner, such premiums paid by the company become taxable income on his personal return. Even with C corporations, some benefits that are tax-free to general employees don't get the same treatment when it comes to owner-employees. The rules involving these benefits are intricate, so talk to your accountant before you decide whether to implement them.

Keeping Things Separate

The most common piece of advice given to (and ignored by) new small-business owners is to keep everything that's personal completely separate from the business right from the very start. In addition to making your bookkeeping job a heck of a lot easier, it can also help you avoid some potential legal and financial pitfalls. While it may seem like a convenience to use your personal credit card to pick up office supplies, that momentary convenience can end up costing you both time and money.

The legal issues can be the most troubling. When you've gone through all the trouble of forming your company as one of the liability limiting entities (corporation, LLC, or LLP), you don't want to lose that personal financial protection due to carelessness. Using the company checkbook interchangeably with your own can result in the loss of your limited liability protection. For that reason, it's critical to keep your personal finances completely separate from your business finances except for bona fide loans, owner withdrawals, and salaries.

In some cases, mixing funds can end up costing you money. For example, if you use your corporate checkbook to pay a personal bill, that counts as paying yourself a dividend. If your corporation is a C corporation, that dividend will increase your personal income tax bill. Similarly, if you pay corporate expenses with personal checks, you've just made a capital contribution; the only way to get that money back is to pay yourself a dividend.

Finally, from a sheer accounting perspective, mixing funds is just plain confusing when it's time to record journal entries. Instead of having one set of documents to comb through for transactions, you have at least two: yours and the company's. That's double the work, and it often takes more than double the time to sort everything out. To avoid the extra work, the extra taxes, and the potential to lose your limited liability protection, make sure to keep your personal finances personal and completely separate from your business finances.

Appendix A

Glossary

account
A record used to hold related financial activity and show the impact of increases and decreases.

account balance
The current value of an account.

accounting period
A period of time used to measure and report a company's financial results.

accounts payable
The amount of money owed to vendors for credit purchases made in the normal course of business.

accounts receivable
The amount of money owed to a business for sales that were made by extending credit to customers.

accounts receivable aging
A report that groups accounts receivable balances according to how long they have been outstanding, and is used to help a company improve its collections.

accrual basis accounting
A method of accounting in which revenues are recorded as soon as they are earned, and expenses are recorded as soon as they are incurred, whether any money has changed hands yet.

asset
Anything that has a monetary value and is owned by a company.

balance sheet
A financial statement that shows a company's financial position on a specific date. The statement details the company's assets, liabilities, and equity.

break-even analysis
A formula used to figure out the amount of sales needed for a company to cover all its costs.

capital
A business owner's share of his company; also referred to as equity.

cash basis accounting
A method of accounting in which transactions are recorded only when money changes hands.

cash sales
Sales that result in immediate payment, whether it's in the form of money, check, or credit card.

cash collections
Money received as a result of credit sales made in a prior period.

chart of accounts
A complete listing of the accounts used by a company for bookkeeping purposes.

corporation
A formal business structure that offers the owners personal protection from business debts.

cost of goods sold
The purchase price of products that are resold to customers.

credit
An accounting term used to indicate a right-side entry to an account. Credits result in account decreases for assets and expenses, and account increases for liabilities, equity, and revenues.

debit
An accounting term used to indicate a left-side entry to an account. Debits result in account increases for assets and expenses, and account decreases for liabilities, equity, and revenues.

depreciation
An expense used to reflect the loss in value of an asset over time.

disbursement
Cash paid out by a business.

equity
An ownership interest in a business; also called capital.

expense
The normal costs incurred by a business to produce revenues.

fixed assets
Physical assets that will serve a business for longer than one year.

gross margin
A measure of profitability calculated by dividing gross profits by sales.

gross profit
The amount left over after subtracting the cost of goods sold from sales.

horizontal analysis
A method of evaluating financial statements by looking at the change in account balances between two accounting periods.

inventory
The goods a business either uses in product manufacturing or holds for resale.

journal
A book in which complete business transactions are recorded by date.

ledger
A book that holds each account listed in the chart of accounts, in which transactions impacting that account are recorded.

liability
Debt incurred by a business.

limited liability company (LLC)
An unincorporated business that may be owned by any number of people and that provides personal protection from business debts for each owner.

liquidity
A company's ability to meet financial obligations as they come due.

net profit
The amount left over after deducting all costs and expenses from revenues.

operating expenses
Expenditures unrelated to product costs that are incurred in the normal course of business.

owner's draw
Money taken out of a business by its owners (except in the case of corporations).

partnership
An unincorporated business owned by at least two people.

posting
The act of transferring transaction information from a journal to a ledger.

prepaid expenses
Advance payments for goods or services, treated as an asset for accounting purposes.

retained earnings
Profits that are held by the company rather than distributed to its owners.

sole proprietorship
An unincorporated business owned by one person.

statement of cash flows
An accounting report that details the movement of cash into and out of a company during a specified period.

statement of profit and loss
An accounting report that shows the results of operations for a specific period.

transactions
The economic events of a business.

trial balance
An accounting report used to verify that a company's accounts are in balance.

vertical analysis
A method of evaluating a company's financial performance over a single accounting period.

Appendix B

Small-Business Resources on the Internet

For Tax Forms and Booklets

The Official IRS Web Site

Your one-stop (free) shop for every tax form and booklet you could ever need. If your company has even one employee, make sure to download Circular E; it's basically an employer's guide to everything about federal payroll taxes. On this comprehensive and easy-to-navigate site, you'll also be able to easily find estimated tax payment calculators and coupons (both for individuals and C corporations).

www.irs.gov

For Accounting Software

Intuit

You may already be familiar with Intuit, maker of Quicken and TurboTax. On the small-business front, its accounting package, QuickBooks, is one of the easiest to navigate. If you've already been using Quicken, you can import your files directly into QuickBooks for more robust business accounting options. The program comes equipped with all the standard accounting reports, and you can design special reports on the fly.

www.intuit.com

Peachtree Accounting

Though not quite as well-known as QuickBooks, Peachtree Complete Accounting is a favorite among professional bookkeepers. The software is particularly good for small manufacturing companies, as the "build a product" module is very user-friendly, so you can track finished goods, work in process, and raw materials inventory with a click of your mouse. The company also offers a robust payroll module, if you want to handle payroll in-house.

www.peachtree.com

MYOB Accounting Software

MYOB offers accounting software geared toward small businesses, along with several other small business services (such as direct credit-card processing with your software package). The program includes all the standard features, including bank recs and a variety of report options.

www.myob.com/us

For General Small-Business Guidance

The U.S. Small Business Administration (SBA)

When you're looking into small-business loans, this Web site should be your first stop. Most banks follow SBA guidelines for loan requirements and paperwork submissions, so grabbing that information here can help you navigate the loan process more easily.

✍*www.sba.gov*

SCORE (Service Corps of Retired Executives)

At SCORE, you can find a business mentor, someone who's done what you're doing and has tons of experience to bring to the table. Whether you prefer live online help or face-to-face meetings, this affiliate of the SBA has a mentor for you. The organization will introduce you to one of more than 10,500 volunteers who can help you with virtually any questions you have about your business. SCORE also offers low-cost (and some free) business workshops for fledgling entrepreneurs, and posts dozens of free advice articles on its Web site.

✍*www.score.org*

Entrepreneur.com

This informative Web site offers all kinds of small-business advice, from opportunities and ideas to home office setups to the best ways to market your business. Although this is a commercial Web site (full of ads), it does load very quickly, and most of the content is free.

✍*www.entrepreneur.com*

NOLO

This site is chock-full of legal information, and plenty of it pertains to small businesses. From choosing a business structure to dealing with human resources problems to contracts, you can find free basic information about almost any legal issues your company may face. In addition to software and books, the Web site also offers single legal contract fill-in-the-blank forms for standard agreements, including employment applications and confidentiality agreements.

✍*www.nolo.com*

Index

A

Account numbers, 15, 29–33
Account reconciliations, 56–59
Accountants, 8–12
Accounting cycles, 43–44
Accounting equation, 63–76
Accounting mistakes, x, 41–43
Accounting periods, 163–75
Accounting professionals, 7–12
Accounting schedules, 50–54
Accounting software, 49–50
Accounting systems, 45–62, 79–82
Accounting types, 1–7, 238–39, 244–53. *See also specific types*
Accounts chart, 31–33
Accounts payable, 59, 161–62
Accounts receivable, 58, 84–86, 152
Accounts, setting up, 29–33
Accounts, types of, 13–23, 178–79
Accrual accounting, 28–29, 52, 55, 80–81, 161–73, 181, 188

Adjusting entries, 167–70
Amortization expenses, 111–12
Annual tasks, 54, 174–75
Assets, disposing of, 71–72
Assets, financing, 237–38
Assets, types of, 30–31, 63–72, 185
Assets, understanding, 15–16, 64–66, 75–76
Audits, 6, 60, 242

B

Balance sheet, 21, 173, 178–79, 184–87, 216–19
Bank statements, 137–39
Bookkeeping, 2–4
Break-even analysis, 233–35
Budget, 236–37
Building industry, 251–53
Business entities, 191–202, 204–8
Business expenses, 56, 106, 277–80. *See also* Expenses; Overhead

C

Cash accounting, 27–28, 80–81, 181, 188
Cash flow, managing, 131–40
Cash-flow problems, 139–40, 228–30
Cash flow statement, 21, 173, 178–79, 188–90, 216
Cash journal, 38–39
Cash projection, 133–34
Cash receipts, 135–36, 152
Cash reconciliation, 57–58
Cash sales, 80, 83–84, 86
Cash transactions, 135–39
Certified public accountants (CPAs), 8–12
Chart of accounts, 31–33
Closing entries, 174–75
Collections, 150–52
Commissions, 106
Consignment merchandise, 92, 244
Construction industry, 251–53
Corporations, 192–94, 198–201, 205–13, 273–74

Cost accounting, 246–47
Cost of goods, 91–102
Costs, 18–20. *See also* Expenses
Credit policies, 84–86, 141–52
Credit sales, 79, 80, 82–86, 141–52
Credits and debits, 22–23
Customer credit, 79, 80, 82–86, 141–52
Customer ledger, 84–86, 152
Customer statement, 85, 148–50

D
Daily journals, 34–39
Daily tasks, 50–52, 55–56
Debits and credits, 22–23, 79
Debts, 151–52, 224–25, 227, 230
Decision-making, 228–32
Deductions, 20
Deferrals, 167–70
Depreciation, 70–71, 109–11, 249–50
Discounts, 88, 244–45
Dividends, 275–76
Documents, keeping, 59–62

E
Employee benefits, 121–22, 279–80
Employee duties, 241
Employees, and contractors, 271–73
Employees, and expenses, 112–13

Employees, and internal controls, 239–41
Employees, and retirement plans, 260–67
Employees, payroll for, 115–30
Employer identification number (EIN), 117–18
Entertainment expenses, 108–9
Entities, 191–202, 204–8
Equity, 17–18, 63, 74–76, 230
Estimated taxes, 53
Expenses, and selling costs, 104–6
Expenses, for travel, 106, 277–79
Expenses, of employees, 112–13
Expenses, types of, 18–20, 103–13, 246–47

F
Files, 45–46, 59–60
Financial ratios, 221–26
Financial statements, 173–74, 177–90, 215–30
Fiscal year, 164
Fringe benefits, 279–80

G
General journals, 34–36, 152
General ledger, 33–34, 152
Glossary, 281–83
Goods, cost of, 91–102
Goods sold, 100–102, 244–45

Gross profit, 19–20.
See also Profits

H
High-tech companies, 250–51
Home-based businesses, 107–8, 247–50

I
Income taxes, 203–14, 269–80
Independent contractors, 271–73
Internal audits, 242
Internal controls, 239–41
Internal Revenue Code (IRC), 269
Internal Revenue Service (IRS), 270
Inventory, 88–89, 91–102, 161–62, 170
Inventory accounting methods, 97–99
Inventory reconciliation, 58–59
Inventory, tracking, 79–82, 96–99
Investments, 66, 224–25
Invoices, 85, 148–49, 151, 161
IRAs, 258–60

J
Journals, 34–41, 174–75

K
Keogh plans, 264–65

L

Layaway sales, 88–89, 244
Leases, 214, 238
Ledgers, 33–34, 174–75
Liabilities, 16–17, 31, 63, 72–76
Liquidity, 64–65, 223–24
LLCs, 192–94, 205, 209
Loans, 72–74, 213–14, 230,
    237–38, 276–77

M

Management accounting,
    238–39
Manufacturers, 93, 95, 99–100,
    102, 245–47
Mistakes to avoid, x, 41–43
Monthly statements, 149–50
Monthly tasks, 52–53

O

Organization, 46–48, 59–60
Overhead, 106–7, 246–47

P

Paperwork, keeping, 59–62
    See also Organization
Partnerships, 192–98,
    205–11, 273
Payments journal, 162
Payroll forms, 116–19
Payroll, managing, 115–30
Payroll taxes, 119–30

Percentage-of-completion,
    251–53
Period cleanup, 163–75
Price-setting, 232
Pro formas, 235–36
Product sales, 78. *See also*
    Goods sold
Profit and loss statement, 21,
    173, 178–83, 216–20
Profitability problems, 226–30
Profitability ratios, 222–23
Profits, 19–20, 131–33, 232–35
Purchase costs, 153–62
Purchase orders, 159–60
Purchase problems, 160–61
Purchases, financing, 237–38
Purchases journal, 37–38,
    95–96, 161–62

Q

Quarterly tasks, 53–54

R

Ratios, 221–26
Reconciliations, 56–59, 137–39
Recordkeeping, 47–48, 59–62
Refunds, 90
Resources, 284–85
Retailers, 94, 244–45
Retainers, 89
Retirement plans, 255–67
Returns, 90, 244–45
Revenues, generating, 63

Revenues, recording, 77–90
Revenues, understanding,
    18–20, 31

S

Salaries, 106, 208–13, 273–75.
    See also Payroll
Sales journal, 36–37, 82–83, 152
Sales projection, 134
Sales receipts, 80, 90
Sales tax, 30, 78, 86–87
Sales transactions, 79–82,
    87–90, 244–45
Scheduling tasks, 50–54
Self-payment, 208–13
Selling costs, 104–6
Selling on account, 84–86
SEPs, 262–64
Service-only sales, 78
Shipping terms, 245
SIMPLE plans, 260–62
Software, 49–50
Sole proprietorships, 192–95,
    205–11, 273
Special transactions, 87–89,
    243–53
Statements, 85, 148–50
Success, measuring, 2

T

Tax deductions, 20
Tax planning, 213–14
Tax shelters, 256–58
Taxes, income, 203–14, 269–80

Taxes, payroll, 119–30
Taxes, sales, 30, 78, 86–87
Technology industry, 250–51
Time sales, 88–89
Transactions, recording, 26–29
Transactions, tracking, 25–44,
    80–81
Transactions, types of, 23,
    55–56, 79–82, 87–90,
    135–39, 243–53
Travel expenses, 106, 277–79
Trial balance, 166–67

V
Vendors, 155–61

W
Weekly tasks, 50–52
Working balance, 166–67

Y
Year-end tasks, 54, 174–75

THE EVERYTHING SERIES!

BUSINESS & PERSONAL FINANCE

Everything® **Accounting Book**
Everything® Budgeting Book
Everything® Business Planning Book
Everything® Coaching and Mentoring Book
Everything® Fundraising Book
Everything® Get Out of Debt Book
Everything® Grant Writing Book
Everything® Home-Based Business Book, 2nd Ed.
Everything® Homebuying Book, 2nd Ed.
Everything® Homeselling Book, 2nd Ed.
Everything® Investing Book, 2nd Ed.
Everything® Landlording Book
Everything® Leadership Book
Everything® **Managing People Book, 2nd Ed.**
Everything® Negotiating Book
Everything® Online Auctions Book
Everything® Online Business Book
Everything® Personal Finance Book
Everything® Personal Finance in Your 20s and 30s Book
Everything® Project Management Book
Everything® Real Estate Investing Book
Everything® Robert's Rules Book, $7.95
Everything® Selling Book
Everything® **Start Your Own Business Book, 2nd Ed.**
Everything® Wills & Estate Planning Book

COOKING

Everything® Barbecue Cookbook
Everything® Bartender's Book, $9.95
Everything® Chinese Cookbook
Everything® **Classic Recipes Book**
Everything® Cocktail Parties and Drinks Book
Everything® College Cookbook
Everything® **Cooking for Baby and Toddler Book**
Everything® Cooking for Two Cookbook
Everything® Diabetes Cookbook
Everything® Easy Gourmet Cookbook
Everything® Fondue Cookbook
Everything® **Fondue Party Book**
Everything® Gluten-Free Cookbook
Everything® Glycemic Index Cookbook
Everything® Grilling Cookbook

Everything® Healthy Meals in Minutes Cookbook
Everything® Holiday Cookbook
Everything® Indian Cookbook
Everything® Italian Cookbook
Everything® Low-Carb Cookbook
Everything® Low-Fat High-Flavor Cookbook
Everything® Low-Salt Cookbook
Everything® Meals for a Month Cookbook
Everything® Mediterranean Cookbook
Everything® Mexican Cookbook
Everything® One-Pot Cookbook
Everything® **Quick and Easy 30-Minute, 5-Ingredient Cookbook**
Everything® Quick Meals Cookbook
Everything® Slow Cooker Cookbook
Everything® Slow Cooking for a Crowd Cookbook
Everything® Soup Cookbook
Everything® Tex-Mex Cookbook
Everything® Thai Cookbook
Everything® Vegetarian Cookbook
Everything® Wild Game Cookbook
Everything® Wine Book, 2nd Ed.

GAMES

Everything® 15-Minute Sudoku Book, $9.95
Everything® 30-Minute Sudoku Book, $9.95
Everything® Blackjack Strategy Book
Everything® Brain Strain Book, $9.95
Everything® Bridge Book
Everything® Card Games Book
Everything® Card Tricks Book, $9.95
Everything® Casino Gambling Book, 2nd Ed.
Everything® Chess Basics Book
Everything® Craps Strategy Book
Everything® Crossword and Puzzle Book
Everything® Crossword Challenge Book
Everything® Cryptograms Book, $9.95
Everything® Easy Crosswords Book
Everything® Easy Kakuro Book, $9.95
Everything® Games Book, 2nd Ed.
Everything® Giant Sudoku Book, $9.95
Everything® Kakuro Challenge Book, $9.95
Everything® **Large-Print Crossword Challenge Book**
Everything® Large-Print Crosswords Book
Everything® Lateral Thinking Puzzles Book, $9.95
Everything® **Mazes Book**

Everything® Pencil Puzzles Book, $9.95
Everything® Poker Strategy Book
Everything® Pool & Billiards Book
Everything® Test Your IQ Book, $9.95
Everything® Texas Hold 'Em Book, $9.95
Everything® Travel Crosswords Book, $9.95
Everything® Word Games Challenge Book
Everything® Word Search Book

HEALTH

Everything® Alzheimer's Book
Everything® Diabetes Book
Everything® Health Guide to Adult Bipolar Disorder
Everything® Health Guide to Controlling Anxiety
Everything® Health Guide to Fibromyalgia
Everything® **Health Guide to Thyroid Disease**
Everything® Hypnosis Book
Everything® Low Cholesterol Book
Everything® Massage Book
Everything® Menopause Book
Everything® Nutrition Book
Everything® Reflexology Book
Everything® Stress Management Book

HISTORY

Everything® American Government Book
Everything® American History Book
Everything® Civil War Book
Everything® Freemasons Book
Everything® Irish History & Heritage Book
Everything® Middle East Book

HOBBIES

Everything® Candlemaking Book
Everything® Cartooning Book
Everything® **Coin Collecting Book**
Everything® Drawing Book
Everything® Family Tree Book, 2nd Ed.
Everything® Knitting Book
Everything® Knots Book
Everything® Photography Book
Everything® Quilting Book
Everything® Scrapbooking Book
Everything® Sewing Book
Everything® Woodworking Book

Bolded titles are new additions to the series.
All Everything® books are priced at $12.95 or $14.95, unless otherwise stated. Prices subject to change without notice.